DATE DUE			

CORPORATE QUALITY UNIVERSITIES

Lessons in Building a World-Class Work Force

CORPORATE QUALITY UNIVERSITIES

Lessons in Building a World-Class Work Force

Jeanne C. Meister

ASTD

AMERICAN SOCIETY
FOR TRAINING AND
DEVELOPMENT

1640 KING STREET
BOX 1443
ALEXANDRIA, VIRGINIA
22313-2043

IRWIN
Professional Publishing
Burr Ridge, Illinois
New York, New York

Sponsoring editor: Jean Marie Geracie
Project editor: Denise V. Santor
Assistant production manager: Jon Christopher
Designer: Heidi J. Baughman
Art coordinator: Mark Malloy
Compositor: BookMasters, Inc.
Typeface: 11/13 Palatino
Printer: Book Press, Inc.

Library of Congress Cataloging-in-Publication Data

Meister, Jeanne C.
    Corporate quality universities : lessons in building a world-class
work force / by Jeanne C. Meister.
        p.   cm.
    Includes index.
    ISBN 1-55623-790-1
    1. Employees—Training of—United States. I. Title.
HF5549.5.T7M423   1994
658.3'124—dc20   93–1268

Printed in the United States of America
 3 4 5 6 7 8 9 0 BP 0 9 8 7 6 5 4

*To my husband, Bob,
and our daughter, Danielle,
for always believing in the book*

Preface

The skills and training required of both frontline workers and managers has changed significantly in the past two decades, and will continue to change in the next. Technological advances are only part of the reason. Three broad movements affecting industry—flatter corporate hierarchies, broader roles required of both workers and managers, and a more culturally diverse labor force—have combined to create a workplace unrecognizable from that which existed in the past.

As manufacturing companies have discovered the consumer, and service firms have discovered the benefits of quality control, a new set of demands has emerged for both current and prospective workers. These workers must be able to not only perform the technical aspects of their jobs, but they must also know how to adapt to new technologies, meet and exceed consumer expectations, and react to global competitive pressures.

Employees throughout the organization are gradually seeing their old roles overturned. Lower-level employees are being required to take on more responsibility and cooperate more closely with one another. More importantly, they must be able to see beyond their specific duties to demonstrate a business understanding of how their company and industry work, and how their jobs relate to the large corporate mission. These employees are required to perform more varied roles than in the past and they must be able to draw upon a broader set of skills. In fact, the skills normally associated with managers are now increasingly required of lower-level workers. In turn, managers must now learn to become coaches and facilitators rather than schedulers of work.

Who will train these employees in the skills businesses need to effectively compete in the global competitive economy? Will it be the educational system? Kindergarten through 12th-grade educators most often view their mission as developing college-bound students. Yet, according to the National Center on Education and the Economy, by the year 2000, roughly 70 percent of all jobs in America will not require a college education. These jobs, in areas ranging from retail sales and service to skilled craftsmen, will form the backbone of our economy and will require ongoing training. The job of training these workers will increasingly fall to corporate America. So far though, corporate America invests roughly $530 billion a year in new plant and equipment and only $30 billion in training its workers.

But as the landscape of the American workplace evolves and changes, some American companies are recognizing an urgent need to invest in their human capital. This book profiles more than two dozen companies who are models in training and developing their workers. These companies are meeting the training challenge head-on by shifting their thinking from conducting one-time training events to building a culture of continuous learning within the organization.

What is distinctive about these companies, as a group, is that they are taking a proactive role in developing educational systems and cooperative partnerships to create world-class employees who are able to function successfully within this changing workplace. In many cases, their vehicle is a corporate infrastructure which I call the Corporate Quality University. The name Corporate Quality University does not necessarily imply a building or a campus. In fact, many of the Corporate Quality Universities profiled in this book lack any distinct physical site at all.

Instead, Corporate Quality Universities are an umbrella for a company's training programs which embody a philosophy of continuous learning and ultimately a lever for cultural change. As a group, these Corporate Quality Universities represent a best-in-class effort to train all levels of workers in the skills, knowledge, and competencies they will need to be successful in their current jobs and be able to adapt to future job requirements. Companies focusing their attention and steering their resources into these universities fervently believe that well-trained workers are their most important asset and critical to their competitiveness in the global marketplace. These companies are taking determined steps now to forge a work force excellence that will promote their own future survival.

This book is an in-depth examination of what Corporate Quality Universities teach and the types of partnerships they are building not only with their own internal employees, but also with their suppliers and customers to ensure that all the members of their business chain have the skills needed for success in the global marketplace. The book offers a ringside look at innovative university programs in progress at more than two dozen American companies, including industry leaders known for their long history of training excellence, such as General Electric, Motorola, Xerox, Disney, Intel, and Corning. The book also covers university initiatives launched at smaller privately held companies like the Iams Company—a leader in the premium pet food market—and Computer Management Development Services—an educational software company—where the training and development programs bear all the hallmarks of the university approach. Taken together, the training efforts here are evidence of a movement that is beginning to revolutionize the way American companies are approaching the challenge of work force training.

Corporate Quality Universities had its beginnings in a two-year research project I undertook on behalf of several Fortune 500 companies. Over the course of two years, I personally interviewed scores of individuals from corporations, government, and universities, and attended numerous programs at these Corporate Quality Universities.

This book explores the phenomenon of the Corporate Quality University through a behind-the-scenes look at universities representing the best of the breed. It examines the guiding principles and often innovative methods which distinguish the university approach. Along the way, the book distills the wisdom and the know-how of Corporate Quality Universities into a number of valuable principles and lessons that any company can adapt to fit its own needs. One of the university's primary functions is to serve as a learning laboratory for the company. In their efforts to find ways to improve employee performance and make training more efficient and relevant to the corporate mission, many companies are using their Corporate Quality Universities to experiment with new approaches and practices to help all the members of their business chain learn at "their moment of need."

A number of guidelines have emerged as central to the success of training at many of the Corporate Quality Universities profiled in this book. No matter what your involvement in training within your organization, whether as a CEO, a strategic planner, a human resources manager, or training manager, you'll find that these basic guidelines will serve as a useful starting point for evaluating and shaping your organization's training programs, whether or not you follow the university approach. Some examples of the guidelines revealed in the book include:

- Training at quality-driven companies starts with inculcating employees at all levels with an understanding of the values, culture, and mission of the company. While traditional training has focused on imparting job-specific knowledge and improving skills, Corporate Quality Universities give a first priority to developing corporate citizenship, which involves a thorough understanding of the company's identity and values as well as developing pride in being part of the organization. After employees have this foundation in the company and its values, then job-related training follows. This theme is explored throughout the book using several examples from the curricula of Corporate Quality Universities.

- Effective training is carefully tied to the strategic needs of the business. At one time, companies offered employees a smorgasbord of generic courses and then employees were left to decide the courses they were interested in. But now, offering employees this cafeteria style of training no longer suffices. Progressive companies identify the competencies needed for each job category and then develop a training and development plan for each employee so he or she can improve mastery and productivity linked to these competencies.

- Training has evolved from a one-time event to a continuous process of lifelong learning. This emphasis on developing a spirit of lifelong learning is one which has been borrowed from our Japanese competitors. In Japan, training is more than a means of career advancement, it is imbedded in the work life of all employees. The 30 American companies profiled in this book recognize the importance of instilling within all employees a motivation to learn and continuously improve as the workplace changes over time.

- State-of-the-art training extends beyond the corporation to include key constituencies in a company's customer/supply chain. Corporate Quality Universities are reaching out to form educational partnerships with customers, suppliers, and, in some cases, the universities and even elementary schools that supply the organization with its human talent.

Finally, this book concludes with an appendix which lists 30 Corporate Quality Universities. This can serve as a useful guide for readers to network with other practitioners in identifying ways to enhance their company's training and development programs. While reading this book, it's important to remember the focus of all this effort: to build a world-class work force and, beyond that, to ensure that all the members of the customer/supply chain understand the company's mission and quality vision. How are companies doing this? Corporate Quality Universities have become an important avenue to achieve this goal.

Jeanne C. Meister

Acknowledgments

To write a book that presents readers with a ringside look at how Corporate Universities have evolved and changed over time requires, above all, access to the people who work in these Corporate Universities. This book, first and foremost, acknowledges the time and effort of over 100 individuals from Corporate Universities, government agencies, and colleges across the United States. I am deeply indebted to these people for patiently cooperating with me in either personal interviews or during lengthy telephone interviews. A list of these 100 individuals appears at the back of the book.

I am also indebted to my editor, Jean Geracie, for the vision, perspective, and commitment she brought to this project. Her support and friendship inspired me to keep going through the numerous revisions and edits of the manuscript. I would also like to acknowledge the foresight of Editor-in-Chief Jeffrey A. Krames, for believing in the mission and scope of this book when it was first presented to him. Finally, I owe Maureen Heffernan a special debt and thanks for her heroic efforts in transforming a wayward manuscript into a structured and easy-to-read book. Maureen was a true partner in this endeavor and her contributions to the final shape of this book have been enormous.

Over the past two years, the research for this book has taken me across the United States, visiting and meeting with scores of individuals who manage and teach in the 30 Corporate Universities profiled here. I came away from this journey with a deep appreciation of the continuing reorganization of the workplace and the corresponding need to invest in training at all levels of the work force. As specialized knowledge becomes obsolete at a terrifyingly fast pace, the workers who flourish will be those who make a commitment to continuously learn new skills, knowledge, and competencies. This book can be used as a helpful guide to scores of companies—both large and small—in showing them how model organizations are responding to the challenge of developing their work forces and devising ways of integrating learning into everyone's daily job.

On the administrative side, I owe a special thanks to Nancy Villanueva, Evelyn Cobo, and Karen Feaster, who patiently kept revising each draft of the manuscript and accompanying figures until we were all satisfied with the end product.

Finally, I would not have been able to write this book without the love and support of my husband, Bob Meister, our daughter, Danielle, my stepdaughter, Debbie, amd my parents, Sal and Camille Cioffi. Thanks for this and so very much more.

J.C.M.

Contents

Chapter One

Changes in the Workplace

BROADER ROLES AND BROADER SKILLS

Corporate Quality Universities at companies such as Motorola, General Electric, and Intel represent a class of training initiative far more ambitious and sophisticated than any yet seen on the American business landscape. To understand the significance of the Corporate Quality University as both a state-of-the-art model for innovative work force training and, in a larger sense, a key instrument for cultural change, it's necessary to understand the broad forces which have given rise to this phenomenon. These include the arrival of the flattened, flexible organization; the broadening of workers' roles; and the need to incorporate a more diverse and mobile labor force into the organization. What these three broad trends point to is the emergence of education and training as a key vehicle for creating competitive advantage.

The workplace is undergoing change at an accelerating rate. One of the most far-reaching changes is the evolution of the organization into a form fundamentally different from that which dominated industry during the 1950s and 1960s. The corporate hierarchy, once stable and slow moving, with the "thinkers" at the top of the pyramid and the "do-ers" at the base, is poorly suited to the fast-moving, competitive environment of today. Instead, corporations are opting for a flat, flexible organization, characterized by decentralized decision making. Organizations are struggling to compete and, in the process, putting a premium on speed and efficiency. Whereas the model for the traditional organization was the army, with its rigid cohesive structure and clear chains of command, the new organization often structures

1

itself as a loosely knit confederation of entrepreneurial units and relies on teams to create value and profit. Compared to the corporate hierarchy of past decades, the entrepreneurial organization is distinguished by more ambiguity, fewer boundaries, and more rapid communication between the company and its employees, suppliers, and customers.

The transformation of IBM within the last decade bears witness to this new emphasis on entrepreneurism. In just the last five years, far less of the work force occupies support roles (such as mid-level management and corporate staff), and more are involved in such "direct" tasks as designing, producing, servicing, and selling IBM offerings. In fact, IBM employees involved in direct tasks now account for 57 percent of total employment, up from 43 percent in 1986.

This transformation within IBM, as well as countless other organizations, has had profound implications for employees. There are now fewer managers to oversee workers and, given the new corporate emphasis on speed, flexibility, and competitiveness, employees in all kinds of organizations are seeing their roles become broader. The following three examples show how roles have expanded for various types of employees in the manufacturing and service sectors.

Motorola. In the old-style, traditionally organized company, the responsibilities of assembly line workers usually amounted to performing a set of narrowly defined and routine tasks under close supervision. But now, in many of Motorola's factories, employees, known as cellular manufacturing operators (CMOs), are expected not only to be able to perform their own jobs, but also to understand a range of additional assembly functions so that the flexibility of the team is maximized.

In addition, at many of these Motorola factories, one manager supervises 80 to 90 cellular manufacturing operators, so workers must largely be self-supervising. They work together in informal teams and are responsible for planning their work, controlling quality, and inventing new ways to improve work processes, reduce defects, and shorten cycle time. This self-governance extends even to the issue of new hires: Chief among CMOs' responsibilities is to be able to become mentors for the new entrants joining Motorola's worldwide work force each year.

Fidelity Investments. In the past at Fidelity, the job of customer service was differentiated into the customer contact workers, such as sales representatives, and the support workers, such as back office billing clerks. Each worker had the knowledge and responsibilities specific to his or her separate functions. Sales reps knew the accounts, and the back office staff knew what happened after the trade. Customers with an inquiry often had to undergo the time-consuming and usually frustrating process of dealing with multiple departments.

Witness the 90s' approach at Fidelity, where *seamless service* (Fidelity's term) has become a priority. At Fidelity, the training program for both a sales representative and back office support worker is quite similar: Each worker is responsible for understanding a much broader body of information than used to be the case. The back office folks learn about Fidelity Investments' service strategy and expectations, while the customer contact workers learn about transaction follow-through. The point, of course, is to guarantee that a customer's inquiry is answered the same way by both a sales representative and a support worker in the back office. In Fidelity parlance, this is called the philosophy of developing one skill set. One of the benefits of this type of cross-training is that when a product or process changes, it is much easier for management to update one skill set. Since Fidelity sales representatives and back office staff have to learn about 170 different Fidelity funds, as well as update the regulatory changes to these funds, cross-training employees has become an efficient way to provide Fidelity's seamless service.

First of America Bank. Traditionally, a bank's customer service representative (CSR) performed a series of repetitive tasks: approving checks, answering routine questions, and helping customers reconcile account balances.

Now, the role of the CSR within a growing number of banks—First of America Bank being one—encompasses understanding a wide range of new bank products, from mutual funds to annuities. Also, as the bank empowers its CSRs, they are increasingly expected to advise bank customers rather than just pass along information about various bank products and services. These CSRs must not only know the technical aspects of their jobs, but also know how to process information and engage in consultative selling to recommend an appropriate mix of products and services to the customer.

In addition to assuming expanded responsibilities in their own jobs, workers are expected to assume a greater number of jobs. For example, at Intel, just three years ago, one operator was used per machine in wafer fabrication, assembly, and test operations. Now, each operator runs as many as eight machines, as well as assuming responsibilities for routine maintenance of the machines. According to Dave Hall, Intel's former director of quality technology, employee morale is much higher now because each worker knows more jobs in his or her immediate area.

As the preceding examples show, there's a pronounced difference between workers' relatively limited roles in the past and the much more ambitious and demanding scope of many workers' daily jobs today. What this means to the average worker is an urgent need to be able to draw on a much broader complement of skills than was deemed sufficient in the traditional organization. The link between workers' skills and an organization's competitiveness was brought home by Lester Thurow, dean of MIT's Sloan School of Management, when he said:

> The education and skills of the work force will be the key competitive weapon in the 21st century. The reason: there is a whole set of technologies coming along that will demand that the average office or production worker have skills that have not been required in the past. These skills go beyond the narrow duties of doing one's job to a broad skill set to adapt to new technologies and change in the marketplace.[1]

Throughout the book, I will refer to a set of CORE workplace competencies identified as critical by American companies profiled here. Essentially, these competencies are the specific skills or know-how employees need to successfully operate in the workplace. The specific CORE workplace competencies will be covered in depth in Chapter 4 and include six skill groups: learning skills, basic skills, interpersonal skills; creative thinking and problem solving; leadership and visioning skills; and self-management skills.

THE CORE WORKPLACE COMPETENCIES EMPLOYERS REQUIRE

Learning skills. To keep its footing in a fast-moving marketplace, a company must proactively embrace change. The ability to continually adjust and improve its systems and processes becomes a survival issue. In such an environment, learning skills rank high in importance since a company's power to successfully introduce change depends on workers' abilities to learn new roles, processes, and skills. Employees must be able to apply existing knowledge to new situations; learn new material efficiently; experiment with learning from a variety of sources, such as co-workers, customers, suppliers, and educational institutions; and build this learning into their everyday lives. The goal is for continuous improvement to become a natural part of how an employee thinks and behaves on the job. Comments from two observers underscore how learning skills are taking precedence as the work force continues to change and evolve. Says Ed Bales, Director of External Systems at Motorola University, "The competitive edge will go to the corporations who have the best mindware." Secretary of Labor Robert Reich comments, "Forty years ago we considered labor to be a cost on the balance sheet. Now we think of labor as an asset, hopefully able to identify problems and then solve them."[2]

Basic skills of reading, writing, computation, and cognitive reasoning. Employers expect all levels of employees to have a solid foundation in reading, writing, math computations, and cognitive reasoning skills. Some companies, such as Motorola, actually devote almost 10 percent of their total training budget to basic skills training. For example, in 1991, basic skills training amounted to roughly $7 million out of a total training expenditure of close to $70 million. In 1991, the American Society for Training and Development (ASTD) estimated that, as a group, U.S. employers spent $300 million on basic skill training, up from virtually zero 10 years ago. These basic skills are no longer narrowly defined as the ability to read, write, and perform mathematical computations at a specific grade level. Instead, workers in this changing workplace are being trained in cognitive reasoning skills in order to apply the information they read and take action on the job.

Interpersonal skills.   When good job performance meant doing a set of prescribed and repetitive tasks to satisfaction, the most important skill set consisted of the technical skills associated with each particular job. With teams moving to the fore as the vehicles of performance within flexible organizations (as Motorola's example shows), individual effectiveness is increasingly linked to well-developed interpersonal skills. These include not only the traditional interpersonal skills of listening and communicating effectively with co-workers, but also such skills as knowing how to work in groups, successfully resolving conflicts, using influence to gain cooperation from peers, and networking within the organization.

Creative thinking and problem-solving skills.   In the past, a paternal management took on the responsibility of devising ways to increase worker productivity. Today, lower-echelon employees are expected to figure out for themselves how to improve and streamline their work. Today's worker is expected to give constructive input on everything from how to ensure the quality of raw materials used to make the product to how to improve processes and procedures. This requires that they be able to draw upon a set of problem-solving skills, which include being able to analyze situations, ask questions, seek clarification of what they do not understand, and think creatively to generate options. Also, because the flexible organization must be able to respond quickly to local market conditions and cannot wait for decisions from the home office, employees must increasingly make decisions at the point of production or at the point of the sale. Hence, they need to have developed the creative thinking and problem-solving skills to handle situations effectively without direction.

Leadership and (visioning) skills. In the workplace of the past, the key skill and activity was managing. Directives for the company emanated from the top, and work was managed (i.e., administered and controlled) down through the ranks and translated into action. In the flattened organization, leadership and visioning are eclipsing managing as the keys to getting things done and moving the organization ahead. In such an organization, all employees are encouraged to be active agents of change, instead of passive recipients of instructions; employees at all levels need to develop abilities to envision an improvement or a new direction and elicit the active commitment of others in order to realize the vision. This is particularly the case in companies with participatory management practices where employees throughout the company must be able to create a vision of how to improve their work areas and live out the company's quality vision in their day-to-day jobs.

Self-development and (self-management) skills. Finally, the skills of self-development and self-management stress the need for employees to take charge of their careers and manage their own development. As the skills needed for the workplace continue to evolve and change, employees at all levels must become committed to ensuring that they have the requisite skills, knowledge, and competencies for both their current and future jobs. The ability to manage one's professional life is now considered a learned competence—one that is the necessary condition for all the other workplace competencies.

What is striking about a number of these workplace competencies is how closely they resemble what was traditionally regarded as management-type skills. Essentially, what is happening is that new, flexible, decentralized organizational structures are pushing responsibility and authority downward in the organization, from managers and staff engineers to the rank-and-file workers. These workers must now know how to interpret information and apply it to their work. In other words, they must increasingly think and behave as managers. As the workplace flattens and the gap narrows between those in leadership positions and those responsible for producing and delivering the product or service, the role of the individual employee is becoming increasingly managerial in nature.

Figure 1–1, "Changing Organizational Patterns in U.S. Industry," describes a number of broad implications of the new organizational structures in terms of changed processes, practices, and requirements in companies. Among the implications shown for workers are broader roles and more demanding skill requirements. For example, a characteristic of the old-style organization is many job classifications, with each job being narrowly focused. But today there is multiskilling, job rotations, and fewer job classifications. Also, in the flat and decentralized work environment of today, the whole notion of basic skills is enlarging. Where having a command of the basic skills (i.e., reading, writing, and math) was once the primary objective, now basic skills are only the platform for developing the higher-order competencies increasingly necessary for survival, such as communicating with co-workers and customers, solving problems, leading a team to success, and ensuring one's career security as opposed to focusing on one's job security.

In addition to these changes impacting the rank-and-file worker, the role of manager is also undergoing a transformation. For managers, the emphasis is shifting from administering and controlling work to coaching and facilitating. The old style manager maintained and protected the bureaucracy. But today, a new breed of leader must be able to creatively dismantle an organization and then rebuild it. Figure 1–2 draws comparisons between the traditional and emerging functions of the old style manager and new breed of leader. Whereas managers were once used to having all the answers, they now must be able to assess which questions are most important. Further, they must be willing to experiment with new ways of learning to develop the capacity of those they supervise to come up with answers themselves. Importantly, they must shift from focusing internally on the organization to directing their energies externally and developing a mindset that is tuned into the bigger picture of what is going on in their business.

The dramatic transformations of roles and skill requirements throughout the organization affect the kind of education and training employees need. Indeed, in the 90s and beyond, the

FIGURE 1–1

Changing Organizational Patterns in U.S. Industry

Old Model *Mass Production,* *1950s and 1960s*	*New Model* *Flexible Decentralization,* *1980s and beyond*

Overall Strategy

- Low cost through vertical integration, mass production, scale economies, long production runs.
- Centralized corporate planning; rigid managerial hierarchies.
- International sales primarily through exporting and direct investment.

- Low cost with no sacrifice of quality, coupled with substantial flexibility, greater reliance on purchased components and services.
- Decentralization of decision making; flatter hierarchies.
- Multimode international operations, including nonequity strategic alliances.

Product Design and Development

- Internal and hierarchical; in the extreme, a linear pipeline from central corporate research laboratory to development to manufacturing engineering.
- Breakthrough innovation the ideal goal.

- Decentralized, with carefully managed division of responsibility among R&D and engineering groups; simultaneous product and process development where possible; greater reliance on suppliers and contract engineering firms.
- Incremental innovation and continuous improvement valued.

Production

- Fixed or hard automation.
- Cost control focuses on direct labor.
- Outside purchase based on arm's-length, price-based competition; many suppliers.
- Off-line or end-of-line quality control.
- Fragmentation of individual tasks, each specified in detail; many job classifications.
- Shopfloor authority vested in first-line supervisors; sharp separation between labor and management.

- Flexible automation.
- With direct costs low, reduction of indirect cost become critical.
- Outside purchasing based on price, quality, delivery, technology; fewer suppliers.
- Real-time, on-line quality control.
- Selective use of work groups; multiskilling, job rotation; few job classifications.
- Delegation, of shopfloor responsibility and authority to individuals and groups; blurring of boundaries between labor and management encouraged.

(continued)

FIGURE 1–1
Changing Organizational Patterns in U.S. Industry

Hiring and Human Relations Practices

- Workforce mostly full-time, semi-skilled.
- Minimal qualifications acceptable.
- Layoff and turnover a primary source of flexibility; workers, in the extreme, viewed as a variable cost.

- Smaller core of full-time employees, supplemented with contingent (part-time, temporary, and contract) workers, who can be easily brought in or let go, as a major source of flexibility.
- Careful screening of prospective employees for basic and social skills, and trainability.
- Core work force viewed as an investment; management attention to quality-of-working life as a means of reducing turnover.

Job Ladders

- Internal labor market; advancement through the ranks via seniority and informal on-the-job training.

- Limited internal labor market; entry or advancement may depend on credentials earned outside the workplace.

Training

- Minimal for production workers, except for informal on-the-job training.
- Specialized training for craft and technical workers.

- Short training sessions as needed for core work force, sometimes motivational, sometimes intended to improve quality control practices or smooth the way for new technology.
- Broader skills sought for all workers.

Source: Office of Technology Assessment, U.S. Congress, *Worker Training: Competing in the New International Economy*, Washington, D.C., Government Printing Office, 1990.

Concluded

issue is not simply training employees to learn another skill, but rather retraining them to perform broader roles in the workplace.

We've seen that the flattening of the organization and the resulting broadening of workers' and managers' roles are two fundamental workplace changes carrying important implications for corporate training approaches in the 90s and beyond. Yet another

FIGURE 1–2
The Old and New Roles

Old Style Manager	New Leader
The manager has all the answers.	The leader experiments with new ways to learn.
The manager has an internal focus.	The leader has an external focus—working with customers, suppliers, and universities.
The manager schedules and manages the work.	The leader coaches, facilitates, and "greases the wheel."
The manager has a handful of direct reports.	The leader calls on a myriad of teammates.

Courtesy of Quality Dynamics, Inc.

major challenge for companies seeking to build a world-class work force is the changed nature of the labor force itself.

LABOR MARKET DYNAMICS

Demographic measures indicate that the size and growth rate of the U.S. work force has changed dramatically over the past decade. The baby boom bulge is past and labor force growth has slowed. The U.S. Office of Technology Assessment estimates that the civilian labor force grew by nearly 3 million people each year during the 1970s, but has grown by only about 2 million during the 1980s.[3] In the next 10 years, the American labor force will expand more slowly than at any time since the 1930s. At the same time that fewer people are entering the labor force, the country is growing older. In fact, by the year 2000, the average age of the American worker will be 40 years, compared with 36 years today. Retraining these workers will become more important as the work force continues to age, especially as larger percentages of workers become subject to early retirement and seek to start second and even third careers in an increasingly demanding workplace. What's more, the number of 16- to 24-year-olds, the traditional source of entry-level workers, is shrinking (although this decline will reverse itself by the mid-1990s as children of baby boomers begin entering the labor force). In fact, the Office of Technology Assessment estimates there will be 27 percent fewer 16- to 19-year-olds in 1995 than there were in 1975.[4]

In addition, a growing percentage of the new entrants to the work force in the decade ahead will be minorities. The Office of Technology Assessment estimates that minorities will represent about 23 percent of the work force by the year 2000. Since minorities have traditionally been underserved by the educational system, they will undoubtedly pose a challenge for employers.[5]

While the makeup of the work force is changing, labor mobility is still high. The Office of Technology Assessment estimates that at least 15 percent of the work force may need some form of training each year simply because of job mobility.[6] Indeed, statistics show this churning in the American workplace to be exceedingly high. Of the nearly 20 million Americans who take a new job each year (in a civilian labor force approaching 117 million), only about one quarter claim previous experience in the same occupation. These tend to be teachers, managers, and technical and professional workers. American workers move from job to job, entrepreneurs start new companies, and existing companies grow and promote people. The resulting job mobility in the economy occurs with much greater frequency in the United States than in Western Europe or Japan. American companies, therefore, are faced with the need to continuously integrate new workers into their organizations.

These three broad challenges for companies—pressure to adapt to a more decentralized way of life in corporate America, broader roles required of workers, and a more diverse and more mobile labor force—have prompted innovative companies to focus on training and retraining their work forces as a means to achieve a competitive advantage in the global marketplace.

AMERICA'S COMMITMENT TO TRAINING THE WORK FORCE

The ASTD estimates that American businesses spend an average of $30 billion dollars on training, or roughly 1.4 percent of their payrolls. This less than 1 percent of the 1991 Gross National Product and averaged across the employed U.S. work force of 117 million, this employer-sponsored training is, at most, $385 per worker.[7] What's more, this $30 billion dollars represents an amount spent by 15,000 employers or one half of one percent of all American companies. Furthermore, the ASTD estimates that the bulk of the $30 billion training dollars is targeted to professional and managerial workers. Figure 1–3 breaks down the training expenditures by job category, showing that about two thirds of training dollars are spent on upgrading the skills and knowledge of college-educated workers with only one third spent on the noncollege-educated work force.

However, the far bigger issue is not the amount of money that American companies spend on formal training and development programs. It is, rather, the growing recognition of the importance of informal training and learning programs where training is integrated with work on the job. For example, when employees undergo on-the-job training, participate in peer training sessions or employee quality councils, or teach a training course, they are certainly learning new skills and new roles. These activities, however, blend seamlessly into employees' daily work and they are not separately accounted for or given a dollar measure. According to the ASTD such informal training is growing in importance, as companies realize that an increasingly large percentage of learning ideally will happen on the job and not be available for measuring and tracking.

Therefore, a number of innovative companies have begun to set a new measure: the amount of work time an employee spends learning new skills, either formally in a classroom or informally on the job. Currently, it is estimated that the average time an American employee devotes to training at a Fortune 500 company is 2.5 percent of work time.[8] However, this is the average, with some companies allocating much more than 2.5 percent of an employee's work time to training and others, none at all. Compare this to Japanese and German companies who regularly allocate about 8 to 10 percent of an employee's work time to training and development, and we begin to understand the advantage these countries have had in both productivity and competitiveness.[9]

FIGURE 1–3
Two Thirds of Company Training Dollars Go to the College Educated

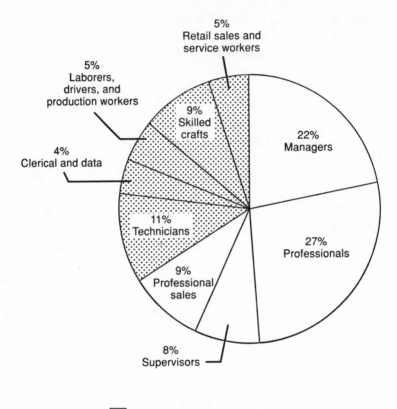

Distribution of $30 billion formal training expenditures

College-educated jobs (30%)

Noncollege-educated jobs (70%)

Source: American Society for Training and Development.

America's Commitment to Training Compared to German and Japanese Competitors

For comparison, it's enlightening to take a look at just how different our economic rivals, Germany and Japan, view training and developing their work force. While German and Japanese companies rely on vastly different training systems to train their workers, the net effect is much the same. Companies in both countries stress a strong culture and tradition of learning and training, employees are trained to do more than one job, and, most important of all, companies in these countries view training and learning as a continuous process whereby learning happens as part and parcel of every worker's job rather than in an isolated formal training program.

For example, in Germany companies embrace broad, ongoing training as a way to enhance productivity, quality, and competitiveness. The average amount devoted to training totals $633 per worker. Key to this investment by German companies is their common practice of pooling resources with the country's strong industry and trade associations to share the costs and benefits of training. In Germany, a partnership of employer associations, labor unions, and the federal and local government agencies design, deliver, and pay for apprenticeships and retraining. While the training curriculum for these apprenticeships is set by the federal government on the advise of employers and labor union officials, the practical implementation is on the local level, in the hands of the Chamber of Industry and Commerce, to which all German firms belong and pay dues. How is this extensive training paid for? The country's 4 percent payroll tax—half charged to the company and half to the employee—goes to the Federal Employment Institute. While most of the Institute's budget is used to support unemployed workers, about 20 percent is targeted for training and retraining of the West German work force.[10]

In fact, Germany's apprenticeship programs are often thought to be the best of any major economy. As the book *Made in America*, by Michael Dertouzos, Richard Lester, Robert Solow, and the MIT Commission on Industrial Productivity, points out, West Germans enjoy the benefits of impressive established transition programs that help young people make the transition from school to the job through a mix of education within companies and special vocational courses.[11]

Indeed, an estimated 60 percent of the German work force participates in some type of apprenticeship program. Germany, with a quarter of America's population, boasts 1.7 million apprenticeships in more than 400 occupations where on-the-job training is combined with classroom instruction often lasting up to three years. In addition, the curriculum of each apprenticeship program is developed by officials from government, employers' associations, and trade unions and is regularly revised to keep it up to date with changes in technology and competitive forces.[12]

But as Ray Marshall and Marc Tucker illustrate in their book, *Thinking for a Living*, the German apprenticeship system does not operate in isolation. Its foundation is a combination of a first-rate educational system and jobs structured so that young German apprentices have an opportunity to show off their high skills. These German apprentices not only receive an outstanding academic preparation as students, but they are trained early in a skills-development program called *Arbeitslehre* where they learn various skills and requirements needed by local businesses. This solid preparation is then combined with jobs structured so that German apprentices can use a broad array of problem-solving skills, which lead up the career ladder.[13]

In other words, German apprenticeship programs do not solely produce better-trained workers, but workers who can and do work at more demanding jobs, ultimately resulting in productivity growth. As Marshall and Tucker point out, investing in training and apprenticeship programs is really only one part of the human capital puzzle. The equally bigger challenge is to design high-performance work systems, as well as systems for child support and public health, which assure the development of a first-class work force.

Another culture in which training is given high priority is Japan. There, education and training are integrated into an employee's work life. In Japan, training represents far more than a means for career advancement. In a culture which exalts lifelong learning to the highest degree, training is a continual pursuit. In Japan, job training is planned and provided by each individual company, instead of being organized by national programs, as in Germany. Both large and small Japanese firms pursue training with unmatched zeal and enthusiasm. They see skill acquisition as a way to develop an employee's human capabilities over the long term and, only secondarily, as a means to prepare employees for specific jobs.

The chief objective of much of Japanese training is to spread the philosophy, culture, and traditions of the company and then to impart skills related to specific jobs. Companies use line managers and supervisors to deliver much of this training. (This approach is slowly being adopted by such companies as Motorola, Corning, Xerox, Intel, and others interviewed for this book.) This approach has been enormously successful in not only teaching job skills, but spreading the corporate culture and corporate values throughout the organization.

In addition to motivational and on-the-job training programs, Japanese companies provide training through job rotation. For example, all new engineers hired at Sanyo must spend some time in sales and in rotations between research and manufacturing.[14] Furthermore, Japanese companies organize a myriad of informal learning programs. Employees participate in councils and suggestion programs organized to explore ways in which employees' work lives can be improved. Perhaps the most documented of these Japanese employee suggestion systems is the Toyota suggestion system where, according to Yuzo Yasuda in his book *40 Years, 20 Million Ideas*, Toyota workers are trained in the how-to's of making suggestions to improve their work areas; this has resulted in more than 20 million ideas generated from employees. Making improvements to one's job has been considered one of the keys to Japanese industrial strength.

Probably, however, the biggest distinction between American and Japanese companies with regard to training is how they view the training experience—whether delivered in a formal program or informally on the job. Japanese companies view training as a lifelong endeavor necessary for competitive dominance in the global marketplace. As Marshall and Tucker illustrate in *Thinking for a Living*, both Japan and Germany have become societies whose *members think for a living*, and where the skills of the work force are perceived to be a vitally important asset.[15]

This is in sharp contrast to many American companies, who often take the narrow view that training is a finite activity to develop a specific skill. In fact, historically, when young Americans received training by their employers, the focus has been on refining or upgrading a specific skill that could be put into service immediately. This practice has tended to produce narrowly skilled workers who are vulnerable to rapid obsolescence. In addition, vocational training has traditionally been given a much lower priority here than elsewhere. American apprenticeship training, for example, has been limited in scope, reaching only 0.1 percent of the work force and mostly in unionized construction and manufacturing jobs. Often, American apprenticeship programs are not viewed as a viable preemployment training system and, in some cases, just having participated in some vocational programs in the United States can often stigmatize a worker in the eyes of a prospective employer. But this attitude is changing and will continue to change as American politicians take a renewed interest in developing stronger vocational educational programs.

In fact, the issue of vocational training is an interesting one in light of some surprising statistics regarding the educational requirements of American jobs published in a 1990 report by the National Center on Education and the Economy. The report held that, while most Americans hold a college education in high esteem, by the year 2000, 70 percent of all jobs will not require a college education.[16] The issue of vocational training will receive increased attention as employers grapple with how to help young Americans entering the work force make a successful school-to-work transition.

While German apprenticeship programs are often viewed as the model for developing American school-to-work transition programs, these programs cannot simply be borrowed or glued on to our training system. Instead we must carve out a uniquely American approach that seeks to experiment with a range of models for apprenticeships, preapprenticeships, career academies, and other types of vocational education programs. One of the important lessons we, as a country, can learn from German apprenticeship programs is the sense of urgency held by all the participants (i.e., German employers, labor unions, schools, and government officials) in experimenting and ultimately developing smooth school-to-work transition programs. The range of German apprenticeship programs have shown us that we can do much more to provide career options for our young people.

The Mission, Scope, and Nature of Training Is Expanding in America

Traditionally, American companies have focused their employee training on upgrading the skills and expertise of professional employees. During the 50s, 60s, and 70s, corporate classrooms sprang up in both large and small companies to teach professional workers how to do their jobs better. These educational infrastructures within corporations proliferated across the United States and became known as corporate universities, institutes, or colleges (not to be confused with Corporate Quality Universities). The goal was, in most cases, to keep professionals abreast of developments or, better yet, ahead of them.

The most sophisticated programs evolved in companies with large investments in technology. As Charles DeCarlo and Ormsbee Robinson stated in their book, *Education in Business and Industry,* "The most advanced corporate education programs are found in those industries which have the highest investment in R&D and where new R&D processes created the need for training and retraining of professional workers."[17]

These corporate universities spread across industries, and now it is estimated that at least 400 businesses presently include a building or campus labeled "college, university, institute, or education center."[18]

The programs offered at these corporate universities often included a cafeteria curriculum of hundreds of courses in new management, marketing, and financial practices and principles. In a sense, companies put a rich smorgasbord on the table for professional managers to choose the types of courses that "were right for them." Often, these focused on upgrading technical skills or knowledge for the company's managerial elite.

While professional and managerial ranks received abundant opportunities for training, other groups did not. Largely overlooked were the frontline workers who make a lasting impression with customers and, more often than not, determine a company's competitive advantage. As the ASTD showed (Figure 1–3), these frontline workers—the clerical workers, the receptionist, and the customer service representatives—have traditionally received the least amount of formal training and retraining. Whatever training they did participate in was occasional and usually tied to some event, like the installation of a new personal computer, a seminar on a company's new benefit policy, or orientation and safety regulations for new hires.

Gradually, though, as more American companies experimented with empowering their workers through total quality management programs and high-performance work teams, workers at all levels became more and more valued. Increasingly, frontline workers are being seen as a critical form of differentiation for an organization. In fact, a growing number of companies are now recognizing the need for excellence *across* the work force, not only in the professional managerial ranks. The theme coming out of a handful of companies in the mid- to late-80s was that increasing productivity is every worker's goal, not just the challenge of professional managers or the expert consultants. Hence, a growing number of companies have begun to perceive a need to shift their training and corporate education efforts from simply training one segment of their work force—managers—to training everyone in the organization and then going one step further by making every employee accountable for continuously learning new skills in the workplace.

Gerry Parker, senior vice president at Intel, presents a compelling example of this mindset shift. According to Parker, the point of corporate leverage has shifted from producing quality products to improving processes to improving the quality of the work force. As Parker sees it, "In the old days we inspected a product's quality with standards not nearly as rigorous as they are today. You see, what happened is the Japanese came in and quite frankly started shipping a better quality product. So, our customers put pressure on us to ship product at that quality level. To be honest, it was our customers and competitive pressures that ultimately forced us to change." Parkers goes on to say that the next emphasis was on the processes. "We quickly came to realize that we could no longer rely on our people to inspect for product defects. Instead, we had to revise our goal from catching mistakes to preventing them through a better process and that meant training the entire work force to continuously look for ways to improve the process."

This obsessive dedication to pursuing customer satisfaction and the need for process improvement, not simply product inspection, has become increasingly prevalent in a growing number of companies. This, combined with the realization that continuous improvement is everybody's business, is now leading companies to focus on the employee as the critical link in delivering customer satisfaction and ultimately profitability. To remain competitive in a global marketplace, many companies have realized that they must think of their employees as their most valuable assets and provide them with opportunities for continuous learning.

Increasingly, this realization has translated into companies taking a more strategic view of training. Corporate classrooms are moving away from offering a cafeteria curriculum of hundreds of courses to concentrate on offering training and self-development programs (in a variety of alternative technologies) aimed at developing the organization's core competencies. This emphasis on competency-based training is what will enable companies to surpass their competitors. Training within this context moves beyond an end in itself to a means of achieving lifelong learning for the entire organization.

Also, in this scenario, employees at all levels must learn to take more responsibility for their own self-development. Instead of waiting for their supervisors to sign them up for training, they must develop, in concert with their supervisors, their own individual development plans, outlining the range of competencies they need to be successful at their current jobs and those future jobs they may wish to be considered for within the organization. As employees become more dependent on skill development than on any one employer, the ability to manage one's career will grow in importance.

CORPORATE QUALITY UNIVERSITIES EMERGE

Some of America's most forward-looking companies are meeting the training challenge head on. The 30 companies profiled in this book (see appendix for a listing of these companies) share a common goal: to train their entire business chain, not just their professional managers, and to view training as a way to inculcate key stakeholders in the vision, values, traditions, and culture of the organization. These companies are expanding their Corporate Universities into Corporate Quality Universities, a term I have coined to refer to the expanded focus of training from simply upgrading the technical skills of professional managers to ensuring that all employees as well as key customers and suppliers understand the company's quality vision, and develop the skills and competencies needed for success.

Signature Characteristics of Corporate Quality Universities

While the Corporate University of the past decade existed primarily as a campus, today the Corporate Quality University consists of a process rather than simply a physical classroom. While some Corporate Quality Universities profiled in this book do have the trappings of a campus setting, like Motorola University, General Electric Management Development Institute, and Disney University, they have evolved to also reflect a corporate process for linking training to the organization's competitive advantage and to expand the target audience for training even beyond the entire work force to the members of the company's customer/ supply chain.

In essence, this Corporate Quality University umbrella for training has become a means of streamlining and systematizing the corporate education effort, as well as providing all the links in the organizations' employee/customer/supply chain with a core foundation in the company's values and quality vision. The goal has become to instill the entire chain with an understanding of the company's quality vision as well as a passion to continuously learn, so that learning happens as a part of an individual's job, either at a computer work station, working with a team of suppliers, in customer forums, or alone via a self-paced workbook or audio/videotape. The emphasis on promoting a spirit of continuous lifelong learning is what makes Corporate Quality Universities so different from the traditional corporate classrooms of the past decade.

In addition, the curricula at Corporate Quality Universities have evolved from a selection of generic business school courses to an integrated program built around the CORE workplace competencies that define the organization's competitive advantage. In numerous examples presented throughout the book, the curricula at these Corporate Quality Universities focus on the three Cs—imparting Corporate citizenship; providing a Contextual reference to the company and its customers, competitors, and suppliers, and the "best practices" of others; as well as developing CORE workplace competencies. While the specific competencies vary from company to company, a set of CORE workplace competencies have been identified across companies and industries interviewed for this book. They include the six skill sets identified earlier in this chapter—learning skills, basic skills, interpersonal skills, creative-thinking skills, leadership skills, and self-management skills. These CORE workplace competencies will be examined in greater detail in Chapter 4.

Essentially, the Corporate Quality Universities profiled in the book have expanded the scope and mission of training from enhancing technical skills to:

- Building a competency-based training curriculum for each job classification.
- Providing all levels of employees with a common shared vision of the company and its values and culture.
- Extending training to the company's entire customer/supply chain—including customers, suppliers, and even the universities that supply the company with its human talent (i.e., the company's new hires).
- Finally, serving as a learning laboratory for experimenting with new approaches and practices for the design and delivery of both formal and informal learning initiatives.

Now, let's take a look at two Corporate Quality Universities in particular, the General Electric Management Development Institute, launched in the early 1950s and reputed to be the first corporate university, and American Express Quality University^{SM}, launched in 1989. Each has come to play a central role within the corporation and illustrates several aspects of the University model of training.

General Electric Management Development Institute: "The Harvard of Corporate America." *Fortune* magazine has called the Management Development Institute "The Harvard of

Corporate America." But to the General Electric managers who came to Crotonville, New York, in 1955 for the first month-long program, the program was much like a "boot camp," where GE managers lived and worked together for the entire month without even being allowed to go home and see family and friends.

Ralph Cordiner, the president of GE in 1950 and later appointed its chairman and chief executive officer in 1958, is often called the "father" of Crotonville, as the Management Development Institute is referred to by many insiders. Cordiner realized that decentralization would most likely not take effect within GE unless GE managers had broad managerial skills. So, Cordiner's answer was to create "a place" where the top hundred or so GE managers could debate the nature of the company, discuss good management practices, and upgrade their skills in marketing, finance, and leadership. Robert Slater, in his book *The New GE: How Jack Welch Revived an American Institute*, says that Crotonville was originally created much like a command and general staff school to disseminate the virtues of decentralization.[19]

The early days of Crotonville were the personification of the Corporate University as a residential experience for the company's managerial elite. Essentially, the curriculum, back in the 50s, was a straight business school curriculum. In fact, the original textbooks created for Crotonville back in the 50s became legendary in the business world. The founding professors, which included the likes of Peter Drucker and some of the best and brightest from the Harvard Business School, ended up writing eight volumes on professional management, known simply as the "blue books." These blue books later went on to form the basic curriculum at many of America's leading business schools.

Today, Jim Baughman, director of the Management Development Institute, describes Crotonville as having gone through a radical transformation. Instead of aiming to build up the knowledge inventories of GE's top managers, Crotonville targets its training to all levels of employees—from entry-level college hires workers to top managers. The training itself no longer focuses on upgrading the technical aspects of one's job, but instead instills within GE employees a firm understanding of the GE culture, with its emphasis on speed, simplicity, and self-confidence. The hoped-for result of this training is not necessarily to learn a new, advanced skill, but to learn a process whereby all employees can become agents for change within their respective jobs.

The major shift in the Crotonville mindset has been from training directed to developing an individual employee's cognitive understanding, to active workshops where teams of employees come together to work on real issues and pressing business problems. The hoped-for result is not just skill enhancement, but the development of action plans to help solve business problems. Along the way, workshop participants grapple with unresolved, real-life problems, rather than case studies from Harvard Business School. In the final analysis, the measure of a program's success shifts from participants' evaluation of how good they feel about the learning experience, to how the experience impacts their particular organization back on the job.

In addition to expanding the mission and scope of training, Crotonville has also expanded its audience from GE college recruits all the way up to the CEO. In fact, customers and suppliers are also invited to participate in the workshops at more senior levels. As Baughman states, "The introduction of customers and suppliers forces us to deal with real issues, and we often start by addressing one simple question: "What if we were one system instead of company/supplier—how could we improve our productivity?"

Finally, the third major shift at Crotonville has been the development of a CORE sequence of learning, which is timed to key transition points in people's careers, such as joining GE as a college recruit, becoming a frontline manager for the first time, and so on. Rather than present each employee with a smorgasbord of course offerings, Crotonville has implemented a CORE development sequence that begins with new hires learning GE's values and extends through to the top GE officer population.

Indeed the payoff of this re-engineering of employee development has been impressive. Productivity, which GE measures by dividing real revenues (with price increases factored out) by real costs (after discounting for inflation) has risen 5 percent in 1991, according to Jack Welch in an interview conducted by *Fortune* magazine.[20] In the interview, Welch goes on to say that much of the increase in productivity can be traced to the company's emphasis on tying training to the strategic vision of the organization and then providing all employees with the tools for creating positive change and improvement in their areas.

This transformation of the GE Management Development Institute over the last 40 years is representative of what other companies interviewed for this book have experienced as well: an expansion of the mission, scope, and nature of corporate education and a commitment to no longer focus on the place where employees "go to get trained" but on the process of developing core competencies and using the training experience as a means for creating change within the organization.

American Express Quality University[SM]**: training starts with the Blue Box Values.**   If GE Management Development Institute illustrates a shift of thinking from training as an event to a process, American Express Quality University[SM], the training arm for American Express Travel Related Services (TRS) division, launched in 1989, illustrates the shift from simply teaching job-related skills to inculcating employees in the quality vision and values of the company. Probably one of the best analogies to understand the American Express Quality University[SM] is to think back to your days as a college freshman. You spent your first two years taking core courses and getting a foundation before moving on to pick-a-major area of specialization—American Express Quality University[SM] was designed in much the same way.

A CORE curriculum was created to be the "educational glue" binding together all of the training within American Express Quality University[SM]. This core curriculum trains all levels of employees within the American Express Travel Related Services division in the common goals, beliefs, and values that drive exceptional customer service. This dual emphasis of training in both the values of the company and technical skills is clear in the following quotation from Ellen Randolph Williams, senior vice president of American Express Travel Related Services, appearing in Quality University's 1992 catalog.

> One of the tools for success and professional growth is Quality University[SM]. In many ways, Quality University[SM] is unique. Like other training programs, it offers the opportunity to learn skills necessary to perform our jobs. However, it also provides an extra edge, that ad-

ditional key that gives us the opportunity to strive toward perfect customer service. This is accomplished by developing a curriculum that includes more than procedures, more than how to operate a terminal. Importantly, it features programs that highlight the values of American Express Travel Related Services which include providing exceptional service to both our internal and external customers as well as a spirit of entrepreneurship and quality.[21]

The launch of Quality University[SM] grew from American Express's desire to achieve exceptional quality and customer service. American Express recognized that, while the Travel Services Group was successful at training employees in the technical skills needed to perform their jobs, no official means existed to train all levels of employees about quality in the broadest sense of the word, like understanding how to handle each moment of truth with a customer, how to make decisions which always put the American Express customer first, and how to surpass customer expectations. So, Quality University[SM] was conceived based upon American Express's knowledge that employee growth and development are critical to attaining high levels of customer satisfaction.

Quality University[SM] delivers all of its courses packaged in a core curriculum followed by several specialty programs of study. The overall intent of this core curriculum is to provide American Express Travel Related Services employees with all the skills necessary to empower them back on the job to manage each customer transaction to the highest level of satisfaction. For example, the core curriculum is made up of several courses introducing American Express employees to the Blue Box Values of the company (see Figure 1–4), as well as training them in how to coach, work in teams, and manage for *Amexcellence*, American Express's quality vision. These American Express employees progress through Quality University[SM] much as they would through a traditional university. They take the core curriculum first and become well grounded in the common goals, values, and beliefs of TRS customer service. Then, they enter one of the advanced schools, depending upon their particular job requirements (these schools include the School of Customer Service, School of Leadership, School of Sales, and Academy of Travel and Tourism). The net hoped-for result of both the core curriculum and the ad-

FIGURE 1–4
*American Express Blue Box Values**

All our activities and decisions must be based on, and guided by, these values.
- Placing the interests of **Clients and Customers** first.
- A continuous **Quest for Quality** in everything we do.
- Treating our **People** with respect and dignity.
- Conduct that reflects the highest standards of **Integrity.**
- **Teamwork**—from the smallest unit to the enterprise as a whole.
- Being **Good Citizens** in the communities in which we live and work.

To the extent we act according to these values, we believe we will provide outstanding service to our clients and customers, earn a leadership position in our business, and provide a superior return to our shareholders.

---

*The values are known as Blue Box Values because they appear within the blue box of the American Express card.
Courtesy of American Express Quality University^SM.

vanced schools at American Express Quality University^SM is for employees to bond with the company and then learn specific competencies to make improvements back in their jobs.

The mission of American Express Quality University^SM is best summed up by the current manager of American Express Quality University^SM, Deb Robbins, who says, "The challenge for Quality University^SM is to be able to ultimately build a network of employees who share an attitude and philosophy about quality that enables them to turn it into a way of life in their jobs."

The two Corporate Quality Universities briefly profiled here, as well as the remaining ones profiled throughout the book, show the implementation of a new view of training, one that sees training as a process of learning how to create change and improve performance back on the job.

Increasingly, the theme emanating from the companies examined in the book is the need to move away from thinking about training as something done "to or for employees." Rather, training must be viewed as a continuous learning process where all the critical links of a company's employee/customer/supply chain develop a coherent view of the company's vision and values. As more companies think of their employees as human capital deserving of development and their customers and suppliers as key contributors also needing training and development, the Corporate Quality Universities profiled here will become models for scores of other companies to learn from and then adapt to fit to their particular businesses.

Chapter Two

The Organizing Principles of a Corporate Quality University

HOW THE UNIVERSITY MODEL WORKS

At the heart of each Corporate Quality University profiled in this book is a basic tenet that defines the University approach as:

> A Corporate Quality University is a process where all levels of employees, as well as key customers and suppliers, are involved in continuous lifelong learning to improve their performance on the job.

Corporate Quality Universities come in many shapes and sizes. Some, such as Motorola University, have a campus setting at each major Motorola site worldwide. Others, such as CMDS Teams University, First of America Quality Service University, Intel University, and Sprint's University of Excellence^{SM}, have no campus at all. Instead, these companies hve committed to the university model as an expression of their training philosophy and commitment to continuous learning. As a group, Corporate Quality Universities provide a state-of-the-art learning environment for their own employees and, in many cases, for select members of their customer/supply chain: customers, suppliers, and even the educational institutions that supply the company with its human talent.

To build a top-flight work force, companies such as those profiled in this book have adopted the university model as a way to systemize and streamline their training and development efforts. Just as each state relies on some form of the traditional university model to systemize higher education and avoid unnecessary duplication, companies with Corporate Quality Universities employ the corporate university model to organize their training activities into one cohesive, purposeful whole.

The Corporate Quality Universities profiled in this book are in various stages of development and maturity. Some, such as Motorola University and Disney University, are several decades old and are widely regarded as models for the university approach to training. (Indeed, both companies now offer seminars to outside companies.) Others, such as the Quality Service University of The First of America Bank Corporation and Target University of Target Stores, are more recent arrivals on the scene, having been launched by their respective organizations within the last three years.

While these Corporate Quality Universities differ in many of their more-surface aspects, they tend to organize themselves around similar principles and goals in pursuit of their overall objective—to serve as the vehicle for developing a best-in-class work force. These clear-cut goals and principles seem to lie at the heart of Corporate Universities' power to galvanize employees into the kind of first-rate work force envisioned.

The following five core principles form the foundation of the University infrastructure:

- Link training to the strategic needs of the business.
- Train the entire customer/supply chain. This includes key customers, product suppliers, and schools who provide tomorrow's workers.
- Design the curriculum to incorporate the three Cs: Corporate citizenship, Contextual framework, and Competencies.
- Consider the University model to be a process rather than a place.
- Experiment with new ways of learning and postlearning reinforcement.

Now, let's take a close look at these principles in action.

Design Competency-Based Training

The University model is competency-based and links training to the strategic needs of the business. In the 1980s,

Motorola dramatically increased its commitment to training all levels of employees, from managers to manufacturing operators. The company's return on this investment increased much faster than the expense. Why? Because the training at Motorola University supported the core competencies required for Motorola's quality vision of achieving total customer satisfaction. Bob Galvin, Motorola's chairman of the executive committee, claims the training really had no real up-front cost because it paid off in improved performance so quickly and effectively. As Galvin says in the book, *Quality or Else*, "Executives must engage in an act of faith that training will not cost them any money. They will rotate some dollars to a line item called training in the budget, but they will get benefits back which far outweigh the cost put in."[1] While Galvin calls the dollars spent on training and education an investment, Bill Wiggenhorn, the president of Motorola University, has the numbers to confirm this statement. "In the plants where Motorola workers learned the core competencies and where managers understood and supported the program," says Wiggenhorn, "every $1 spent on training returned about $33."[2]

In essence, Motorola deliberately set out to design a training strategy to develop, maintain, and update the core competencies needed to sustain their competitive advantage. In the case of Motorola, the company has staked out its competitive advantage by emphasizing manufacturing efficiency through quality and cycle-time reduction. In turn, Motorola has translated this objective into a series of competency centers set up to train Motorolans as well as select customers and suppliers in the company's core competencies which include manufacturing technology, software, management, executive education, sales/marketing, and product engineering, quality and culture (culture is defined as both training Motorolans in the company's culture of prudent risk taking as well as translating Motorola University's training programs into various countries around the world). Each competency center then puts together a team of instructional design professionals, developers, and subject matter experts to develop a specific training program around the core competencies.

Secretary of Labor Robert Reich reinforces the importance of linking training to the strategic needs of the company when he says, "The only real competitive advantage a company has in the 90s is the knowledge and competencies of its work force."[3]

Clay Carr, in his book *Smart Training,* expresses a similar idea:

The ability of any firm to compete in today's dynamic economy stems from its ability to develop, maintain, and increase the competence necessary not only to preserve its current position but to identify and respond successfully to the new opportunities the market presents.[4]

It is critical to remember an organization's core competencies are dynamic and will change as the competitive marketplace changes. Companies must realize that the process of defining core competencies required in workers is an iterative one. They must continually identify, refine, and update their core competencies and adjust their training and development programs accordingly.

Effective training is systemwide training, that is, it addresses not only employees, but also key members of the company's customer/supply chain, which can include customers, product suppliers, and local schools, such as K–12 school systems, as well as colleges and universities.

Effective Training Is Systemwide. The term *systemwide training* may sound like just another grand-sounding slogan for the 90s, but the concept behind the idea is a powerful one. A systemwide approach involves proactively training and educating the key participants in the company's customer/supply chain. The reasoning behind this practice is that, if all the critical members of the chain understand the company's vision, values, mission, and quality goals, as well as the individual workplace competencies supporting its competitive advantage, the company is better able to meet its business objectives.

This systemwide approach is continuous and open-ended. In other words, rather than offering X-amount of training and then thinking the job of training is over, companies who adopt this approach develop a learning system which enables employees, customers, suppliers, and key universities to continually engage in learning and development opportunities.

The combination of an internal and an external focus inherent in the University philosophy often redefines the nature of relationships between a company and its product suppliers, customers, and educational suppliers. For example, in many companies the traditional view of product or material suppliers holds them more as adversaries than partners, a view that can create mistrust, fear, and frustration on both sides and impede long-term quality improvements. The supplier training programs now offered at places like Motorola University and Intel University address a fundamental fact: often, many of a company's quality problems are really specification and design issues that can be alleviated by bringing suppliers into the development loop at an earlier stage and offering them training to better understand the company's quality mission.

Companies with Corporate Quality Universities have recognized that the success of their suppliers and their customers is critical to their own success. Instead of treating suppliers as adversaries or, worse yet, like disposable diapers to be discarded when their function is accomplished, many companies are taking a far more enlightened view of the need to build partnerships with key links in their business channel.

Motorola provides an excellent example of how Motorola University has become a vehicle to establish an open dialogue with suppliers, learning from them and even teaching them the corporation's religion of Six Sigma.*

In an interview in the book *Quality or Else*, Bob Galvin uses the example of a plastics supplier to make a point about the need for such dialogues. A Motorola designer, he argues, will know what the plastics part must do, but the plastics manufacturer will have ideas on how to make it more efficient, more reliable, and less expensive because that's his or her business.[5] Now, Motorola University sponsors forums in which in-house personnel listen to suppliers as the experts in their fields and gain new ideas from them regarding issues ranging from new-product development to cost-reduction opportunities.

Evidence that this systemwide approach to training is gaining adherents can be found in the increased number of suppliers at-

---

*Six Sigma refers to six standard deviations from a statistical performance average. In plain English, Six Sigma translates into 3.4 defects per million opportunities, or a goal of 99.99966 percent error-free transactions—be it on the production line or in the legal department. In effect, the Six Sigma process means changing the way people do things so that products and services are error-free.

tending programs at Corporate Quality Universities. Take Motorola University as an example. By the end of 1991, 500 suppliers were trained each month and this represented a 25 percent increase over the 1990 supplier training participation. Adherence to Six Sigma has become the battle cry for both employees and suppliers at Motorola.

Corporate Quality Universities also target for training those on the other side of the customer/supply chain: the company's customers and intermediaries who sell the products to end-users. Corporate Quality Universities have become the focal point for building partnerships with dealers, distributors, and retailers and, importantly, designing programs aimed at helping them to become more successful in their businesses. The belief behind such training is that, as more products meet quality standards, the competitive advantage will go to those companies that have the best-trained work force—whether they are the company's own customer contact workers or the sales forces of its customers.

An example of this is the creation of Ford Heavy Truck University (detailed in Chapter 6). This University targets the Ford dealer network of principals, salespeople, and sales managers. Its mission is to increase the professionalism of all those who come in contact with end-users. In other words, by enhancing the success of its dealer network, Ford is creating a form of competitive advantage in selling its trucks. According to Jeff Kahn, director of Ford Heavy Truck University, training the dealer network is now viewed as a long-term business strategy, the goal of which is to develop the best-trained dealer team within the car industry.

Saturn Corporation is another example of a company focusing its efforts on training the dealer network. In fact, Saturn Corporation believes so strongly in training the entire dealer team—from the dealer principal to the vehicle attendant—that new dealers are required to pay for training up front, when they purchase a Saturn franchise. For example, after a Saturn dealer (called *retail partner* within Saturn) comes on board, the retail manager attends a three-day course, "The Saturn Difference", at Saturn's Spring Hill, Tennessee, training center. Here, retail managers learn not only how Saturn cars are manufactured, but also learn and practice such soft skills as active listening, problem

FIGURE 2–1
IAMS University Distributor Program

Distributor Sales Person	Distributor/Administration
Orientation	
Orientation to distributorship	Orientation to distributorship
Animal well-being	Job rotation: sales, telephone,
Animal nutrition	warehouse
Knowledge	
Iams product line	How to survey customers/accounts
Retail selling and merchandising	Build competency standards for jobs
Telephone prospecting	Small business management skills
Application	
Account development strategies	Effective staff meetings
Professional selling skill building	Performance appraisals
Enrichment	
Active listening	Analyze the competition
Negotiation skills	Coaching teammates

Courtesy of The Iams Company.

solving, and interpersonal communication techniques. Then, these retail managers return to their locations and train the entire retail team in the key elements of being "Saturnized."

This emphasis on customer training is not limited to companies the size of the Ford Motor Company or Saturn Corporation. The Iams Company, a $300 million privately held company serving the premium pet food market, has developed Iams University specifically to provide training to select members of the Iams business channel, including pet store owners, distributors, veterinarians, and breeders. Iams University conducts a year-long training program for distributors which initially focuses on providing them with skills and knowledge in animal nutrition and the Iams product line, and then goes on to train them in sales management, account development strategies, and negotiation skills. Figure 2–1 profiles the Iams University program targeted to distributor salespeople as well as the owner/distributor. Iams

University Director Jack Tootson believes this commitment to customer training is Iams's way of ensuring their customers' success and, in the process, their own success.

This notion of creating alliances with suppliers and customers is borrowed from the Japanese and is called *keiritsu*. In Japan, keiritsu refers to multicompany groups anchored by cross-shareholdings. (In the United States, companies are not going so far as developing these cross-shareholdings, but they are building alliances with customers and suppliers in order to ensure their overall success.) Such an emphasis on teamwork between companies and their suppliers and customer-control links in the marketplace will over time lead to innovation, better quality, and greater productivity.

Perhaps the most pioneering innovation evident at several Corporate Quality Universities is their use of the university to create alliances with the educational institutions that supply them with their new recruits each year. Why this increased emphasis on forging alliances with local educators? American companies engaged in global competition are discovering that they are competing not only against a better-trained work force abroad, but also one that has a stronger tradition of lifetime learning.

Therefore, the most forward-thinking companies, such as Motorola, Intel, IBM, and Xerox, to name just a few, are designing programs which impact the quality of the local school systems where they have a significant market presence. What these companies are essentially doing is considering the K–12 school systems and the local colleges as suppliers—similar to product suppliers—and they are taking steps to manage the quality of the end product, in this case the students. These companies are bringing local educators together with community leaders and their own business executives to suggest ways to improve the quality of teaching and, importantly, to ensure that the local schools and colleges teach the types of skills, knowledge, and competencies needed in the workplace of the 21st century. The goal of many companies profiled in this book is to create an awareness among the student population, from the earliest age possible, that continuous lifelong learning will be a reality of their entire adult lives.

One of the critical findings among the 30 companies examined here is that the local schools and colleges can no longer focus on just ensuring that students acquire the basic skills of reading, writing, and math. As Chapter 1 pointed out, these basic skills are merely the foundation for more learning. What is deemed increasingly critical for workers of the future is to develop higher-order skills and competencies such as problem solving and knowing how to learn. Robert Smith, professor of adult education at Northern Illinois University, explains, "Knowing how to learn involves possessing, or acquiring, the knowledge and skills to learn effectively in whatever learning situation one encounters."[6] Brenda Sumberg, Director of Quality at Motorola University, makes an important point about the need for such learning skills when she says, "Our workers will probably change careers about five or six times during their forty-year work lives."

These learning skills are at the heart of retraining and job redefinition programs. Since learning skills are best developed early in life, companies like Motorola, Intel, and Xerox are developing extensive partnership programs with select K–12 school systems and with colleges whose graduates will fill the ranks of their corporate work forces. They want to ensure that these academic institutions not only teach students the competencies they will need for tomorrow's jobs, but also the skills of how to learn and adapt to changes not yet foreseen in technologies and job functions. Some of the most innovative partnerships are, in fact, happening at the K–12 level. Motorola and Intel are two examples of companies going beyond providing scholarships and donating equipment to focusing on building systemwide improvements at the local primary school district level. These improvements aim to increase the quality of teaching and learning at the schools located in the target communities where these companies have major plant locations. Several specific examples of K–12 initiatives are outlined in Chapter 6.

Focus the Core Curriculum on the Three Cs

The curriculum of the University focuses on three Cs— developing Corporate citizenship, providing a Contextual frame-

work to the company, and building CORE workplace competencies among employees. One of the most striking features of the Corporate Quality University model among the companies profiled in this book is the increased emphasis on formally training all levels of employees in the values, beliefs, and culture of the corporation. Intel University features the Intel Culture Course; American Express Quality University^SM's program includes a course called "The Spirit of American Express." Regardless of the name or even how the course is designed or packaged, the goal is similar across many companies: to inculcate all levels of employees—from the clerical assistant to the senior vice president—in the culture and values that make the organization a unique and special place and then specifically define behaviors which enable employees to "live the values."

This emphasis on supplying training in the company's culture before addressing specific job know-how springs from a recognition that employees must "bond" with the company, understand the values, and know how to live by them so they can live out the company's quality vision from their hearts rather than just follow a set of instructions and formulas.

One of the goals of the Corporate Quality University has been to provide a vehicle for training all levels of employees in the corporate culture and values, so that they become a guiding force and, in a sense, provide a road map for employees to follow in their day-to-day jobs.

Intel Corporation, the Santa Clara, California-based chip and computer maker, provides an excellent example of how values can provide a central focus not only for training, but also for an entire organization's performance and reward system. Craig Barrett, Intel's chief operating officer, was recently interviewed on CNBC. During the interview, Barrett said, "Total quality is not new to Intel. When we started out in business 24 years ago, we had a set of clearly articulated values, and our definition of total quality is performance to these values in everything we do."[†] (See Figure 2–2.) Barrett went on to stress that, "We make a complex product and participate in a fiercely competitive market-

---

[†]These values include risk taking, discipline, quality, customer orientation, results orientation, and making Intel a great place for employees to work. A complete listing of these values and the behaviors associated with them is shown in Figure 2–2.

place, competing against the Japanese, Western European companies, and leading U.S. semiconductor firms, so we have had to take a continuous improvement emphasis to our business from day one."

Recently, Intel was awarded the Zero Defect Award from one of their major customers, NEC, in recognition of the fact that they shipped products over a 12-month period without a single defect. This was the first time NEC gave the award to an American company.

It is impossible to speak with an Intel employee without the topic of the "Six Values" entering into the discussion. As one walks around the Intel facility in Chandler, Arizona, one sees the Intel values displayed everywhere—on posters in employees' offices; in the company magazine, *Quest;* and even on the flip side of each employee's photo ID.

Training in these values is just the beginning for Intel employees. The values have become the lifeblood, the very soul, of the company. As Dick Ward, director of Intel University, says, "Many companies introduce employees to the corporate values in a day-long orientation program which also covers the corporate benefits, policies, and procedures. Often, this may be the last time the employee hears about the values of the company. But this is not the case at Intel. "We make a conscious effort to build the values into the fabric of the company," says Dave Hall, Intel's former Director of Quality Technology. Intel does this by stating in detail the behaviors that produce performance in line with Intel's values—behaviors the company encourages its employees to build into their day-to-day way of thinking and acting on the job. The specific behaviors tied to each Intel value are outlined in Figure 2–2.

Intel's performance review system makes innovative and effective use of the Intel values. Now, when an Intel manager writes a performance review on each employee, he or she must evaluate the employee's behaviors against the Six Values. Intel's Dave Hall is a fervent believer that the values and their corresponding behaviors must be continually reinforced throughout the company's ongoing performance management system.

In addition to reinforcing these values in the performance system, Intel also reinforces them in their reward system. While a

FIGURE 2–2
Intel's Six Core Values

Risk Taking

To maintain our innovative environment, we strive to:
- Embrace change.
- Challenge the status quo.
- Listen to all ideas and viewpoints.
- Encourage and reward informed risk taking.
- Learn from our successes and mistakes.

Quality

Our business requires continuous improvement of our performance to our Mission and Values. We strive to:
- Set challenging and competitive goals.
- Do the right things right.
- Continuously learn, develop, and improve.
- Take pride in our work.

Discipline

The complexity of our work and our tough business environment demand a high degree of discipline and cooperation. We strive to:
- Properly plan, fund, and staff projects.
- Pay attention to detail.
- Clearly communicate intentions and expectations.
- Make and meet commitments.
- Conduct business with uncompromising integrity and professionalism.

Customer Orientation

Partnerships with our customers and suppliers are essential to our mutual success. We strive to:
- Listen to our customers.
- Communicate mutual intentions and expectations.
- Deliver innovative and competitive products and services.
- Make it easy to work with us.
- Serve our customers through partnerships with our suppliers.

Results Orientation

We are results oriented. We strive to:
- Set challenging goals.
- Execute flawlessly.
- Focus on output.
- Assume responsibility.
- Confront and solve problems.

Great Place to Work

A productive and challenging work environment is key to our success. We strive to:
- Respect and trust each other.
- Be open and direct.
- Work as a team.
- Recognize and reward accomplishments.
- Be an asset to the community.
- Have fun!

Courtesy of Intel Corporation.

number of companies now require each business unit to perform a self-assessment using the Malcolm Baldrige criteria, Intel goes one step further. The newly created Intel Quality Award challenges each department to not only achieve a minimum score of 500 points on the Malcolm Baldrige Self-Assessment, but also to demonstrate a consistent understanding and role modeling of Intel's Six Values. The reason to inculcate employees in the vision, values, and culture of a company is a simple one—to develop a bond between the employee and the company.

This emphasis in values training is expressed by Connie Remenschneider, Corporate Quality Service Manager at First of America Bank, and one member of a team which spearheaded the launch of Quality Service University in 1990. Remenschneider says, "Since the inception of QSU three years ago, employee pride in being a member of the First of America Team has soared. As our employees have learned more about First of America's quality vision, values, traditions, culture, and, importantly, how the bank holding company stacks up against its competitors, they have reported a much deeper sense of belonging to the corporation and, in turn, greater satisfaction in their jobs."

Developing corporate citizenship, which is at the heart of what Intel and First of America Bank are doing, is modeled after practices at many successful Japanese companies. In Japan, many production workers go through a one-week, off-the-job motivational program to learn the company's values, beliefs, and traditions, often directly from the founder. The purpose of this motivational program is to build employee pride and bonding between the employee and the company. The focus of such training is more than a means of career advancement; it is targeted to building an employee population which *wants* to meet the company's strategic business objectives, rather than to be merely job caretakers.

Perhaps Motorola University is the ultimate example of building this corporate citizenship. At Motorola University, there are four functional curricula: engineering, manufacturing, sales, and marketing, and each of the four is divided into three areas: interpersonal skills, technical skills, and business skills. All programs begin with training in Motorola's quality vision, values, culture, history, and traditions. The goal is for everyone at all levels within Motorola to understand the company's mission: the

FIGURE 2–3
Motorola's Total Customer Satisfaction Card

OUR FUNDAMENTAL OBJECTIVE
(Everyone's Overriding Responsibility)

Total Customer Satisfaction

 **MOTOROLA**

KEY BELIEFS—*how we will always act*
• Constant Respect for People
• Uncompromising Integrity

KEY GOALS—*what we must accomplish*
• Best in Class
  — *People*
  — *Marketing*
  — *Technology*
  — *Product:* Software. Hardware and Systems
  — *Manufacturing*
  — *Service*
• Increased Global Market Share
• Superior Financial Results

KEY INITIATIVES—*how we will do it*
• Six Sigma Quality
• Total Cycle Time Reduction
• Product. Manufacturing and Environmental
  Leadership
• Profit Improvement
• Empowerment for all. in a Participative.
  Cooperative and Creative Workplace

Courtesy of Motorola, Inc.

achievement of total customer satisfaction. While the managers and engineers learn the specifics of Six Sigma quality, the security guards learn how to translate this objective of achieving total customer satisfaction to their job function. After being formally trained in the vision and values of the company, each employee receives a total customer satisfaction card (see Figure 2–3). Everyone at Motorola carries this card along with his or her corporate ID.

In fact, senior managers at Motorola have been known to start meetings by asking all the participants if they have their cards with them. As one Motorola executive says in the video, "In Search of Quality," "The principles listed on the card are integral to the way we want our employees to approach their work—not every now and then, but all the time. Total customer satisfaction must be the common language of the corporation."[7] The training Motorolans receive in the values, beliefs, and traditions of the corporation is essentially targeted to accomplish one fundamental goal: to provide all levels of employees with a common vocabulary in pursuing total customer satisfaction in their particular jobs.

Another important objective built into the curricula of Corporate Quality Universities is to provide workers with an understanding of the contextual framework the company operates in. This means that companies are actually designing courses in their Corporate Quality Universities to focus on providing employees with a background in how the company makes money; who the customers, suppliers, and competitors are; what the best practices of other companies are; how the features and benefits of the company's products differ from competitive offerings; and, importantly, how each employee's job fits into the larger corporate mission. This contextual reference provides employees with a big picture framework so they can understand how important their roles are in meeting the company's business objectives and profit goals.

Finally, the curricula of Corporate Quality Universities provide employees with training in a number of CORE workplace competencies that support and help define the company's competitive advantage. These CORE workplace competencies are a combination of the basic skills, interpersonal/communication skills, learning skills, and advanced technical know-how that employees must have to function successfully in a flexible organization. The specific skills included in these CORE workplace competencies are outlined in detail in Chapter 4, along with examples from the curricula of leading Corporate Quality Universities.

Design a Process, Not Necessarily a Place

Design a process, not necessarily a place. Corporate Quality Universities do not have football teams, cheerleaders, or grant degrees. In fact, many, like Sprint's University of Excellence[SM], Intel University, and First of America Quality Service University, to name just a few, do not even have a campus setting. But, in many other respects, they fit the model of a university described by Cardinal Newman some 150 years ago in his book, *The Idea of a University*. Newman wanted his ideal university "to mold individuals who could master any subject with facility."[8]

Corporate Quality Universities aspire to a somewhat similar goal. They seek to increase employees' aptitude for learning by instilling within each individual employee a *commitment* to life-long learning, and by providing ease of access for learning and improvement. A Corporate Quality University doesn't necessarily involve a large campus, or even an elaborate infrastructure. It is a corporate philosophy, a mindset, which focuses on providing all levels of employees with opportunities to continuously learn new skills and broader roles in order to improve their performance on the job. Traditional training looks at the learning process along a continuum with a beginning and an end. The focus has been on delivering X-amount of training and then the job of training is over. But the emphasis at Corporate Quality Universities is on encouraging employees to strive to continuously learn new skills during their entire working lives and, importantly, be accountable for learning these new skills.

But why call this a university? The companies that have packaged their training and development programs under the university model have decided the university approach conjured up the sort of expectations that matched the company's objectives. They wanted a university umbrella to systematize the training effort and centralize its development and administration, while experimenting with new ways for employees to learn on the job. These companies also wanted the university theme to create high expectations among their employees, as well as within the local community. As Bill Wiggenhorn says about Motorola's decision to create Motorola University, "The response from local educators in the public schools and universities was not only positive, it was enthusiastic. They took this to mean that we were serious about education, not just enthralled about our bottom line."[9]

Finally, some companies choose the university approach because it lends a certain cachet to the corporate training effort that is attractive to employees. Bill Wiggenhorn drives this point home in his article about Motorola University in the *Harvard Business Review* when he says, "Training, it appears, is not something we can deliver like milk and expect people to consume spontaneously. It is not simply a matter of instructing them or even giving them the chance to instruct themselves in home study courses or self-paced workbooks. Instead, you first have to motivate them to *want* to learn, and then to take that knowledge and create change in their respective departments."[10]

Peter Huston, the director of Hart Schaffner & Marx University (HSMU), believes the university theme has been successful in creating this cachet for the participants of HSMU. This is especially important to Hart Schaffner & Marx because the target audience for the university is not Hart Schaffner & Marx employees, but rather the retail salespeople who sell Hart Schaffner & Marx suits in retail stores. Huston reflects on this when he says, "Our students are the sales associates of our customers—like Dillard's or Jordan Marsh. Since they are not our employees, we realize how important it is to build a training program that creates excitement among these retail associates." Houston then draws the following analogy: "What's that line by Kevin Costner in the movie *A Field of Dreams*, 'If you build it, they will come.' Well, in our case we believe that, 'If you build it, they must *want* to come.' " Since retail selling is often regarded as an interim career, with retail associates supporting themselves with a sales job so they can ultimately obtain some form of higher education, attending Hart Schaffner & Marx University, which is eligible for continuing education credits at Eastern Illinois University and hopefully, one day undergraduate credits, gives these retail associates a status and cachet they do not have in their current jobs on the sales floor of Macy's or Dillard's.

While these Corporate Quality Universities have many of the accoutrements of a traditional university—a course catalog, a distinctive logo, and even, in some cases, graduation certificates and a ring—they have become much more than a way to package corporate training. Rather, they have become an important vehicle for a company's internal employees as well as its suppliers and customers to continuously learn the broader skills necessary to compete in the global marketplace.

Finally, the name *University* creates an ideal avenue to communicate with the universities of higher education. This is what many Corporate Quality Universities are currently in the process of doing. They are forming alliances with local K–12 schools and colleges to lead reforms in local school systems and in some cases to design training programs which are eligible for either continuing education credits or, in some cases, like American Express

Quality University^{SM}, college credit. (Specific examples are given in Chapter 6.)

Some Corporate Quality Universities carry the analogy to a real university one step further by forming a board of regents. If you think of the "product" of the Corporate Quality University as training which renders employees capable of improving their job performance and achieving better corporate results, then the board of regents or board of directors, as it is sometimes called, is simply an outside body set up to continually ensure that the product achieves its goals. Essentially, a Corporate Quality University's board of directors functions in a similar fashion to an outside board, by monitoring the overall direction of training to ensure that it is tied to the company's strategic goals. At Ford Heavy Truck University, for example, the Board of Regents includes Ford managers, dealer principals and, importantly, a core group of former students who have gone through training programs at Ford Heavy Truck University. It is this group of seasoned professionals which ensures that the training offered at Ford Heavy Truck University is continually improved and ultimately linked to the company's strategic business objectives.

Motorola has established several groups to oversee training at Motorola University. Each group has a specific role and a makeup appropriate to that role. The Executive Advisory Board is composed of members of senior management and corporate staff. This board formulates policy, sets priorities, and allocates resources based on the company's strategic direction. A steering committee, made up of senior training professionals from Motorola University and throughout Motorola, meets monthly to review the performance of Motorola University against the corporation's strategic plan. Motorola University also uses input from separate advisory councils from the areas of engineering, manufacturing, sales, and management, to provide strategic direction and give "from the field" advice on the educational needs of employees and the corporation and specifically how these needs can be met by Motorola University.

The University umbrella, in a nutshell, is the organization's attempt to promote the same spirit of lifelong learning that one finds in a traditional university. Some companies have adopted this university approach without actually naming their training and development effort a university. IBM and Corning are two such examples of companies firmly committed to the principles laid out in this book but do not speak of their approach in terms of a university. Nevertheless, they adhere to the basic beliefs of the university model. The goal of this model was eloquently summarized by William Esrey, chairman of the board of Sprint. Recently, he spoke about the formation of Sprint's University of Excellence^{SM}, saying, "It is more than a place or even an educational system. Rather, it is a living entity composed of trainers, trainees, curriculum developers—all role models committed to the continuous process of learning and lifelong development. Employees cycle through courses, exercises, and updates created by the University of Excellence^{SM} as a means of fulfilling their commitment to self-development."[11]

Experiment with New Ways to Learn

The University model becomes the focal point to experiment with new ways of learning and postlearning reinforcement. While Corporate Quality Universities have extensive programs in place to train all levels of employees in a set of skills, knowledge, and competencies, their real emphasis is focused not solely on training internal employees, but rather on becoming a learning laboratory for all members of the employee/customer/supply chain. These Universities promote learning in both formal training programs, delivered in a classroom or distributed through some type of multimedia, and from a myriad of informal sources: other employees, customers, suppliers, and even the universities that supply the company with its new recruits. Xerox Corporation has coined a phrase to connote this emphasis on learning as part of one's job; it is called *transparent learning*. At Xerox Corporation, transparent learning refers to building a spirit of continuous learning in the workplace so learning occurs as a normal and natural part of each employee's everyday work. The goal is to make learning as much a part of everyone's job as the work product itself.

Chapter 5 is devoted to exploring how some of these Universities experiment with new ways of learning. At the heart of this experimentation is a firm belief that training is much more than

merely passing along new information to workers. Instead, training should encompass learning about how others have taken action and improved productivity—either inside the corporation or
evident in the best practices of innovative companies. Across the
board, the companies profiled in this book share a devotion to
experiment with learning from a variety of sources in order to
build a spirit of continuous learning into the very core of the
organization.

This passion for experimenting with new ways to learn con-
trasts significantly with the emphasis of training in the past,
which has been on designing and delivering the most efficient
courseware to train a company's internal employee population.
This formal type of training, whether delivered in a classroom or
by some alternative means of delivery, such as satellite, video, or
computer, is still only a small piece of the puzzle. Rather, as
Chapter 1 pointed out, the mission and scope of training has en-
larged to include ways for the entire organization to continuously
learn or, as Peter Senge says in his book, *The Fifth Discipline: The
Art and Practice of the Learning Organization,* "to continually expand the capacity of the organization to create its future."[12] Companies must therefore go beyond concentrating resources on just
designing and delivering state-of-the-art training. Rather, they
must focus on providing abundant opportunities for all employees as well as key members of the company's customer/supply
chain to learn new skills and, importantly, to assume broader
roles in the workplace.

One technique for helping an entire organization to learn is
General Electric's Workouts. (Workouts are explained in greater detail in Chapter 5.) Essentially, Workouts are town meetings in
which a cross-section of 30 or so General Electric employees, from
senior and junior managers to hourly workers, meet together to
discuss ways to make improvements in their business. According
to Jim Baughman, the "father" of Workouts and the current director of General Electric's Management Development Institute,
the concept of Workouts was borrowed from New England town
meetings which give citizens a forum for discussing their concerns
with local politicians. Baughman stresses that the town meeting
format of GE Workouts was conceived in 1988, long before Ross
Perot popularized the concept of electronic town meetings.

The purpose of Workouts is to bring together General Electric employees, from various functions and levels, to devise ways to get more speed, simplicity, and self-confidence (i.e., the Key General Electric values) into their respective operations. Think of Workouts as structured ways for rank-and-file employees to meet with their managers and dream up improvements in their business operations. But is this training? Certainly not in the traditional sense of learning by listening to a subject-matter expert. But it is very much learning-by-doing and, in the process, tinkering with the organization's modus operandi.

Companies with Corporate Quality Universities are not only exploring new ways for employees at all levels to learn, as in Workouts, but also experimenting with ways to reinforce learning on the job. In the words of Judy Simmons, training manager at Sprint's University of Excellence^{SM}, "One of our most significant future challenges is to develop new ways to efficiently transfer learning to the workplace." To address this issue, all of the programs offered at Sprint's University of Excellence^{SM} include, in Sprint parlance, a Before-During-After (BDA). This means that each program offered at the University of Excellence^{SM} has a set of discussion issues the participant must consider Before enrolling in the training program, then, During the training program, the participant is encouraged to focus on these key issues and, finally, After the training program is over, a set of discussion guidelines is given to both the participant and the supervisor so they can jointly address how the participant will use this new learning in his or her current job. This BDA approach (see Figure 5–3) is credited with assisting Sprint employees in transferring learning to their jobs.

Executives at Corning go one step further in this postlearning reinforcement by encouraging each individual to self-manage his or her own career. Once a Corning employee completes a formal training program, he or she is responsible for rating his or her behaviors on an ongoing basis in a self-assessment questionnaire. This questionnaire rates whether one exhibits the behaviors in one's job consistent with the company's CORE workplace competencies. The thinking behind this emphasis on self-management is a simple one: The skills, knowledge, and competencies needed to succeed in a global marketplace will continue to evolve and change as companies go after new customers and new markets. Therefore, each individual employee must be responsible for ensuring that he or she is acquiring and improving upon his or her set of CORE workplace competencies. The company's emphasis on continuous learning must start with each individual employee within the organization so that the entire organization can become, in the words of Senge, "a learning organization." Ultimately, the success of an organization's efforts to learn will be judged on how well each individual employee redefines his or her work and achieves customer satisfaction either through his or her own efforts or in combination with co-workers.

In addition to helping each employee become more proactive in the learning process, Corporate Quality Universities also experiment with how to best cascade individual employee learning and successful best practices throughout the organization. One of the ways of passing along learning is to formalize the concept of role-modeling. Just as parents role-model for their children, demonstrating, by their actions (which are often louder than their words), what they believe and value, managers should also be effective role models for their employees.

The first company to popularize the concept of role-modeling was Xerox Corporation. Xerox Corporation pioneered the concept of cascading the message of training down from the top of the organization in its Leadership Through Quality effort. The cascading concept at Xerox means that as each level of management is trained, the managers become the leaders in training those who report directly to them. This means that Xerox managers are essentially involved in training on two occasions—first, as members of the manager's family group and then, second, as leaders of their own family groups. Xerox believes the benefit of this heavy involvement of Xerox managers is twofold—first, employees see their managers' involvement and realize their participation is more than mere lip service and, second, when managers are involved in the training effort, they can bring real-life examples and situations into the training environment. Training then becomes more than some intellectual exercise—it becomes an opportunity to share knowledge, learning, and, importantly, the "war stories" about how things really get done within the organization.

Many of the companies profiled in this book are taking the role-modeling concept and expanding upon it to include bringing successful peers into the training classroom to inspire and motivate the rest of the employee population. Take the example of Evelyn Schultz. She is a team specialist in the American Express Travel Related Services division and a 1990 winner of the American Express Great Performers Award. She is frequently asked to be a guest speaker in the American Express Quality University^{SM} orientation program entitled "The Spirit of American Express." This class focuses on exposing all American Express employees to the Blue Box Values (see Figure 1–4). The real benefit of having Schultz as a speaker in the class is to inspire new hires so they can see and hear how a truly outstanding American Express performer has lived the Blue Box Values in her day-to-day job responsibilities. Schultz's message to these new hires is to "Always look for alternatives in solving customer problems and never be satisfied with the first "NO" you get . . . always push on to really try to satisfy the customer." Schultz's can-do attitude led her to get money to a cash-drained college student in Moscow when Soviet officials would not allow American Express to send money into the country on behalf of their customer.

In Motorola's Manager of Manager leadership training program for middle-level managers, the highest-ranking executives, George Fisher, Gary Tooker, and Chris Galvin, from the office of the CEO, participate in the program as guest speakers to share their experience. The class, affectionately known as MOM, is an opportunity for Motorola's middle managers to learn firsthand about top management's expectations for leadership. Bill Faust, the program manager for MOM says, "In essence, the three top Motorola executives nurture, support, and encourage these Motorola middle managers to try a few new behaviors back on their jobs to energize and motivate their people."

These Motorola middle managers receive an opportunity to learn from the company's highest-ranking executives about how to drive the company's quality vision down and across the organization. Bill Faust, who manages this program at Motorola University, says, "Employees must understand that our emphasis on quality is really a new way of thinking, acting, managing, and working. And when they see the highest-ranking executives as role models of this vision, it comes alive for them."

This emphasis on role-modeling at Xerox, American Express, and Motorola has the effect of opening up an employee's mindset, of encouraging employees to proactively explore and innovate on the job. Ultimately, the goal is for training to become transformed into learning how to make improvements in one's work environment.

Essentially, the companies applying the principles inherent in a Corporate Quality University are creating a continuous learning system where the entire organization is learning and tinkering with new processes and new solutions. This "tinkering" is what Peter Senge calls the ability to run experiments in the margin. In Senge's article, "The Leader's New Work: Building Learning Organizations," he recalls a study commissioned by Shell Oil which examined the changes in the firms appearing on the Fortune 500 list. The Shell Oil study found that one third of the companies listed on the Fortune 500 list in 1970 had vanished by 1983. In fact, the lifetime of the largest industrial firm was estimated to be less than half the average lifetime of a person in an industrial society. But the bright light this study found was that those firms which survived for 75 years or longer made a point of continually experimenting and exploring new businesses and creating new sources of growth.[13]

Companies applying the principles evident in Corporate Quality Universities are doing the same thing—looking beyond just offering a finite amount of training for one target population—the internal employees—to building a learning system which brings together the key constituencies in the company's employee/customer/supply chain in the pursuit of continuous learning. The challenge, as expressed by these companies, is to create a learning environment where all the links in the company's business system understand the importance of continuously learning, so that learning new skills becomes part of everyone's normal way of thinking and acting on the job.

Chapter Three

The First Priority: Hire Smart

I ncreasingly, companies are beginning to realize that training employees in a set of CORE workplace competencies, outlined in Chapter 1, on its own will not guarantee improvements in job performance. While employees can be trained to enhance their basic and interpersonal communication skills and to upgrade their technical skills, the effectiveness of such training depends as much on the aptitude of the employee as on the quality of the training. What is required are attention, planning, and resources targeted to ensure that the *right* individual is hired into the company so he or she can reap the fullest benefit from the extensive training programs offered at Corporate Quality Universities. Accordingly, progressive companies who have committed to the sophisticated training epitomized by Corporate Quality Universities are exercising greater scrutiny in their hiring practices for all levels of the work force.

The reason for this increased emphasis on employee selection as the critical precursor to training at Corporate Quality Universities rests squarely with the changes in the workplace. The workplace of the past was a lot like the board games popular in the 60s and 70s. Remember Monopoly? A player went around the board, gradually accumulating hotels and properties along the way. A wrong move could lead to losing a turn or two. The pace was one of steady movement until finally someone accumulated the most money and property and won the game. Today, the business environment is much more dynamic and competition is a "war of movements." In a sense, it is much like an interactive video game, where the movements are fast-paced and the penalty for not anticipating enemy moves and obstacles is being wiped off the screen and disappearing forever, instead of merely losing your turn. Workers of the future need to understand that being flexible, multiskilled, and knowing how to think and adapt in the workplace is the modus operandi.

The common theme here is that the average employee will be required to contribute much more than in the past. The increase in workers' skills in America, driven by a combination of technological changes and increased participative management practices, has created the need for a new type of worker—one with a broad set of skills and attitudinal traits previously required only of managers and supervisors. As more employees assume management-type roles, companies are increasingly concerned about hiring the *right* individual.

Corning Incorporated, Motorola, and Saturn Corporation present three good examples of employing a scientific approach to employee selection for all levels of workers. These three companies have designed employee selection practices to make sure the people they hire will reap the fullest benefit from their training and development programs.

The challenges of hiring at Corning, Motorola, and Saturn are the same ones every company faces. How does a company identify and select employees who can thrive in today's demanding work environment? How does the company determine beforehand who is flexible, who has initiative, and, importantly, who possesses a can-do attitude which is the basis for persistence and perseverance? Historically, companies have felt it was impossible to judge attitudinal traits accurately. Hence, while everyone has long acknowledged the importance of such attitudinal traits in prospective employees, many companies have failed to build employee selection processes to deliberately screen for these traits. Instead, the usual practice has been to assess the more easily measured math, reading, and technical skills and to rely on reference checking as the primary means for uncovering important information about a candidate's attitudinal and work behavior on the job.

However, the companies cited here are breaking new ground in employee selection on two fronts. First, they are becoming as sophisticated in assessing their applicants' attitudinal traits and work habits as their mathematical and reading competencies.

Hence, they are making a science of zeroing in on specific behaviors and traits and then asking detailed questions to determine the presence or absence of key attitudinal traits. Secondly, they are applying these scientific employee selection practices to frontline employees, not just professional managers. So now, the assembly line worker as well as the engineer is going through an extensive selection process to ensure that the company hires the best candidate. Then, when this candidate comes on board, he or she can become a business partner to the company, instead of simply a hired hand.

MAKE A SCIENCE OF SELECTING EMPLOYEES

The task of transforming raw human talent into committed, eager recruits able to succeed in a flexible workplace begins with each company's employee selection process. The best employee selection processes incorporate three practices which have largely been ignored by many companies. They include:

- Outlining exactly the CORE workplace competencies the company is looking for in applicants and then designing an interview process which assesses each applicant's hard skills as well as his or her soft skills.
- Providing applicants with a preview of the nature of the job and exactly what to expect when they begin work at the company.
- Providing training to line workers in interviewing and employee selection so they can take on a major role in the employee selection process.

Let's see how some companies have applied these practices.

CORNING'S CORE COMPETENCIES
DOMINATE THE INTERVIEW PROCESS

Corning Incorporated likes to think of a competency as any knowledge, skill, set of actions, or thought pattern that distinguishes superior performers from average ones. In other words, a competency is what superior performers do more often and in more situations and with better results than average performers do.[1] Corning has gone to great lengths to identify the hard and soft competencies, as well as the associated behaviors that go along with these competencies, needed by the corporation. In the case of Corning, the human resource department spearheaded a competency project that started by conducting 240 interviews with top performers (these included both exempt and nonexempt Corning employees recommended by their Human Resource Manager) representing all businesses, all functions and all levels within the organization. The goal was to target the critical success factors for hiring, retention, career development, and succession planning. The result of the study was a definition of 26 CORE workplace competencies falling into three categories: key human traits, leadership skills, and operational attributes. These are outlined in Figure 3–1 and are known as Corning's Competencies for Excellence.

It's the key human traits—the first category—that Corning managers believe is the most enduring across various career stages. These attitudinal traits encompass such areas as an individual's self-confidence, persistence, and flexibility. Since these traits are recognized as vitally important precursors to achieving higher-level competencies in the leadership and operational areas, the Corning employee selection process starts by identifying individuals who have a predisposition to these key attitudinal traits. Uncovering such traits is taking on an increased importance at Corning and several other companies interviewed for this book as employees organize into teams to carry out work assignments.

One of the key tools used in uncovering each individual's attitudinal traits is the performance-based interview. Essentially, the performance-based interview asks prospective employees to describe situations, actions, and results in which they have demonstrated the range of traits the company looks for in workers.

The performance-based interview at Corning begins with questions specifically designed to identify prospective employees who have demonstrated in their past jobs a predisposition toward flexibility, persistence, and a high degree of initiative. Many human resource professionals agree that the best predictor of the future is the past. In other words, the "flexible" workers of tomorrow have a track record of being flexible or having a can-do attitude in various work and school assignments they have today.

Let's take a look at some of these interview questions to get an indication of just how sophisticated the employee selection process has become at Corning. For example, one of the key human

FIGURE 3–1
Corning's Competencies for Excellence

Key Human Traits
- Achievement orientation.
- High self-confidence.
- High commitment..
- Initiative risk taking.
- Persistence.
- Flexibility.
- Honesty and integrity.

Leadership Skills
- Accurate self-assessment.
- Relationship building.
- Information utilization.
- People development.
- Valuing diversity.
- Networking.
- Team building.
- Integration.
- Change facilitation.
- Innovation.
- Strategic influence.
- Strategic thinking.
- Visioning.

Operational Attributes
- Market/customer orientation.
- Planning and organizing.
- Problem solving and decision making.
- Priority setting.
- Quality results orientation.
- Technological curiosity.

Courtesy of Corning Incorporated.

traits that Corning, along with other companies, deems important is flexibility. But how does an employer know from the onset who is flexible? The following questions act as a guide to help interviewers assess the degree of flexibility in prospective employees.

Can you share with me an example of a time when you had to take on new responsibilities when you already had a full plate? How did you react to the request? What impact did it have on your performance?[2]

Next, Corning looks for individuals who are self-starters and who take advantage of opportunities as they arise. The following questions from Corning's interview process evaluate this trait in prospective employees.

Can you share with me an experience where you went the extra mile to accomplish a critical priority? What specifically did you do? What happened as a result of your actions?[3]

Clearly, what Corning is looking for are prospective employees who have demonstrated flexibility and initiative in their normal ways of thinking and acting on the job. In other words, they do not require "training per se" in how to be persistent or flexible. Instead, they have demonstrated time and again in previous school or work assignments that they are flexible and can initiate and complete the task at hand.

The recruiting lesson from Corning is a simple one: Know what you are looking for in prospective employees. Then, intensively recruit candidates—both professional managers and entry-level workers—who have demonstrated in previous jobs, extracurricular activities, and the roles they played in professional societies and organizations that they have a predisposition toward the types of attitudinal traits and competencies your company needs to survive in the marketplace. While a worker's hard competencies and technical skills are, of course, still critically important, more often than not it will be his or her ability to demonstrate persistence, flexibility, and initiative on the job that will give a company its competitive edge in the marketplace.

MOTOROLA'S QUALITY FOR HIRE PROGRAM

Motorola's Quality for Hire program got its start in Motorola's Arlington Heights plant in the late 1980s. The Arlington Heights plant, a facility which makes and ships Motorola's cellular phones, was opened in 1985 as a pilot site for a new, flexible style of assembly management. The making of cellular phones is an intricate process that requires plant workers to operate and maintain sophisticated new equipment and facilities to a near-zero defect standard. In fact, these plant operators are expected to know enough about the machinery they operate and the products they produce to troubleshoot problems. Where, in the past, industrial engineers would have been called to the rescue, now it's the Motorola plant operator who is supposed to do the troubleshooting. To help these workers handle the increased demands of their jobs, Motorola managers have adopted a participative leadership style of management where high-performance work teams work closely together on identifying problems and then solving them.

These changes in the workplace necessitated a new approach to hiring. The broader skills and roles required of employees at the Arlington Heights plant pointed to the importance of ensuring that the *right* employee was selected for each position. Bill Wiggenhorn, president of Motorola University, notes that, "In the old days, we simply asked employees, 'Do you have a good record of showing up?' 'Are you motivated to work?' We did not ask prospective employees if they could solve problems or work on a team. We just asked them to show up for work and be productive for so many hours."[4]

Motorola's Quality for Hire program was launched to ensure that both the current and prospective production workers had the workplace competencies Motorola needed to stay ahead of global competition. The Quality for Hire program differs from Motorola's old approach to hiring production workers. Now, instead of being asked rote questions about attendance habits and work experiences, production workers are carefully assessed for proficiency in the skills and competencies needed to succeed in a team-based manufacturing environment and to master as many as 11 different jobs within the Arlington Heights plant.

Sue Thompson, personnel manager for the Arlington Heights plant, estimates that Motorola now devotes as much time and attention to detail in hiring its *cellular manufacturing operators* (the Motorola term for assembly line worker) as the company does in selecting its engineers.

Essentially, the Quality for Hire program seeks to select production workers who have:

- Basic skills, defined by Motorola as being able to read, write, and perform mathematical calculations needed for the job of a cellular manufacturing operator. This includes such skills as being able to read written instructions; write instructions for co-workers; and compute decimals, fractions, and percentages. In addition to having these basic skills, Motorola cellular manufacturing operators must also have cognitive reasoning abilities to apply the information they need to the job.
- Problem-solving skills to reason and solve practical problems, follow written and oral instructions, and deal with situations in which there may be several variables.
- Interpersonal skills to deal with and work cooperatively in a team environment, be reliable and punctual, and understand and commit to continuously learning on the job.

How Quality for Hire Works

Motorola's Quality for Hire program starts with proactively targeting and sourcing prospective employees, rather than just placing an ad in the newspaper. Motorola's Thompson works with community organizations and agencies in the Chicago area, counseling on the types of skills, knowledge, and competencies workers must have both now and in the future. In a sense, Thompson is building a series of alliances with these community organizations and their members to help them understand what is needed for success at Motorola's Arlington Heights plant.

For example, one of the groups that Thompson works with is the Spanish Coalition for Jobs in Chicago. Thompson has invited several job placement counselors from the Spanish Coalition to tour the Arlington Heights plant and attend a seminar on the types of skills required of new employees. By establishing an open dialogue with the Spanish Coalition for Jobs and other referral sources, Motorola's Thompson is increasing the likelihood of identifying applicants who have the basic skills and knowledge needed at Motorola.

Once prospective employees have been identified, Motorola goes on to develop a number of screening procedures to assess each applicant's hard and soft skills. Hard skills, such as reading, math, and problem solving, are assessed when applicants take a three-hour basic skills test. But even before applicants take the test, they are screened when they complete their job applications. In the past, applicants for a cellular manufacturing operator's job came to the plant for an application and then went home and returned with the application completed. But Motorola personnel managers never knew if, in fact, it was the applicant who completed the application. Now, Motorola requires prospective employees to complete applications on-site; then they are invited to take a three-hour basic skills test.

Once applicants complete the hard skills portion of the application process, they move on to a soft skills test probing their work habits and interpersonal skills. Motorola's Quality for Hire program is built around a belief that a prospective employee's work habits and predisposition to work in teams with co-workers needs to be assessed along with his or her hard skills. The "Quality for Hire Work Habits" video does just that. It is a 45-minute video consisting of 15 hypothetical scenarios that might, in fact, occur at the Arlington Heights plant. The video was created based upon input from both production workers and their supervisors. The video presents hypothetical scenarios containing a dilemma and applicants are required to make choices about how they would react to discovering a product defect or resolving a conflict with a co-worker. The prospective employee watches each hypothetical work scenario and then answers a multiple choice question which attempts to uncover an individual's work habits on the job. Grading is then based upon what a group of Motorola supervisors expect in terms of optimal performance in the workplace. It is this 45-minute video which tests an employee's work habits that executives such as Nancy Rus, Motorola's vice president and corporate director of Organizational Development, point to as being particularly successful in identifying candidates who have a set of workplace behaviors suited to work in high-performance work teams.

Finally, the last enhancement associated with Motorola's Quality for Hire program is the way prospective employees are interviewed for a job. In the past, potential new production workers were given a short interview by the plant's personnel manager. But now, as more employees work in high-performance work teams at Motorola, teammates are increasingly conducting the lion's share of the interviews with prospective employees. This heavy involvement of frontliners in the employee selection process has benefits for both the current teammates and prospective employees. Current team members get a chance to participate directly in a decision which affects them; who will join their team. In addition, prospective employees get an opportunity to see their work environment, meet future peers, and understand what is expected of them before joining the team.

This heavy investment of time and resources in peer interviewing has yet another outcome. It puts the job of selecting a new employee where it should be—with the teammates with whom the new hire will be working closely on the job. These teammates are closest to the everyday work and have a better sense of the mix of attitudinal traits and skills a prospective employee must have in order to operate successfully. So, as peers become actively involved in the recruiting process, their judgment is on the line and ultimately it's up to them to help the new hire become a successful teammate.

Henry Turner, who leads the empowerment effort at the Arlington Heights plant, believes that these cellular manufacturing operators, in the final analysis, feel flattered to participate in interviewing peers. Turner says, "Our results with employee satisfaction surveys show that as our team members become more involved in various aspects of their work life, they become more satisfied on the job."

The employee selection process used at Motorola's Arlington Heights plant has been so successful in targeting and selecting production workers that a modified version has been designed for other employee populations at the company, such as technicians, secretaries, and clerical workers.

Motorola's Nancy Rus believes that the Quality for Hire program has achieved its original objective: to identify prospective employees who have the *right* mix of interpersonal skills and competencies needed to be successful in a Motorola manufacturing facility. The program has also accomplished something else. It has helped Motorola forge solid relationships with various local community organizations (e.g., Spanish Coalition for Jobs), and these organizations have become better informed as to the types of key human traits, skills, knowledge, and competencies Motorola is seeking in prospective employees. Ultimately, Motorola hopes to build a core group of referral sources who know precisely what the company is looking for in applicants across various job categories.

Rus points to rather significant results to prove just how successful the Quality for Hire program has been, especially when it is coupled with Motorola's history of participatory management. For example, Rus says that employees who have gone through this extensive program in employee selection and screening achieve up to 80 percent productivity within three or four days of training. Previously, it has taken new employees up to 60 days of working in their jobs and undergoing training to achieve this level of productivity.

In addition, many employees who have gone through the Quality for Hire program are able to solve problems at levels that were previously expected of technicians, supervisors, and engineers. This point is especially important because, as Motorola's plants move from five to six layers of management to, in some cases, one to two layers, the ability to take the initiative and solve a problem at hand is crucial to continue achieving increases in productivity. To date, Motorola has reported 78 percent productivity increases companywide from 1987 to 1991.

These results are not totally the outgrowth of the Quality for Hire program. But the employee selection program, coupled with Motorola's efforts in quality, cycle-time reduction, training, and participatory workplace practices, have largely been responsible for these dramatic improvements in productivity. In essence, what the Quality for Hire program has done is to help Motorola select the *right* employee so that continuous and consistent training can have its fullest impact on productivity.

SATURN'S EMPLOYEE SELECTION SYSTEM

The Saturn Corporation was launched in 1990 as a new subsidiary of General Motors charged with building a world-class economy car to effectively compete with Toyota and Honda. Saturn Corporation, General Motors's $3.5 billion gamble, was born. At the time, Saturn set out to create both a new kind of car company and, in the process, a new system to hire and train employees.

Saturn began with an advantage in being able to start from scratch in selecting its employees. While the labor contract did require the company to select its work force from current and laid-off GM workers, Saturn was able to choose freely from these workers instead of having its choices mandated according to seniority.

At Saturn, the work force is organized into teams, and Saturn empowers each team to manage everything from its own budget and inventory control to screening, selecting, and hiring teammates. Since each Saturn self-managed work team is the primary unit of performance, teammates actively participate in an intensive peer interviewing process.

What are these Saturn teammates looking for? A comment by Michael Bennett, president of the UAW Local 1853, contains clues. He says:

> There is something unique about the Saturn associates (i.e., employees). These people are risk-takers. They are the kind of people who want an opportunity to make a difference.[5]

This desire to contribute appears to be a common trait among workers who thrive in an empowered work environment. They want to make an impact and they try to really live the company's values and quality vision in their day-to-day jobs.

But how does a company go about identifying prospective workers who want to make a difference? Saturn has developed several techniques which make its employee selection system as sophisticated and scientific as its training and development programs. The basic elements of Saturn's employee selection system include: (1) providing applicants with a preview of the nature of a career in the automotive industry, (2) asking applicants to complete a rigorous paper-and-pencil test, as well as a face-to-face interview, and (3) having applicants participate in a two-hour production simulation which mirrors their actual job responsibilities working on a Saturn assembly line. Underlying these three employee selection practices is a firm understanding of the hard and soft skills Saturn is looking for in prospective employees.

Larry Nelson, Saturn's team leader in the human resources area, believes "Knowing what you're looking for is nine tenths of the job associated with hiring a new employee." Nelson certainly speaks with experience in the area of Saturn's employee selection practices. He was part of Saturn's Task Force 99, the team of 99 GM and UAW employees assigned to pilot the founding of Saturn. According to Nelson, one of their first initiatives was to study the employee selection practices of such world-class companies as Honda, Nissan, Toyota, and Mazda in an attempt to find the common thread in these companies' screening and selection processes. The thread uncovered among these companies was a strong commitment to a scientific employee selection process for both entry-level frontline employees and managers. In other words, these companies had a clear idea of what they wanted in all levels of employees and then went about selecting employees who matched their vision.

In Saturn's case, the Task Force 99 was able to boil down what Saturn was looking for in employees into four crucial skill areas. These are broadly defined as:

1. *Teamwork skills*—being able to communicate and interact with teammates.
2. *Problem-solving skills*—being able to prioritize tasks and use creativity to solve a problem.
3. *Openness to change*—being open and flexible to new technologies and new work systems.
4. *Customer orientation*—wanting to exceed the expectations of both internal and external customers.

Each prospective Saturn associate is then rated along a nine-point scale in the specific behaviors that go along with each skill area.

After Saturn defined exactly what it was looking for in new employees, company officials identified prospective employees by holding informational forums in local communities across the United States. These forums bring together Saturn line managers and representatives from the local Saturn retail network (i.e., the dealers) with prospective employees to openly discuss what's involved in the day-to-day job of a Saturn associate. By holding these forums, instead of simply placing an ad in a local newspaper and interviewing those responding to the ad, Saturn officials create an opportunity for prospective employees to learn about Saturn and what's involved in a career at the company.

It's here that prospective employees first learn about the Saturn Customer Philosophy, which revolves around creating Customer Enthusiasm.

> We, the Saturn Team, believe the single most important element of our business is the Customer . . . therefore, we must be Customer-focused in everything we do.
>
> To be truly successful, our sights must be aimed beyond providing Customer satisfaction, we must exceed Customer expectations and provide an unparalleled buying and vehicle ownership experience that results in CUSTOMER ENTHUSIASM.
>
> If a Saturn Customer requires information or assistance, we believe it provides us an opportunity to demonstrate that SATURN CARES about them.
>
> **Above all else, treat Customers the way they wish to be treated.**
>
> By continuously operating in accordance with our philosophy, we will stimulate positive word-of-mouth advertising, achieve conquest sales, create strong owner loyalty, and, most importantly, achieve CUSTOMER ENTHUSIASM.[6]

By giving prospective employees this type of detailed preview of the Saturn vision and customer philosophy, company officials hope to identify applicants who understand, even before they start work, the type of enthusiasm and dedication to the customer that are needed for success at the company.

After prospective employees have had this preview, they are asked to take a paper-and-pencil test measuring their hard skills in the areas of reading, math, writing, and mechanical and spatial relations. Then, after the written test, they participate in a two-hour production simulation testing their soft skills in such areas as teamwork, interpersonal communication, and a commitment to continuous improvement. The two-hour production simulation essentially involves one task: assembling the headlight of a car. But the simulation is structured in such a way as to mirror what it's like to work on a Saturn assembly line. Applicants actually assemble this headlight and then meet with teammates (i.e., other prospective employees) to suggest ways to improve the quality of the product and the work process itself. During this simulation, applicants' on-the-job performance is rated according to Saturn's four core competencies deemed critical to success—teamwork, problem solving, openness to change, and customer orientation.

Who rates the applicants? At many companies where elaborate employee selection processes are practiced, the job of interviewing and rating prospective employees falls to professionals in the human resources area. But not at Saturn. Saturn teammates are the ones who interview and rate applicants during the employee selection process. In fact, Saturn associates undergo two-and-a-half days of training in how to interview and rate applicants and are ultimately "certified" to be interviewers and assess prospective employees during the employee selection process. The major outcome of this heavy amount of peer interviewing, according to Saturn's Nelson, is that team members have a vested interest in ensuring that a new Saturn associate becomes a successful team member.

The three companies profiled in this chapter—Corning, Motorola, and Saturn—all have put into place employee selection practices which seek to "hire smart." In other words, these companies have developed scientific employee hiring practices for workers, whether they work on the assemby line or on the sales floor. While companies have traditionally spent time and resources screening and hiring professional managers, these three companies provide world-class examples of smart hiring practices for all levels of the work force. Notable are the creative ways these companies have devised to select prospective frontline employees, such as Motorola's "Quality for Hire Work Habits" video and Saturn's production simulation. If we truly believe that frontline workers hold the key to a company's competitive advantage, then identifying, screening, and interviewing these workers in a scientific fashion is crucial to building and retaining a world-class work force.

As the demands of the workplace require all levels of employees to take on more responsibilities, a company's hiring practices—especially for its frontline workers—will increasingly come under scrutiny. As these three companies have shown, it's no longer sufficient to look for prospective employees who have the "hard skills to do the job." Now, companies must also screen for employees who possess the *right* mix of soft skills, that is, being able to communicate with teammates, have a customer orientation, and be able to work in teams. Essentially, the smart hiring practices profiled in this chapter attempt to identify individuals who have a predisposition to work in a fluid and fast-changing work environment where soft skills are as important as hard skills.

Chapter Four

Formal Training Programs: What Corporate Quality Universities Teach

THE UNIVERSITY CORE CURRICULUM

As companies face rapidly changing technologies, increased customer expectations, and escalating competitive pressures, the workplace is becoming a dynamic, interdependent one, where thinking and acting must be done at all levels of the organization. These changes point to the need for a flexible work force with high levels of general skills, rather than a repertoire of narrow capabilities that can be applied only to a fixed workplace regimen. Workers operating within this flexible organization must be able to proactively anticipate problems, eliminate bottlenecks, make suggestions for improvements in their work processes, and, above all, ensure quality.

As Chapter 3 pointed out, companies are increasingly using sophisticated employee selection practices to identify, screen, and select individuals who have demonstrated in either their previous jobs or school activities that they have the *right stuff* for success in a demanding workplace. The next order of business is to supply the training that will transform these promising recruits into performers in their jobs.

The Three Cs of the CORE Curriculum

The training programs at Corporate Quality Universities represent an expanded effort to train all levels of workers in the skills needed in today's changing workplace. A key goal of such programs is to start to build among workers the knowledge and skills necessary to support the company's overall competitiveness. While each company's training program differs in its specific course offerings, interviews with directors of Corporate Quality Universities have revealed a set of key themes common to nearly all outstanding University programs. For the purposes of discussion, this set of common themes will be referred to in the remainder of the book as the University CORE curriculum.

Figure 4–1 shows the components of this CORE curriculum. Its overall emphasis has been expanded from simply teaching technical skills to building a set of CORE workplace competencies. This CORE curriculum stresses communicating the corporate culture and values; providing employees with an understanding of the company relative to its customers, suppliers, and competitors; and building within employees a set of CORE workplace competencies that define the company's competitive advantage. In fact, this CORE curriculum is what distinguishes Corporate Quality Universities from traditional corporate universities or corporate learning centers of past decades that have historically focused only on providing employees with the technical skills needed for their immediate jobs. The Corporate Quality University approach recognizes the importance of having a firm foundation in the company's values, culture, traditions, the contextual framework the organization operates in, and the organization's competencies.

Taken together, the CORE curricula of Corporate Quality Universities examined in this book promote employee development in three broad areas, termed here the three Cs. They include:

Corporate citizenship. Inculcates all levels of employees to the culture, values, traditions, and big picture of the company. Implicit in this concept of citizenship is a strong identification with one's company and the values, beliefs, and traditions that are central to the organization. This inculcation in the corporate cultural identity is similar to the approach taken by many Japanese companies.

FIGURE 4–1
The CORE Curriculum

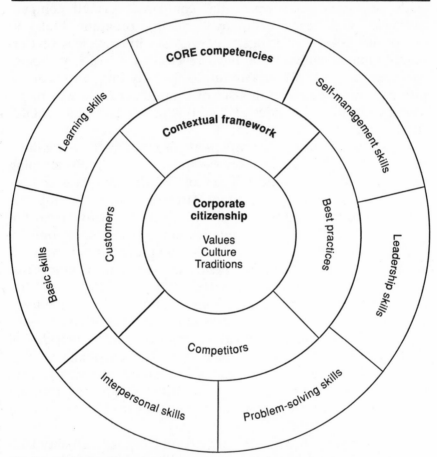

Courtesy of Quality Dynamics, Inc.

Contextual framework.   Gives all employees an appreciation of the company's business, its customers, competitors, and the best practices of others. Employees become grounded in the features and benefits of the company's products and services, how the company makes money, how its line of business stacks up against the competition and, importantly, how to learn from the best practices of world-class companies that determine standards of excellence within an industry.

CORE workplace competencies. Develops a set of specific workplace competencies that define the company's competitive advantage. The common CORE workplace competencies identified by companies interviewed for this book include:

Learning skills. Knowing how to understand and manipulate new information quickly and confidently. Above all, showing a commitment to self-development and constantly improving one's ability to learn new skills and competencies.

Basic skills. Possessing the basic skill set of reading, writing, and mathematical computations necessary to handle the increased demands of all jobs.

Interpersonal skills. Knowing how to listen and communicate with co-workers and customers, resolve conflicts constructively, negotiate, and, importantly, network inside and outside the organization.

Creative thinking and problem-solving skills. Knowing how to recognize and define problems, implement solutions, and track and evaluate results. Above all, possessing the cognitive reasoning skills necessary to transcend sequential thinking and leap to creative solutions.

Leadership and visioning. Being able to empower co-workers and "envision, energize, and enable" a group or team to achieve the corporation's business initiatives. Knowing how to value a diverse work force and, importantly, how to recognize co-workers in a timely and appropriate fashion for a job well done.

Self-development/self-management. Having the ability to proactively manage one's own development and career, rather than to just passively follow a training plan laid out by one's manager.

Let's examine in detail how these Three Cs of the CORE curriculum are translated into action within the curricula of some specific Corporate Quality Universities.

CORPORATE CITIZENSHIP

Know the Corporate Values, Culture, Big Picture, and Traditions of the Company

The concept of ordinary citizenship implies a degree of identification with one's city or country that comes in part from a close familiarity with its values, customs, and culture. Progressive companies want to cultivate in their work forces a similar sense of connectedness and pride, and they are doing this by *formally* training employees in the corporation's unique values, culture, traditions and the specific employee behaviors that go along with "living the values" on the job.

Corporate values take center stage at Intel. Intel's definition of quality is a simple one: performance expressing the company values. At Intel, dedication to values involves a combination of designing programs at Intel University to train all levels of employees in the company values and culture, as well as ensuring that the company's performance measurements reinforce living the values.

This emphasis on values isn't a new phenomenon at Intel. Intel executives have emphasized the importance of its six central values (detailed in Figure 2–2) as a foundation for all training since the inception of the company 24 years ago. Over the years, however, Intel discovered that simply stating its values as a set of generic principles was not enough to produce the kind of work performance consistent with these values. So, over time, Intel senior managers came to understand that in order for employees to really "get it," top management had to paint a vivid, detailed picture of the type of organization they wanted Intel to be.

Over the past few years, Intel has defined its six core values and the specific behaviors that translate them into action, in order to guide employees in their day-to-day decision making. For example, one of Intel's values is Customer Orientation. Employees are given a specific breakdown of exactly the type of behaviors required to actualize this corporate value.

Intel's definition of customer satisfaction

- Listen to customers and suppliers
  Carefully listen to input and requests from customers and suppliers.

Actively seek feedback to learn from customers/suppliers.
Directly address customer problems and issues.

• Communicate mutual intentions and expectations
Communicate which needs can be met and which cannot.
Look for solutions.
Conduct updates on a regular basis.
Make clear and mutual agreements.

• Deliver innovative and competitive products/services
Meet or exceed customer expectations.
Demonstrate a sense of urgency.
Emphasize customer satisfaction in all aspects of business.
Deliver products and services on time.
Help the customer find the right answer to meet his or
her needs.

• Make it easy to work with us
Be responsive and courteous to customers/suppliers.
Treat customers/suppliers fairly.
Honor commitments.[1]

Each of the six values is as detailed as the preceding customer
orientation one. Intel employees then spend a total of 10 classroom hours over their first 15 months with the company discussing these values with co-workers and trainers (in most cases, the
trainers are Intel senior managers), and specifically examining
how to live these values in their day-to-day jobs. This training in
values does not stop with exposure in the classroom. Intel line
managers managing new employees are also brought into the
loop. They are encouraged to spend the first month orienting the
new employee to the organization, its values, and, specifically,
how the annual performance evaluation measures employees'
performance against the six values. In other words, managers inculcate employees in the Intel values before they focus them on
their immediate job duties.

Finally, these values are built into the performance evaluation
process so employees and their supervisors can track an employee's performance against the designated behaviors associated
with each Intel value.

Focus on values from day one: Intel's orientation process.
Intel's orientation process is the vehicle for painting a vivid picture of the company and the values that lie at its heart. Intel's

orientation spans the first 15 months of a new hire's tenure with the company and seeks to inculcate in new employees the values, vision, and culture of the company in a way similar to orientation practices at many Japanese firms.

Indeed, Intel's present orientation process came out of a study Intel executives made of orientation practices at Japanese companies. At the time of the study in the early 80s, the typical assembly worker in the United States was receiving four to five days of orientation and training when hired. Intel was running about double this, offering their employees about two weeks of orientation and training at the beginning of their tenure.

Intel's executives were astounded to see how Intel's orientation, which they considered extensive, paled in comparison to efforts at Japanese firms. The average Japanese production worker receives six months of orientation and training at the beginning of his employment with the company. After hiring in, Japanese production workers typically begin with a week or so in an off-the-job motivational program. These programs are intended to impart the essentials of the company's history, values, beliefs, culture, and philosophy—in many cases, based on the thoughts and beliefs of the original founder.

The Japanese system instills a remarkable sense of pride among new hires in working for the company. Japanese orientation programs are directed to the "hearts" of employees before they learn the specific skills needed for their jobs. Then, gradually, these employees participate in a series of on-the-job seminars, job rotations, and formal training programs along with some production work. So by the end of six months of orientation and training, these new hires at Japanese firms understand not only their own and the other workers' job, but also how all the jobs fit into the overall corporate mission and scheme.

Since conducting its study, Intel has revised its orientation process. Intel employees participate in seven orientation seminars offered under the Intel University umbrella, enrolling in each one at designated points during their first 15 months with the company. What makes these seminars particularly valuable for new hires is that about 90 percent of the facilitators conducting the seminars are Intel senior and mid-level managers. So, these courses are more than just passing along information about the company and its history. New hires hear from the horse's mouth how to get things done within the company. Taken together, Intel's seven orientation seminars total nearly 30 classroom hours and include such courses as:

What makes Intel, Intel. A four-hour course detailing the company's history, products, procedures, quality initiatives, and culture.

Intel operating philosophy and economics. A three-hour course covering Intel's history, corporate objectives, how the company makes money, its management structure, and its decision making by peers.

All about Intel: Marketing and the customer. A four-hour course outlining Intel's principles of marketing and how Intel sells its products—key markets, customers, and distribution.

Intel management by objectives. A four-hour course during which Intel employees learn how to write their objectives and the key results they want to accomplish within their departments.

All about Intel: Components and systems manufacturing. A four-hour course which takes Intel employees through the manufacturing process of an integrated circuit. This is a basic know-and-understand-the-business type of course targeted to nonmanufacturing personnel.

All about Intel: The Intel product line. A four-hour course explaining the history of product development at Intel, as well as current and planned product lines.

The Intel culture course. An eight-hour course examining Intel's unique culture, its values, and how the company does things. Specifically, the course gives new employees an understanding of Intel's philosophy of constructive confrontation and the need to use constructive confrontation in working effectively within high-performance work teams.[2]

Intel's strategically focused orientation differs significantly from the more perfunctory, bland checking-in process characteristic of orientations at many U.S. companies. Gradually, more companies are revising their approaches to orientation, especially those committed to building a world-class work force. Instead of a half-day event that is often characterized by paper shuffling and benefits briefings outlining everything from vacation days to retirement policies, orientation is increasingly seen as a strategic activity and, importantly, as an opportunity to immerse the employee in the company's quality vision, culture, and traditions. This new model of orientation works to lay the foundation of employee empowerment and achievement of the company's total quality vision.

Companies who are giving new priority to orientation are doing so in part for practical reasons. First, employers are concerned about the cost of turnover. According to a study cited in the February 1991 issue of *Training & Development Journal*, 50 to 60 percent of all new hires leave their jobs within the first seven months. With the average cost to hire a new employee running at $6,000 per person, companies are realizing they must do something to retain new employees long enough to make their tenure worth underwriting.[3] Secondly, employers point to demographic trends which project that, by the year 1995, there will be 27 percent fewer 16- to 19-year-olds available for work than were available in 1975.[4] Since this traditional source of new workers is forecast to be shrinking through the year 2000, employers recognize they now must focus on how to retain employees.

Economic considerations notwithstanding, companies who are developing a more strategic approach to orientation are motivated by a conviction that by doing so they strongly enhance the organization's customer-service culture. They believe that employees who feel they've been treated well will, in turn, treat customers well. What better way to leave an indelible positive first impression on employees than through a carefully scripted orientation process? It all but guarantees that new employees start out on the right foot.

Courses paint the company's big picture.   In addition to building the company's values and culture into the training programs at Corporate Quality Universities, the companies profiled for this book are going one step further by supplying employees with the big picture of the company. A company widely known from having pioneered this practice of interweaving history and traditions into its now legendary employee training program is Walt Disney. Disney University was launched in 1963 to train all Disney employees, known in Disneyese as cast members. Disney University offers "Traditions I," a day-and-a-half program that prepares Disney cast members to deliver exceptional customer service. These new recruits learn the language and traditions of Disney before they learn the specifics of their jobs. Shelley Lauten, Disney's training manager, believes that "Traditions I" is where pride in Disney takes hold. Lauten adds, "Employees routinely deliver quality service and go the extra mile for the customer because they are proud to be working for the company. "Traditions I" ignites employee pride by giving each cast member—from the ticket taker at the gate to the senior vice president—an in-depth view of the culture, values, and traditions of the company, in many cases using clippings from Disney classic films and speeches from Walt recalling his vision for a theme park. It is intended that cast members leave this day-and-a-half course feeling a strong bond to the Walt Disney Company.

While Disney University may have been the first to include its history and traditions in formal employee training programs, a number of Corporate Quality Universities have expanded on this to design specific courses sharing the company's big picture with all levels of employees. Both Apple Inc. and MBNA Corporation, a bank holding company with 1991 assets of $6 billion, have developed such course offerings at their Corporate Quality Universities. For example, at Apple University, the Biz seminars are a half-day program developed to help all levels of employees better understand the company and the larger issues—competition, customer groups, and the economy—which impact the company's quality vision and corporate goals. Jim Cutler, director of Apple University, is fond of saying that, "The Biz seminars are not a motivational or 'feel good' program, but rather a wake-up call to present the critical issues Apple faces to its middle managers so they understand how these issues affect their departments and the departments' goals." While many top managers may know why achieving the quality vision is critical to the success of the corporation, often this macro understanding does not filter down to all management levels. The Biz seminars assist Apple employees in understanding Apple's external business environment and internal business direction so they can make more informed business decisions in their day-to-day jobs.

MBNA Corporation's primary line of business is consumer credit cards. Its Customer College offers a similar one-day course to Apple University's Biz seminars where employees at all levels receive training in the credit card industry and, specifically, MBNA's role, its product offerings, and competitive advantages of its product line. Ron Obstfeld, MBNA's vice president of corporate education, believes supplying employees with this larger business perspective has played a critical role in helping them understand the big picture of the industry and the specific advantages of MBNA's product line.

Traditions come alive in corporate museums. Finally, some companies, such as Motorola and Intel, have started to bring their values, culture, and the big picture of the company alive in the form of a corporate museum. Victor Danilov, in his book *Corporate Museums, Galleries and Visitor Centers*, tells us that the number of companies opening corporate museums is clearly on the rise.[5] Historically, the emphasis of corporate museums has been on memorializing the historical objects, records, and photographs of the founder. But today, corporate museums are being used to enhance the bonding process between employees and the company. In addition, these museums are becoming more professional, relevant, interactive, and important to companies, as a vehicle to showcase their corporate traditions to a growing audience of employees, guests, customers, and the general public.

The Motorola Museum of Electronics is perhaps the best example of this. The museum, which opened on September 3, 1991, is a place where employees, interested community members, and elementary school students can trace the course of Motorola's growth as a company while also learning about the electronics industry's development and growth. What's more, new employees are given time off to visit the museum.

Motorola Museum has become the incarnation of the dream Bob Galvin had 30 years ago. He envisioned an institution which would preserve and tell the ongoing story of Motorola, communicating both the great moments in Motorola's history and lessons learned from the business initiatives which were not successful. Motorola Museum has accomplished just such a feat. Motorola's culture of prudent risk taking and tinkering shows through in exhibit after exhibit within the halls of Motorola Museum. For example, employees learn that Motorola's first product was a battery eliminator, enabling radios to operate directly from household current. But within one year, that product was obsolete and Paul Galvin, Motorola's founder, was back to the drawing board to design another new product. Next came the car radio, inspiring the name "Motorola" to suggest "sound in motion."

But what's particularly interesting about the Motorola Museum is that it displays *both* Motorola's successful products and products which have not been successful. For example, visitors can view the gasoline-powered car heater. This invention was abandoned after nearly $1 million in investment but yielded many important lessons for the company. Displaying this type of abandoned business initiative lets Motorola get across a valuable message linked to its promotion of prudent risk taking: that learning comes from understanding one's successes *and* failures. Overall, Motorola Museum has achieved a prominent role in supplementing the company's formal training programs covering Motorola's values, cultures, and traditions.

The companies with Corporate Quality Universities make a deliberate attempt, through formal course offerings in the company's values, culture, and big picture, to develop a strong sense of corporate citizenship among all members of the work force. Rather than rely on employees to learn about the company in a haphazard fashion the companies profiled here consider the assimilation process a critical first step in building a world-class work force. In many ways, this is similar to training and development practices used by Japanese companies, where training is broadly defined as a way to inculcate workers in the foundation and roots of the company.

CONTEXTUAL FRAMEWORK

Know the Company's Customers, Competitors, and Best Practices of Others

The companies surveyed for this book believe that corporate performance is enhanced when all employees, not just management, operate from a base of shared understanding about the organization's business and the key players within it. Context training, as I have termed this, has become the second component of the CORE curriculum. This training aims to develop in workers a very specific and practical know-how about the company, its customers, and how it stacks up against others within the industry.

But, how does a company "train" employees in essentially what an old-timer instinctively knows about the company and the industry?

American Express employees walk in the shoes of customers. One company that has done an innovative job of training employees in what its customers expect is American Express. Since American Express service representatives do not have face-to-face contact with customers, the job of understanding customer expectations becomes more difficult. So, American Express Quality University[SM] has developed a course simulating what it's like to be a business traveler so employees can walk in the shoes of customers. This course, "Developing a Relationship with Your Customer," is included in the American Express Quality University CORE curriculum and therefore is required of all levels of employees. Essentially, the course goes beyond making employees cognitively aware of the company's quality vision to helping employees understand firsthand what customers expect from the American Express service representative.

One innovative way American Express Quality University[SM] brings the customer into the classroom is through an exercise in which employees use their own experiences as customers to better understand the expectations of American Express customers. As part of the course entitled "Developing a Relationship with Your Customer," American Express employees look at experiences they've had in ordering food in a restaurant or ordering clothes from a catalog to examine some of the best and worst examples of customer service. "When employees think about how they've been treated as customers," says Deb Robbins, manager of American Express Quality University[SM], "they not only learn what customers want, they also discover the skills and attitudes that build stronger customer relationships." These experiences can range from memories of outstanding customer service to the worst customer service experience of a lifetime.

During the course, trainees create a portfolio of positive behaviors which complete the sentence, "When I'm a customer, these things matter to me. . . ." Such positive behaviors can include following up with the customer to resolve a problem and in essence, act as an in-house agent for the customer. Finally, American Express employees are asked to develop an action plan for what they will do in their specific departments to better understand the needs of internal and external customers.

Ultimately, the goal of this course is for American Express employees to develop a strong sense of what's really important to customers. So, by giving employees a chance to share their experiences as customers, they can go beyond routinely applying quality process tools by rote to empathizing with customers and *wanting* to deliver exceptional service.

The Southern Company College trains employees in how to be a "student of the business." While American Express trains customer-contact workers to "walk in the shoes of customers," The Southern Company, an Atlanta-based electric utility supplying energy in Alabama, Georgia, Florida, and southeastern Mississippi, has defined their brand of contextual training as a five-day course focusing on "what it takes to be successful in the electrical utility industry." The course, "The Student of the Business," was designed to give Southern Company employees a foundation in the corporate vision, "We sell efficiency."

Top managers at The Southern Company believe that every employee must bond with the company and take ownership of its vision. In other words, corporate visions cannot be achieved simply by executive mandate, but by the personal involvement and understanding of each employee. Hence, "The Student of the Business" brings together managers and members of the International Brotherhood of Electrical Workers to hear firsthand from senior officers of The Southern Company the major facets of the business, what customers expect, and what specifically drives the company's ability to achieve bottom-line results.

David Connell, the dean of The Southern Company College, describes the college as "our way of ensuring that each employee knows how to live the corporate vision on the job." While in the past, The Southern Company trained employees in the technical skills of finance and economics (with some additional courses concentrating on interpersonal skills), the emphasis now is on how to make faster and better business decisions that support the company's vision of cutting costs and building customer satisfaction—put simply, selling efficiency.

Perhaps the most important development in "The Student of the Business" course is the gradual involvement of union members. Connell felt it was critical to involve and educate all segments of the employee population, including bargaining-unit employees, in how to think strategically about the challenges and changes confronting the electric utility industry, and specially how The Southern Company can strengthen its competitive position. The Southern Company hopes "The Student of the Business" course will enable every employee to make business decisions based upon a "big-picture" perspective.

General Electric's "Best Practices Workshop" at the Management Development Institute.   Best Practices takes the concept of contextual training in a much broader and more strategic direction. Instead of simply focusing on what "makes one's own company tick," some companies are also studying the Best Practices of others and incorporating this into their curriculum. In the words of Jim Baughman, GE's director of the Management Development Institute, "The challenge is to uncover the very secret of another company's success and translate that to your company". The GE Best Practices effort essentially looks outward to explore how select American, European, and Japanese companies are more productive. Among the companies GE targets are Sanyo, Ford, Wal-Mart, Toshiba, AMP, Xerox, Chaparral Steel, and Honda. GE Best Practices teams (including a mix of senior GE managers and consultants) visit each company full time for a couple of weeks. The goal is not to study a particular function but to simply observe and put a finger on the gestalt of the company.

Jack Welch sums up one lesson the GE Best Practices effort uncovered about Wal-Mart when he says, "After our management teams observed the speed, the bias for action, and the utter fixation on the customer that drives Wal-Mart, they came away feeling envious and, ultimately, fiercely determined to do whatever it takes to get that fast and customer-driven."[6]

The outcome of the GE Best Practices effort is to identify themes common across all of the companies included in the study. GE's Best Practices study found commonalities in essentially three areas:

- *Process over product.* How things got done rather than *what* got done was the focus of management's attention.
- *Partnering with suppliers.* Treating suppliers as business partners rather than adversaries was key to increased productivity.
- *Tight inventory management.* Managing inventory so that less working capital per dollar of sales was tied up.

But GE does not stop with just generating findings from the Best Practices study. After the GE Best Practices study was completed, Jack Welch, chairman and CEO of GE, sent Jim Baughman a challenge: Come up with a way to "blow the Best Practices concepts" across GE.[7] Baughman's answer was the formation of Best Practices workshops. The Management Development Institute turned the Best Practices findings into monthly seminars for key representatives from GE's manufacturing businesses. These seminars, in effect, turned into brainstorming sessions where GE employees asked such questions as, "What can GE learn from emphasizing process over product?" and "How can GE suppliers become better business partners to GE businesses?"

The entire area of contextual training—from understanding the needs and expectations of the customer to developing a strong internal grasp of what drives a company to achieve bottom-line results as well as an external understanding of the Best Practices of other companies—is becoming increasingly important as a part of the CORE curriculum at Corporate Quality Universities. The most significant result of contextual training isn't that employees learn facts, figures, or increased technical skills. Far more important, they come away from courses and workshops with such titles as "Developing a Relationship with Your Customer" (American Express), "The Student Of The Business" (The Southern Company College), or "Best Practices Workshop" (General Electric) with ideas for how to do the company's work better and eager to put their ideas into practice. These courses really become a lever for actualizing a culture change throughout the work force.

KNOW AND PRACTICE A CORE SET OF WORKPLACE COMPETENCIES

A *competency* is defined as any knowledge, skill, set of actions, or thought pattern that distinguishes reliably between superior and average performers. In other words, a competency is what superior performers do more often and with better results than average performers on the job. By practicing a core set of competencies, workers have the opportunity to raise the bar in terms of their performance.

As the workplace shifts to a more open paradigm, lower-level workers are required to assume more responsibility and develop broad and interchangeable skills. The flexible organizations of the future need adaptable workers who know how to work in teams and have the self-sufficiency to acquire new skills as the workplace and marketplace change. Hence, it is no longer enough to have workers simply upgrade their technical skills; now they need to develop a core set of workplace competencies which give the company its competitive advantage. But building a work force equipped with these competencies actually involves two separate processes. The first is to ensure that employees who receive training have the *right* attitudinal traits and work ethic needed to reap the full benefits from formal training programs. This, of course, requires that companies have in place smart hiring practices such as the ones used by Corning, Motorola, and Saturn Corporation profiled in Chapter 3.

The next step is to use training to build competencies which lead to improvements on the job. This section takes a look at the kinds of CORE workplace competencies identified as critical by directors of Corporate Quality Universities interviewed for this book. Essentially, these competencies fall into six skill groups: learning skills, basic skills, interpersonal skills, creative thinking and problem-solving skills, leadership skills, and the ability to manage one's development.

CORE WORKPLACE COMPETENCIES

Learning skills. As Chapter 1 pointed out, the workplace has fundamentally changed from that which existed in the 60s and 70s and will continue to change in the coming decade as American companies compete in a global marketplace. In the 60s and 70s, it was possible for an organization to expect its workers to take direction and carry out a series of simple, routine tasks. Now, workers must have a broader set of skills and not only understand their own jobs but also the other jobs in their immediate departments, and continuously think of ways to improve their own work processes. In short, these workers must develop an ability to know how to continually learn new skills and transfer these skills from one area to another. Hence, workers must learn as they work and work as they learn.

The American Society of Training and Development defines the skill of knowing how to learn by breaking it down into four component skills, which include:

1. Asking the right questions and knowing when you have asked enough of them.
2. Identifying the essential components within complex ideas and tasks.
3. Finding informal ways to measure one's understanding of pertinent material.
4. Applying these skills toward the goals of specific job tasks.[8]

It's important to remember that learning to learn is a never-ending process. The companies who have made inroads in instilling a commitment from employees to continuously learn have done so by providing them with a framework for learning new skills plus a vehicle for self-management. At the heart of learning to learn is a process known as *andragogy*, coined by the adult education expert Malcolm Knowles. Essentially, the basic principle of the andragogical style of instruction, as defined by Anthony Carnevale, Leila Gainer, and Ann Meltzer in their book, *Workplace Basics*, is to involve workers in planning, designing, and evaluating their learning needs in order to instill a sense of ownership in the learning process rather than just having them passively attend one-time training events.[9]

Basically, the andragogical style of learning includes the following principles:

- Set the climate for learning: make it physically and psychologically receptive.
- Involve learners in diagnosing their learning needs and give them the opportunity to see the gap between the skills they currently possess and those they need to be successful.
- Involve learners in the planning process, including formulating their objectives and designing their own individual learning plans.
- Involve learners in evaluating/assessing their learning.[10]

One company interviewed for this book that has made significant headway in promoting this commitment to involve the learner in the learning process is Corning Incorporated.

Corning's approach is to provide employees with a framework for evaluating how they are doing in terms of possessing the corporation's CORE competencies. This framework is known as Corning's Self-Assessment Questionnaire. Corning employees complete this questionnaire on a quarterly basis. The questionnaire asks them to rate their behavior against standards for successful behavior tied to each of Corning's CORE competencies.

For example, employees are asked to think about how often they exhibit behaviors that define each of the company's CORE competencies and then rate themselves on a 1–7 scale which is as follows:

			Scale			
1	*2*	*3*	*4*	*5*	*6*	*7*
Never exhibit the behavior			Sometimes exhibit the behavior		Consistently exhibit the behavior	

Now, let's take a specific Corning CORE competency such as Networking. At Corning, this competency is defined essentially as knowing how to use key people both within and outside the organization to get things done.

The Corning Networking Competency

		Rating Scale 1–7
A.	I understand how decisions are made and use the Corning culture to get things done.	
B.	I develop a personal reputation and credibility across functions and organization levels.	
C.	I make frequent connections with key people in the customer's organization and in my own organization.[11]	

Corning employees use the Self-Assessment Questionnaire to rate themselves on specific behaviors associated with being able to network both inside and outside the organization. What's the benefit of this self-assessment tool? Corning's Gail Baity, manager of Strategic Corporate Education, sums it up in the following way: "The goal of learning new skills does not end with completing a formal training class. Instead, Corning employees must continuously build new skills into their behavioral repertoire and then make a commitment to assess themselves on a regular basis to see how well they have incorporated these behaviors into their normal way of thinking and acting on the job."

The common theme at Corning and other companies interviewed for this book is clearly focused on the need to develop processes and tools to help employees "know how to learn." Continually learning in the workplace and evaluating one's personal performance will become more important as companies adopt a flexible organization and shift employees between jobs and responsibilities. Knowing how to learn will become the foundation for all the higher-order workplace competencies.

Basic skills. In the past, several layers of management could act as "translators" for workers who had difficulties with basic skills such as reading, writing, and understanding directions. But today, each and every worker must possess the fundamental reading, writing, and computational skills needed to understand and perform his or her job independently. The introduction of approaches such as statistical process control (SPC) demand higher mathematical skills. In addition, workers who deal with customers must be proficient at reading and writing in order to move ideas through the workplace.

A report in the October 5, 1992, *Wall Street Journal* documented the mighty efforts American companies are making to increase the basic skills of the work force. The article states:

> A growing number of businesses are . . . trying to do educational makeovers of their own work forces. Unable to wait for public schools or vocational schools to catch up with their corporate needs, these employers are taking on the role of educators. They are pouring millions of dollars and thousands of man-hours into high school equivalency courses and other basic-skills training.[12]

According to Anthony Carnevale, chief economist of the ASTD, who was quoted in the article, companies spent an estimated $300 million on basic-skills training in 1991, up from near zero only 10 years ago.[13]

Motorola is an example of a company which has made a serious commitment to training all levels of employees in basic skills. In 1991, out of the $70 million Motorola spent on formal training and development programs, about $7 million was targeted for basic-skills training. Much of this training occurred at Motorola University.

Bill Wiggenhorn, president of Motorola University, stresses the importance of basic skills when he says, "Our country is going off-shore for brain power, not for low-cost labor."[14] Motorola has set out to ensure that all its employees can read, write, problem-solve, and do mathematical calculations necessary for their respective jobs. At Motorola, the specific basic-skills set required varies depending upon the job requirements. But what is important is that Motorola has gone beyond just requiring employees to be proficient in reading, writing, and math at a particular grade level to constantly evaluating the changing requirements of specific job categories and training employees in the skills needed to do their current jobs as well as future jobs within the company.

This emphasis on basic-skills training is not limited to companies the size of Motorola. In *Fortune*'s May 4, 1992, cover story, "The Truth about the American Worker", manufacturing plants as small as 500 people were engaged in basic-skills training using computer-based learning systems, known as Wicat Systems educational software, to teach vocabulary, reading, and math.

David Brennan, the owner of one such manufacturing plant, estimates it will take about three years at two hours a week of company time to get workers at his plant up to the basic-skills competency level needed for their jobs, at a total cost of roughly $3 million. Another company cited by *The Wall Street Journal*, the Georgia-based carpet manufacturer Collins and Aikman, invested a reported $1,200 per worker in basic-skills training.[15]

Brennan argues that the cost is worth it. "I wouldn't hesitate to spend the same amount of money on a machine that five years from now is going to be increasing my productivity by $1 million a year, so why not spend this amount on my workers?"[16]

Employers in flexible organizations simply cannot compete effectively without a work force that has basic academic skills. But probing further, employers need employees with good academic skills and "much more." The much more includes knowing how to communicate with co-workers and customers, being able to think on your feet and solve problems, knowing how to lead a team to meet the organization's business initiatives, and, above all, being able to manage one's development.

Interpersonal skills. While reading, writing, and computation are essential, it is the activities of communicating, negotiating, managing conflict, and networking that keeps the work force humming smoothly. These interpersonal skills, or, as they are frequently referred to, *soft skills*, are growing in importance within the flexible organization.

The importance of the ability to communicate as a prerequisite for nearly all jobs is being increasingly understood by employers. Linked to this is a growing emphasis on the component skill of listening. Compelling statistics compiled by the ASTD regarding the types of interpersonal skills workers use on the job indicate why. According to the ASTD, the average worker spends 8.4 percent of his or her communications time writing, 13.3 percent reading, 23 percent speaking, and a whopping 55 percent listening to others.[17]

Ironically, when we think of listening, we assume it is basically the same as hearing; this, however, is a dangerous misconception, leading us to believe that listening is an instinctive ability. On the contrary, listening is a learned skill, demanding energy and discipline. It is also a necessity for employees who work in quality-driven companies, where workplace practices, such as team-building and coaching, are being required of greater numbers of employees.

Who teaches workers to communicate with and listen effectively to others? It is not American primary and secondary schools, who currently offer little instruction in oral communications or listening. The scant instruction they do provide in oral communications is often in the context of a drama or debating class, with virtually no instruction in listening. So, companies have had to take up the slack in training workers in these interpersonal, or soft, skills.

While effective listening and communication programs have been offered at companies for quite some time, they are now showing up with a new twist. Increasingly, listening and effective communications programs are being customized to give employees practice in effectively handling day-to-day interactions with customers and co-workers. One program offered at American Express Quality University[SM], "Communicating with Success," allows American Express employees to create their own role-play situations in which they practice solving customer problems they frequently experience in their jobs. In practice sessions, these employees have the opportunity to try out their listening skills, while the other members in the class are the official observers. "What happens in the class," says Mark Schrooten, senior design specialist for American Express Quality University^{SM}, "is that our employees get an opportunity to observe how they interact with customers and co-workers, and then pinpoint the barriers to communicating effectively."

Another company that has made a major commitment to training its frontline staff in interpersonal skills, active listening skills, and team-building is Target Stores, a Minneapolis-based discount retailer and a division of Dayton Hudson Corporation. The retail chain now operates 506 stores in 32 states and plans to open as many as 250 more outlets and add over 100,000 frontline workers. With all this growth coming down the road, Target Stores has focused on training as an important way to transform a hierarchical culture into one that invests employees with the power to please the customer.

Target University was launched in 1990 after Larry Gilpin, senior vice president of customer, team, and community relations returned from three days of training at Disney University. Essentially Target University was created to help frontline workers deliver superior customer service. As Gilpin says, "Training has evolved at Target Stores from 'fill out the form this way and key in the register that way', to building teams, teaching customer contact workers to actively listen and helping them devise ways to please the customer." Whenever Target opens a new store, it sets up a Target University, a movable course that is usually conducted by a veteran store manager from the chain.

Classes at Target University use novel approaches to build team work. For example, sales clerks participate in exercises with hula hoops to remind them that Target Stores is supposed to be "fast, fun, and friendly." All this training, conducted on-site in a mobile classroom, has had a dramatic effect on employee turnover. Traditionally Target's turnover has averaged about 120 percent per year (including the part-timers). But in 1990, the first year of operation of Target University, turnover dropped to about 75 percent.

Interpersonal-skills training at other companies includes skill-based training in how to negotiate with co-workers and successfully manage conflict in the workplace. Saturn's Gary High cites one course from Saturn's Training Center, "Managing Conflict at Saturn," as an example of how interpersonal-skills training builds from training in how to listen and communicate effectively to instruction in how to manage on-the-job conflicts. "Managing Conflict at Saturn" is an eight-hour course given to all Saturn associates. It teaches Saturn associates to focus on the issue and not on the person to achieve positive results. High notes, "We have a lot of conflict at Saturn. It comes from the commitment of our work force and their open expressions of wanting this organization to be everything it can be. Things that are not well understood or seem wrong are often challenged by associates."

Saturn's careful training, however, helps ensure that conflict works as a constructive, not destructive, force. One clear piece of evidence is the small number of grievances filed. According to High, there have been a total of only *nine* grievances written by the Saturn work force of over 5,000 people since its inception two years ago. High points to this as evidence that Saturn associates, who are trained in how to manage conflict on the job, can and do find ways to resolve their differences.[18] Of the 30 companies with Corporate Quality Universities profiled in this book, many, if not all, have included courses, workshops, and seminars on how to manage conflict in the workplace. Why? As the workplace shifts to one with ambiguity and fewer boundaries, more workers will be required to identify problems and know how to work with co-workers to reach a consensus on solutions.

Another interpersonal competency identified as critical by a number of quality-driven companies is the ability to network with co-workers, customers, and suppliers. In fact, this networking competency is now considered so important that it is being embedded as a theme in a number of soft-skills training programs at Corporate Quality Universities. Corning recently enhanced its soft-skills training programs with a series of seminars on how to network within the organization.

You might be thinking, "Is networking really a skill?" It is, if employees learn how to make connnections with peers, customers, and suppliers and in the process increase their productivity. At Corning, this is just what happens in networking seminars. Engineers learn how to network with peers across functions and organizational levels to improve their work processes. As employees are required to assume broader roles in their organization, there will be an increased need for networking and sharing Best Practices.

Creative thinking and problem solving. Employees must be able to think creatively to offer suggestions to improve their work environments and to solve problems that arise with co-workers and customers. Nearly all the Corporate Quality Universities train employees in how to identify and solve problems. But the challenge is to go beyond simply teaching employees the five or seven steps to solving problems and to seek out heroes and share stories about how they have used creativity to solve workplace problems. Rus Robinson, a recent graduate of Motorola University's middle managers leadership program (known as Manager of Managers, or affectionately, as MOM) is just such a hero. Robinson, an operations manager in the Land Mobile Products department, was profiled in Motorola University's *Opportunities*, a monthly newsletter published for and about Motorola training and education, for his creative and nontraditional solutions to implementing quality improvements in the workplace. These improvements resulted in a 61 percent quality improvement or, in Motorola's language, a 5.67 Sigma level. (As mentioned in Chapter 2, Six Sigma represents near error-free performance.)

But it is how Robinson used nontraditional thinking and creativity that makes his improvements in quality so impressive. Historically, when Motorola associates (factory workers) completed formal classroom training in quality tools and techniques, the job of training was over. But Robinson found that formal training alone was not adequate to really drive home the quality message.

Robinson supplemented formal training programs with creative on-the-job reinforcements to build a spirit and enthusiasm for quality improvement. For example, Robinson developed a series of 13 flash cards, similar in size to baseball cards, with each card containing a review of quality tools and techniques and how to use them on the job. Each flash card outlined a separate quality concept (e.g., pareto charts) along with an example from the factory floor. Then each week, at random, Robinson would walk around the factory floor and ask an associate to define a specific quality tool. If the associate gave the right answer, he or she instantly received a small reward—a calculator. Then, at the end of the 13 weeks, Robinson asked for volunteers to take a written quiz using examples of the quality tools and, of course, giving all the volunteers a reward for taking time to take the quiz. The participation rate was astounding—about 60 percent of the associates signed up to take the quiz. Robinson's explanation: The associates had fun learning and applying the quality concepts on the job and reviewing these concepts using the flash cards.

The next application of nontraditional thinking was Robinson's crusade to build team spirit within his department. While all the associates completed traditional formal training in how to work as a team, Robinson decided to take this one step further by instituting a nontraditional technique for building team camaraderie: a talent show among the associates. What does a talent show have to do with implementing Six Sigma on the factory floor? "Everything," says Robinson. "Only when associates truly believe they are a team, and experience feelings of trust and camaraderie toward each other, can empowered work teams happen on the factory floor. Until then, the training is simply compartmentalized." Robinson was amazed that associates spent time after work at each other's houses preparing for the talent show. This talent show for the Land Mobile Products department has now become a regular annual event at the factory.

What's the moral of the Robinson story? Rus Robinson has become a folk hero within Motorola for his use of creative and nontraditional techniques in building team spirit. Robinson has proven that empowerment on the factory floor is more than just memorizing the quality how-to's learned in a formal training class. Instead, empowerment involves using new techniques and nontraditional ways of thinking, behaving, and managing to build team spirit.

Leadership and visioning. Perhaps one of the most important distinctions of the past decade has been the emphasis in Corporate Quality University curricula on leadership courses as opposed to management courses. It is critical to understand the difference directors of Corporate Quality Universities see between leadership and management.

Management entails a control process of delegating, directing, motivating, and evaluating the work of others. Leadership, on the other hand, encompasses all the competencies required of managers, yet goes beyond them. For example, leadership involves the ability to empower, influence, and inspire team members to value and draw forth the strengths of a diverse work force and to give recognition in a skilled, yet sincere, way that reinforces learning and improves productivity. Increasingly, the curricula of Corporate Quality Universities offer programs in leadership because an increasing number of employees will be asked to assume leadership and visioning roles as the workplace continues to flatten.

One interesting approach to building leadership and visioning skills in the work force is taken by Texaco Quality Institute. Texaco starts by training employees in the how-to's of creating a vision. Jeanne Chatigny, program manager, believes that employees are intimidated when their supervisors ask them to create a vision for their work areas. Instead, Texaco's Create a Vision training program helps employees understand that visions in their work lives are similar to those they have in their personal lives, like building extensions on their houses or going on a family vacation. These are all presented as examples of real-life visions that employees have on a day-to-day basis. The Create a Vision training program at Texaco Quality Institute hones in on how to turn this capacity for dreaming dreams into visions for improving a department or work area.

Perhaps the most innovative program in this area is Motorola University's MOM course in leadership and visioning, cited earlier. This program is unique because of the high level of top-management involvement. While many Corporate Quality Universities offer an academic approach on leadership, presenting the advantages and disadvantages of various styles of leadership, Motorola's MOM brings Motorola's three top senior executives, George Fisher, Gary Tooker, and Chris Galvin, all from the office of the CEO, into the classroom to share their expectations of successful leadership. The substantial commitment of time and effort from Motorola's senior managers is impressive and makes all the difference to attendees. As Bill Faust, program manager for MOM, says, "The opportunity to see, hear, and share ideas with these senior-most leaders of Motorola is one of the important benefits of MOM".

In the classroom, these top executives discuss the importance of not just routinely adopting a specific leadership style, but trying to envision, energize, and enable team members to manage change in the organization. "In essence, the three top Motorola executives nurture, support, and encourage these middle managers to try a few new behaviors back on their jobs, such as having a vision, communicating this vision, and energizing their people with success stories," adds Faust.

Valuing diversity is another leadership skill which is increasingly offered within the core curricula of Corporate Quality Universities. The reason for the emphasis on knowing how to value diversity is primarily due to the changing demographics of the labor market. With more workers who are women, minorities, and recent arrivals from the Asia-Pacific Rim, Latin America, and other countries, business leaders must learn how to mold a diverse group into a successful cohesive team. At Bristol-Myers Squibb Pharmaceutical College, where over 40 percent of incoming Ph.D. candidates differ in age, race, and gender (with a large proportion from the Asia-Pacific Rim), the challenge to managing a diverse work force starts with carving out a human resource strategy for how to integrate a multicultural work force into the organization. The two-day course, "Managing Diversity," is the outgrowth of the Bristol-Myers Squibb commitment to understand how members of such a diverse work force can communicate effectively and work together to achieve business results.

Finally, the CORE curriculum addresses what has emerged as a key component of leadership: the effective use of recognition. Progressive companies are viewing recognition with new eyes; not merely as a sign of thoughtfulness or a pat on the back, but as a key skill to be defined, mastered, and deployed to improve productivity. Chapter 7 takes an in-depth look at recognition training developed and implemented at Texas Quality Institute.

Self-development. The final CORE workplace competency is self-development, corresponding to the responsibility all employees have to manage in their own careers. You can think of this competency as the skill possessed by individuals who are self-starters. Two of the most general of these competencies are the ability to set realistic career goals and to manage time over the long term in accordance with these goals. Perhaps the need for this competency is best described by Peter DiToro, a 45-year-old middle manager who has survived a half dozen rounds of layoffs at Computervision, a Bedford, Massachusetts-based computer company. DiToro had this to say about the importance of self-management in a recent *New York Times* interview:

> *"Job security is gone forever," says DiToro. "I expect a revolution in my career every five to seven years. So, I now believe I am the corporation and it's my responsibility to manage my career."*[19]

This theme of self-management is echoed in Apple University's course catalog. The catalog opens in the following manner:

> Apple employees are responsible for their own development. Apple, through Apple University and other internal training organizations, is responsible for providing employees with focused resources to continuously increase their effectiveness in their current jobs and prepare them for future jobs.[20]

Many companies profiled here with Corporate Quality Universities have taken a firm stand on the importance of having employees understand that it is their responsibility to manage their own development. The assumption made by these companies is that once the company sets the direction and defines the CORE workplace competencies, each and every employee must assess if he or she has these competencies and, if not, how can they be developed.

But is it as easy as taking a course in self-development? Some courses do, in fact, exist in this area. Specifically, IBM, through its subsidiary, Skill Dynamics, an IBM Company, has developed a number of course offerings entitled "How to Manage Your Future." This course, delivered in a variety of multimedia vehicles, stresses the importance of continuously learning and managing one's career.

However, more important than completing a course offering is the need for employees to be proactive in searching out ways to ensure that they develop the skills they need for lifetime employ-ability. On this score, companies must first identify competencies tied to each job category and then develop tools like Corning's Self-Assessment Questionnaire (mentioned earlier in this chapter) so employees can continually rate themselves on the skills they possess versus the ones needed by the corporation.

COMPETENCIES TAUGHT IN CORPORATE QUALITY UNIVERSITIES REFLECT LARGER WORKPLACE NEEDS

The CORE competencies taught in Corporate Quality Universities are the ones companies profiled here have concluded are most important to their continued competitiveness. Independent research also supports that these competencies are becoming more critical in the labor force at large as the workplace changes. One recent major study, conducted at Stanford University, sought to predict the skills that workers of the future will need. The skill sets identified in this study closely parallel the CORE competencies found in the University CORE curriculum.

Stanford University's Study: Educational Requirements for New Technologies and Work Organization

Stanford University's study, conducted under the direction of Professor Henry Levin, examined the soft skills and, more specifically, the human traits needed in the workplace of the future. The purpose of the study was to identify a set of skills required in work settings characterized by different types of technologies as well as different forms of workplace organization. On the basis of personal interviews with numerous companies, Professor Levin came up with a set of 13 skills that he believes workers need to function effectively in a workplace which stresses participative management practices.

Figure 4–2, "Competencies for the Modern Workplace," outlines the skills Professor Levin concludes are necessary in workers of the next decade. This list contains many of the com-

FIGURE 4–2
*Competencies for the Modern Workplace**

---

1. *Initiative.* The drive and creative ability to think and perform independently.
2. *Cooperation.* Constructive, goal-directed interaction with others.
3. *Working in groups.* Interaction in work groups that is directed toward both short-term goals of efficient task or activity accomplishment and the long-term goal of group maintenance.
4. *Peer training.* Informal and formal coaching, advisement, and training of peers.
5. *Evaluation.* Appraisal, assessment, and certification of the quality of a work product or service.
6. *Communication and listening.* Appropriate uses of spoken, written, and kinesic communication as well as good listening, reading comprehension, and interpretive skills for receiving messages.
7. *Reasoning.* Evaluation and generation of logical arguments, including both inductive and deductive approaches.
8. *Problem solving.* Identification of problems, generation of alternative solutions and their consequences, selection of an alternative, and implementation of a solution.
9. *Decision making.* Employing the elements of problem solving on an ongoing basis in the workplace.
10. *Obtaining and using information.* Deciding which information is relevant, knowing where to obtain it, obtaining it, and putting it to use.
11. *Planning.* Establishing goals as well as scheduling and prioritizing work activities.
12. *Learning skills.* Cognitive and affective skills that facilitate the acquisition of new knowledge, as needed.
13. *Multicultural skills.* Understanding how to work with persons from other cultures in terms of language, communication styles, and different values.

---

*These competencies were outlined by Dr. Henry Levin of Stanford University in the research paper entitled "Investing in People: A Strategy to Address America's Workforce Crisis."

petencies covered in the University CORE curriculum: interpersonal skills, learning skills, and problem solving.

Professor Levin notes that previous studies of the skills needed in the workplace have tended to focus more on the effects of changes in technology than on the effects of changes in workplace organization.[21] Consequently, companies who use these studies as guidelines for developing training tend to preoccupy themselves with training employees primarily in the basic skills. In other words, many companies are putting their efforts into defining the specific reading and math levels workers in future jobs must attain to master new technologies rather than focusing on developing broader skills needed in the flexible workplace. Professor Levin supports the premise that jobs in the workplace of the future will require both higher-level cognitive skills and a repertoire of broad soft skills such as cooperating with others, communicating and listening, problem solving, and obtaining and using new information in the workplace.

Interestingly, these competencies for the modern workplace are not, to a large extent, the standard ones stressed in elementary and secondary schools in the United States. For example, most schools teach traditional academic disciplines, such as math and science, through rote learning and memorization in classroom settings that emphasize individual competition. But the schools, much like the corporate training programs, will have to broaden what they teach their students. In addition to teaching the three Rs, the schools must also begin to train students in the six skill areas outlined in this chapter and increasingly required by employers.

Indications are surfacing that our educational institutions have seen the writing on the wall and are beginning to shift their focus. Indeed, *The Wall Street Journal*, reporting in its September 11, 1992, issue on the trend toward what is called *active learning*, tells how a number of progressive schools throughout the United States are preaching a new brand of student engagement.

This new approach casts students in the role of workers and teachers as coaches. Instead of having information spoon-fed to them in lectures and texts, students take greater charge of the learning process for the entire group. Required material is covered through students digging for knowledge and then communicating it to the class, often in oral presentations, debates, and team projects. By developing many of the very skills discussed throughout this chapter, active learning seeks to prepare students for the real world and workplace they'll encounter when they graduate.[22] This is a positive development for employers, as it means that they will be able to hire workers from the outset who have the broad skills required in the workplace of the future.

The Stanford study and the growing emphasis within a number of school systems to focus on active learning indicate an important direction for worker training throughout U.S. industry in the next decade. More and more, the companies interviewed for this book have designed their corporate training programs to reflect a growing emphasis on developing broad, interchangeable skills and a corresponding deemphasis on training simply in the narrow technical skills needed to do one's immediate job.

Companies realize that workers at the turn of the century will be much more involved in teaching, training, and motivating teammates than just executing the technical aspects of their jobs. The companies profiled here have perceived a growing complexity of jobs at every level of the organization. They've observed that work is becoming less task oriented and more people oriented, requiring workers who can think critically, make decisions, solve problems, and effectively communicate with both coworkers and customers. The university model for training has become their means of "upskilling" their work forces to meet these new demands. They provide an important example for other companies to follow. The common theme emanating from the CORE curricula of numerous Corporate Quality Universities is the need to develop workers who are broadly skilled and closely attuned to the identity and strategic mission of the organization.

The CORE curriculum outlined here reflects the challenge of transforming a diverse working population into a powerful and cohesive work *force* worthy of the name. But, it's important to remember that training under the Corporate Quality University umbrella doesn't end with the formal training represented by the CORE curriculum. This approach seeks to promote learning as a continuous process. Learning happens not only in the formal classroom session, but also in informal situations: at one's workstation, in groups—wherever and whenever the opportunity arises. Chapter 5 examines a myriad of creative ways Corporate Quality Universities stimulate continuous learning.

Chapter Five

The Corporate Quality University Becomes a Learning Laboratory

The Corporate Quality University provides a natural testing ground for trying out new ways for the entire organization to learn. So far, we have looked at the guiding principles and the types of programs found at many Corporate Quality Universities. But, over time, classroom-based corporate education and training programs, as we know them today, will be only one part of an organization's overall strategy for training and educating its work force.

As all jobs within the organization become more complex and the skills required of workers become broader, the traditional assumptions underlying corporate training and development programs will be increasingly called into question. These assumptions have held that training is an event targeted to a homogeneous audience of roughly the same age, cultural background, and values. The instructional format of choice has been one trainer standing up before a classroom of 15 to 20 trainees. And since training has usually been carried out away from employees' jobs, the responsibility of ensuring that trainees transfer new knowledge and skills back to the job has rested with the supervisors.

As Chapter 1 points out, the workplace has been beset by profound changes. The work force is becoming less homogeneous and more multicultural, with workers differing by age, gender, skill level, and learning styles. What's more, the globalization of the marketplace, as well as the fast pace of technological change, means that the skill mix of employees must be updated continually in response to new opportunities and advances in technology. Employees at all levels of the organization will be called upon to have broader yet deeper and more specialized skills to meet the changing needs of global customers. Meanwhile, companies are called upon to continually assess the current skills of their workers, measure these skills against their changing business needs, and provide training and learning opportunities to close the skill gap.

As a result of these changes in the workplace, companies with Corporate Quality Universities are challenging traditional assumptions about training and adopting new ones. Companies are experimenting with new ways for employees to learn—both in the classroom and at the work site. Training is no longer viewed as a way simply to help employees develop cognitive understanding and acquire a smorgasbord of new skills, but rather as a means to achieve improvements on the job. Figure 5–1 looks at some of the ways the companies profiled here are experimenting with learning. These companies hope that when the pieces of the learning puzzle are put together, employees will ultimately make improvements in their jobs. The old approach of dispensing knowledge for knowledge's sake has given way to experimenting with ways to increase employee productivity. Some of the ways the companies profiled here are experimenting with learning fall into the following categories:

Corporate storytelling. Corporate storytelling has emerged as an important and viable way for employees to learn how things "really work" within a company. While this is not necessarily a new concept in and of itself, what is new is how a company like Motorola uses it: detailing both company successes and failures to pass along important lessons learned by Motorola managers.

Learning by doing. Instructional design methods must emphasize "learning by doing" over "learning by listening." Learning by doing means that employees actively participate in the learning process. In other words, they get an opportunity to become involved in real-world problems, propose solutions, and then implement them in their jobs.

FIGURE 5–1
Experiment with New Ways to Learn

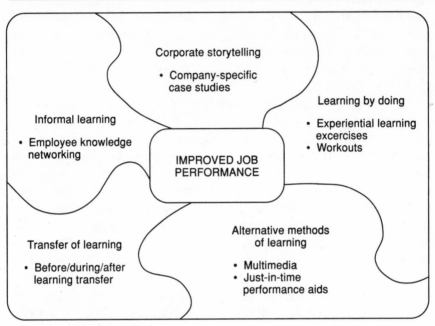

Courtesy of Quality Dynamics, Inc.

Alternative methods of learning.   A growing percentage of learning will happen outside of a traditional classroom. Therefore, new methods must be found which are on demand and individualized. Corporate Quality Universities are becoming laboratories for researching and testing how training can be distributed in short bursts that are available on demand, rather than just delivered in bulk, to employees in a course format. The goal here is for employees to learn new skills just before they put them to use on the job.

Transfer of learning.   Employees must take advantage of and contribute to knowledge transfer. Companies are now designing formal postlearning reinforcement tools and techniques so employees can more effectively transfer new skills and knowledge back to their jobs. The old adage, "What happens on the job is the supervisor's responsibility", is no longer viable. Instead, companies and individual employees are now working in partnership to devise ways for transferring knowledge to the workplace.

Informal learning. Employees at all levels must be continually developing themselves so they can meet new challenges in the workplace and in the marketplace. Companies are recognizing the importance of informal yet intentional learning as another way to increase an employee's productivity on the job. Some companies are devising processes to help employees take advantage of many informal learning avenues they come across every day.

As Corporate Quality Universities challenge old assumptions about training and tinker with new ideas and solutions, they apportion to themselves a new role in the organization: that of a learning laboratory. Just as a scientific laboratory experiments with new methods and theories, Corporate Quality Universities, in their role as learning laboratories, explore different ways to induce desired learning, that is, learning which improves an employee's performance on the job. Thus, the Corporate Quality University serves to foster a spirit of experimentation in exploring new instructional design methods, learning technologies, self-development tools, and the transfer of knowledge to the job so that employees possess the requisite skills, knowledge, and competencies to successfully compete in the marketplace.

This experimentation must be guided, however, by a realistic appraisal of the skills the organization needs and the skills the work force currently possesses so that training and learning activities are developed in concert with the changing needs of customers and markets.

SKILL ASSESSMENT IS THE
FIRST ORDER OF BUSINESS

At IBM, workplace education and training is conducted by one of its companies, Skill Dynamics. What is now Skill Dynamics used to be IBM's own education and training arm from which IBM formed a separate company offering training programs and educational consulting services to outside, as well as in-house, clients. Its president, Ralph Clark, believes fervently that an organization must first examine its workers' skills before developing and experimenting with new course offerings, instructional design methods, or alternative delivery modes. Clark drives this point home when he says:

> If an organization's people are truly its most important asset, then each employee must be viewed as an investment in human capital which must be maintained and nurtured, just as an organization maintains its physical assets. This means that organizations must begin to take inventory of their employees' skills, match these skills against their business needs, and develop education programs and performance aids to close the skill gap.[1]

At IBM, all employees participate in a skill inventory program to address such questions as:

What are the current skills employees have?

What are the skills employees must have to meet the changing business needs?

What is the "gap" between the skills the company needs and the ones employees currently have?

What type of learning opportunities must employees participate in to close this "gap"?

IBM's Skill Assessment model is part of a larger system at IBM known as the Management System For Education (MSE). This system, as shown in Figure 5–2, links the functional skill requirements of the company (i.e., those required to meet business and customer needs) with individual employee skills. The gap between the skills IBM needs and those which its employees currently have is known as the skills gap. To close this gap, employees, in concert with their supervisors, plan numerous learning activities and educational experiences. This plan, called the employee's Individual Education Plan, is quite specific in providing each employee with a road map of instructional modules, courses, conferences, books to read, and individual learning activities to participate in which must all be completed in order for the employee to meet his or her educational objectives.

FIGURE 5–2
IBM's Management System for Education

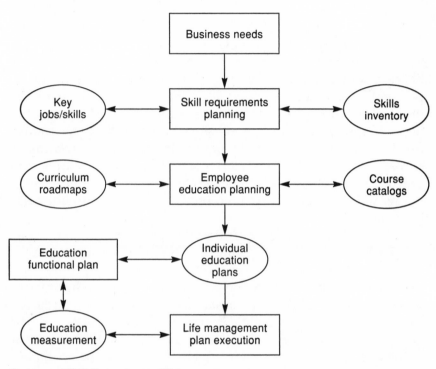

Courtesy of Skill Dynamics, an IBM company.

What makes this process so valuable is that the MSE is able to print out a side-by-side comparison of the skills required for each job within the company along with what it knows so far about the individual employee. The road map which is ultimately created details the specific when, what, and how of meeting the corporation's skill requirements.

Taking an assessment of employee skills will become increasingly critical as companies examine how to best meet the challenges of the marketplace. In other words, before companies embark on training their workers, they must first know what skills they need and then match these against the skills their workers currently have. How else can companies intent on developing a world-class work force be sure their workers possess the requisite skills, knowledge, and competencies needed to meet the emerging business and customer needs?

CORPORATE STORYTELLING

Sharing stories during training usually takes place in an unplanned, uncoordinated, and informal manner. An increasing number of companies, however, are recognizing the power of deliberate and consistent use of storytelling within the training function. Some, like Motorola, have gone beyond just relating the success stories, to include stories about company failures. This practice gives employees perspective about how things can go wrong with a business and then how the problem can ultimately be turned around.

Why are stories so powerful as training vehicles? Stories are chock full of vivid details. Employees often experience the events of a story as if they were there, and apparently this propels them to remember much more of the story than if the same information were presented to them as a statement of fact in a traditional lecture. After all, the reality is that employees usually do not experience more than a small part of the complex and diverse activities of the corporation in which they work. So, company-specific case studies provide employees with greater insight into how things really work in a company.

While stories have always been used within the training classroom to illustrate a point, corporate-specific case studies go further by communicating aspects of the company's history, traditions, successes, and failures within the context of the case study. As Professor Alan Wilkins, an associate professor of organizational behavior at Brigham Young University, says, "These corporate stories really serve as a cultural map. They symbolize a purpose or philosophy in a way that inspires and teaches. Secondly, they provide enough information about the right and wrong way to handle a situation so that employees who are exposed to the case study understand how they should act on the job."[2]

Perhaps the best reason for creating company-specific case studies is outlined in David Armstrong's recent book, *Managing*

By Storying Around: A New Method of Leadership. Armstrong, vice president of Armstrong International, believes that corporate stories are an important part of the company's folklore. His reasons for passing them along include:

- They're timeless. While Total Quality Management and the *One-Minute Manager* may come and go, corporate stories are ageless.
- They're an excellent way to pass along corporate traditions and instruct people in how they should behave.
- They're a way to empower people and lay out guidelines for how to get a job done.
- They're a way to profile the success behaviors so employees have a real "feel" for the types of behaviors that lead to promotions and those that will probably get them into trouble.[3]

The Motorola example which follows is just one way Motorola University uses corporate stories to pass along the culture and values of the company.

Motorola Uses Company Case Studies to Train Managers in Leadership and Change

Motorola University's Manager Of Manager leadership program (MOM) makes extensive use of Motorola-specific case studies as a way to teach lessons about Motorola's successes and failures. What makes this approach so innovative is that Motorola uses three of its senior executives from the office of the CEO to moderate a discussion of these corporate successes and failures.

In the Manager Of Manager leadership program, case studies look at two separate attempts to develop a product from Motorola's semiconductor business—a first unsuccessful attempt during the 1970s and a later one, which meets with success. Both case studies are presented to the Manager Of Manager leadership class participants as real-life stories, with the names of specific individuals disguised.

The case study method allows Motorola managers the opportunity to "live the story" while stepping back in time with Motorola's top executives to examine what happened and how the business was ultimately turned around to be successful.

Case Study I

Bart McCartle, vice president and general manager of the High-Technology Products group, quickly scanned a memo from Vice President Bill Hanson of the Circuits Division. He angrily picked up the phone and called Bill to say, "Are you telling me that the new 40K RAM didn't pass the product test? We've counted on that product in Corporate to make this year's numbers."

Bill Hanson replied, "It's a shock to me and I've called a meeting of the key groups involved to find out what went wrong."

Then, Bill and his assistant, Roger Andrew, went to the meeting. As they entered the room, Hanson turned to the director of Design Engineering, Paul Well, and said, "Let's hear it, what went wrong?"

Paul Well replied, "We gave them a unique technology and they messed it up."

Jack Ramsey, director of Process Manufacturing, was visibly upset and then shouted, "The design was awful; it could not have been manufactured with any of our equipment."

Then Bill Hanson moved to take over the meeting by saying, "This argument isn't getting us anywhere. Let's ask the Marketing Planning area about the viability of this product."

Clarence Reynolds, manager of Market Planning, responded, "We do not have anything to say, because the Engineering Group never asked us about what the customer wanted from this product. It appears to have been designed without taking the customer's needs into account."

At this point, Bill Hanson stands up and says, "I've had enough of this kind of talk where everyone blames the other guy. We are all in a jam and we have to figure out what can be done to save this product. Then he says to his assistant, Roger Andrew, "I'm late for another meeting. Figure this out and put an action plan on my desk as soon as possible."[4]

A Motorola senior executive then leads a discussion about the case and how such a situation can be corrected or avoided.

The second case study picks up where the first one stops, with the added knowledge that the 40K RAM product was finally introduced to the market, but several months late and at a significant cost overrun. But now, Roger Andrew, the assistant from Case Study I, is an empowered middle manager who takes on the responsibility to find a better way to manage new product introductions.

Case Study II

After months of extra effort by the entire Circuits Division, a new product in chip technology (40K RAM) finally made it to market, but at a greatly increased cost to the company. Roger Andrew, assistant to the vice president of the High-Technology Products Sector (Case Study I), is now in charge and believes there is a better way to manage product introductions.

Roger Andrew felt that one major cause of the problem was that the design engineers didn't have the extra discipline of computer software to test design specifications. He also felt that the design engineers, the manufacturing process engineers, and marketing planning should all be part of one new product team. The team recommended by Andrew included Ben Wright of Design Engineering, Larry Black of Process Manufacturing, and Mike Mitchell of Market Planning. This is the group that would lead in the development and manufacture of the 60K RAM. Wright said, "We have a lot of experience with the 40K RAM and really don't need to spend all that time developing computer test software." Larry Black responded, "I'd think about that, Ben, because it would really help us manufacture the stuff if we knew for sure that the design would work." Mike Mitchell quickly responded, "Anything that will help make the design easier to build will cut cycle time."

Ultimately, the software was developed to test the circuitry, and manufacturing had the specifications early in the development process to actually give input on changing some of the specifications.

By May of 1985, Roger Andrew had a call from Ben Wright in Design Engineering. Wright said, "We did it, the 60K RAM chip is ready."

Bart McCartle, Sector Vice President, recognized each employee with a recognition plaque. What's more, Roger Andrew and his team ended up developing a "New Product Introduction Process" Handbook that would be used in the future.[5]

Motorola's Bill Faust, the program manager for MOM, believes that what makes these case studies so valuable is their use of real issues and challenges profiling both the successes and the failures of a Motorola business. There's no doubt that case studies have been used in training for quite some time. But here, Motorolans can identify with the successful outcome of one particular style of management as well as the unsuccessful result of another. Finally, when these corporate stories are moderated by Motorola top managers, the participants learn about the company's values, culture, and traditions in quite a memorable way.

LEARNING BY DOING

In addition to experimenting with new vehicles inside the training classroom, the companies profiled here with Corporate Quality Universities are also exploring instructional design methods which stress active learning rather than passive, traditional, lecture-based classroom instruction.

While traditional lectures just pass along information, active learning demands that employees learn new ways of thinking and behaving while working on real-world problems that closely resemble their current job challenges. One method often used to promote active learning is the experiential learning exercise.

These exercises are designed to help employees see the big picture of their work environment and try new behaviors and new skills on the job. The exercises are essentially a series of situations carefully researched in focus groups with employees and their supervisors to simulate the real world of the employee. Then, participants get a chance to immediately apply their new skills in situations which are quite similar to those they encounter on the job.

Wal-Mart's management development training program for store managers conducted at the Walton Institute is one example of a program that uses the learn-by-doing approach.

Wal-Mart Store Managers Practice New Skills As Store Managers of the Always Store

Wal-Mart has become the number one retailer in the United States and is ranked by *Fortune* magazine as one of the three most admired companies in America.[6] According to Harry Cunningham, founder of Kmart, "The culture created by Sam Walton and running throughout the entire company is really the secret to the whole business."[7]

The Walton culture is best described by Sam himself, in his book *Sam Walton, Made In America,* as a sort of "whistle while you work" philosophy. For example, there's a management singing group called Jimmy Walker and the Accountants. And at the Saturday morning business meeting, the entire home office associate team comes together at 7:30 A.M., and no one is considered too important to lead the Wal-Mart cheer. The cheer goes this:

Give me a W . . . W
Give me an A . . . A
Give me an L . . . L
Give me a Squiggly (here everyone does the twist)
Give me an M . . . M
Give me an A . . . A
Give me an R . . . R
Give me a T . . . T
What's that spell?
Wal-Mart
I can't hear you!
Wal-Mart
Who's number one?
THE CUSTOMER

Some of the culture grew naturally out of Wal-Mart's origins as a chain geared to the needs of the small town, where often the trip to Wal-Mart is the day's entertainment. Wal-Mart understood this and tried every possible way to make shopping fun. It would stage shopping cart bingo, a game in which each cart would be given a number and winning numbers meant an automatic discount on whatever was in the cart. Another Wal-Mart tactic was to give away boxes of candy to the customers who had traveled the farthest distance to get to the store.

This culture of fun and hard work also stresses associate (the individual Wal-Mart employee) development. The Walton Institute, originally founded in 1985 by Helen and Sam Walton, was conceived as a place to which store managers could go to broaden and update their management and business skills. The Walton Institute originally operated much like a traditional university, with managers attending formal classes in basic management development, merchandising, and interpersonal communications. Essentially, these managers sat and learned by listening.

But then, back in 1990, Wal-Mart managers decided the process of associate development should incorporate some of the fun and excitement of the Walton culture, so the emphasis shifted from learning by listening to learning by doing. Now, managers who attend Walton Institute learn new skills and new roles by actually solving problems that occur in a Wal-Mart store.

Hence, Wal-Mart's Always Stores came into existence. Essentially, the Always Store is just like a real Wal-Mart store. It was conceived to give Wal-Mart store managers an opportunity to practice new management development and marketing skills in a real-world environment that closely resembles their store. Its name—Always Store—is actually a play on words, since Wal-Mart's motto is: "Always the Lowest Prices, Always." In the Always Store, the manager gets an opportunity to solve problems and crises that normally happen in his or her job, and then discuss with associates (i.e., other store managers as well as Wal-Mart home office managers) the results of his or her business decisions.

The real-world experiences created in an Always Store start on day one when 36 managers are grouped into work teams and begin their training by sorting through their Always Mailbag (the equivalent of the in-box). The first morning sets the tone for the entire week at the Always Store. For example, the mailbag includes an announcement that a new competitor has entered the Always market area and, over the last two months, has taken away a large share from the Always Store. A set of questions is then posed to these managers concerning this development and other managerial concerns. Such questions include:

1. How can you regain market share from the competitor?
2. How can you curb turnover at your store?
3. How can you improve coaching skills for all your teammates?

These Always managers then group themselves into a team to come up with recommendations to be ultimately presented to the regional vice president of store operations for Wal-Mart. This experiential learning exercise gives each Always store manager an opportunity to be a coach, lead a team, generate solutions to problems—like regaining market share or curbing employee turnover and then implement the solutions.

According to Wal-Mart's Joe Walker, manager of management development and home office training, the situations created for this six-day management development program were carefully researched to simulate what it's really like managing a Wal-Mart store. Walker believes these experiential learning exercises provide Wal-Mart store managers with an opportunity to solve frequently occurring issues, customer concerns, and even crises in a situation closely resembling a real Wal-Mart store. According to Walker, "Because there are no paradigms for solving problems at an Always Store, store managers can practice solving the types of everyday problems and customer requests that normally occur in running a Wal-Mart store." So, instead of learning the "seven ways to solve a customer problem," these Wal-Mart managers go ahead and attack typical customer problems, and then immediately discuss their problem-solving techniques with Wal-Mart's regional vice president of store operations. This combination of practice and feedback reduces the amount of trial-and-error learning new managers will face on the job and helps them assimilate faster. These Wal-Mart managers don't have to wonder, "Well, if I try this new way of solving a problem, will it fly at the home office?" They'll already have valuable experience to use as a guide. This type of learning by doing ultimately gives these Wal-Mart managers the self-confidence they need to try productive new behaviors in their stores.

A Guide to Designing Experiential Learning Exercises

Let's say you want to create a set of experiential learning exercises. Here's some advice in how to create your own real-world exercises:

1. Use real issues employees face on a day-to-day basis in their jobs. Focus groups using employees and their supervisors can provide the input in building an experiential learning exercise.
2. Create a sense of drama and excitement in the experiential learning exercise.
3. Keep the points illustrated in the experiential learning exercise simple—one or two key competencies—that can be easily demonstrated to all the participants.
4. Design the exercise so participants take the responsibility for their actions. Instead of telling a participant to act like he's a store manager, give him all the responsibility and authority store managers have in the company and then let him learn firsthand how he reacts to real-world crises.
5. Conduct both an alpha and a beta test. The alpha test happens early in the design process and tests out the basic assumptions of the experiential learning exercise. The beta test is a live shakedown of the anticipated final experiential learning exercise and allows the designer the opportunity to refine and enhance the simulation.

General Electric's Workouts

General Electric's Workouts take the concept of learning by doing one step further. Workouts are designed to deliver the Crotonville experience to the mass of GE employees. Essentially, Workouts are a way to bring groups of GE employees together with their business leader to work out real problems and issues happening in their departments and propose solutions. Increasingly, Workouts are being used by GE as a vehicle to uncover issues, analyze strengths, and test new ideas.

What has made Workouts so successful is its vast scale. By mid-1992, more than 200,000 GEers—representing over two thirds of the work force—had experienced a Workout in their department. By comparison, GE's Management Development Institute annually reaches just over 10,000 employees, or roughly 4 percent of the work force. Hence, Workouts have literally become the major force in transforming GE training and development from a *place* of learning to a *process* for learning by doing. Now let's look at an example of how General Electric actually uses Workouts to encourage employees to learn by doing and, in the process, to develop the self-confidence to look for bigger and bolder improvements down the road.

The General Electric Answer Center in Louisville, Kentucky, is essentially charged with handling up to four million customer calls per year. But the Answer Center is much more than a facility to answer customer questions. Instead, it seeks to build a bond with customers—a bond that will last many years and ultimately give the company a competitive edge in the marketplace. Its staff of 167 highly trained consumer representatives—essentially the frontline customer contact workers—form the heart of the operation.

As General Electric restructured throughout the 80s, the Answer Center became a much leaner organization. Specifically, the consumer representatives lost many of the layers of management who were primarily responsible for evaluating their performance on the job. So, with the ratio of reps to managers having increased from 10–1 to 20–1, the reps needed a new way to receive ongoing feedback about their performance. The response from General Electric's Answer Center was: Organize a Workout with the reps and the remaining managers and, in essence, "figure it out for yourself."

The Workout session at the GE Answer Center consisted of bringing together a cross-section of consumer reps and supervisors along with their business leader to essentially do just that propose a new way to evaluate the performance of reps in their day-to-day contact with customers. These consumer reps realized that a significant change was in store for them. In the old days (i.e., before the restructuring by management), managers gave the reps daily feedback on both the quality and quantity of their customer calls. Now, with a leaner organization, this was no longer possible. Hence, Workouts were scheduled to propose a new performance appraisal system.

The Answer Center Workout session was organized for a total of three business days, with the first day devoted to learning how to work together as a team. These teams, consisting of about 30 to 40 GE employees, went through a number of exercises learning to build trust with their teammates. The second day was devoted to brainstorming solutions, and the third day culminated in making recommendations to the group's business leader on how a new evaluation and performance appraisal system would work within the Answer Center.

And what did the Workout finally come up with? A revolutionary new way of evaluating consumer reps? Essentially, the criteria for evaluating the reps remained the same, but the process of how to evaluate reps was revised. The primary change was that consumer reps were now required to be actively involved in their own management and development. In other words, instead of waiting to find out from a supervisor "how am I doing," these reps had to now take responsibility for evaluating their performance in their jobs. Each month, they received the tools—in the form of monthly statistics—detailing the quantity and quality of their customer calls. But here's where the difference came—now they were responsible for actually writing down on a piece of paper how they performed their jobs. In turn, they discussed this self-evaluation with their managers.

In theory, the concept of self-evaluation is not new. But, at the GE Answer Center, it is new for nonexempt workers. Bill Waers, manager of General Electric's Answer Center, believes the Workout sessions were instrumental in helping the reps and their managers understand the importance of self-evaluation within a new leaner organization. "Rather than impose a new performance appraisal system on reps, the Workouts helped to give the reps a voice in the design of a new evaluation system," says Waers.[8] And what the reps came up with was not only a new process, but also a list of new skills they needed to develop to make the process work, such as better presentation skills to "present" their performance to a level of management not intimately involved in their day-to-day job responsibilities.

As a formal mechanism for sustaining continuous improvement in the workplace, Workouts are unsurpassed in propelling employees to work on real problems, propose improvements, and in the process become more productive. But companies who are tempted to try Workouts must realize they were built on an already successful transformation within General Electric that sought to empower employees and eliminate unnecessary work throughout the organization.

ALTERNATIVE METHODS OF LEARNING

As Corporate Quality Universities expand their role beyond the classroom, they are beginning to test and experiment with ways to provide on-demand, individualized instruction. Barry Arnett, an education consulting services executive with Skill Dynamics, an IBM company, provides a compelling perspective on this phenomenon:

> The traditional corporate training program of the past decade was a formal course in a classroom lasting between one and two days. But by the year 2000 and beyond, the average training program will be an instructional module and will probably take between five and ten minutes and happen right at an employee's work station.[9]

In fact, as Arnett sees it, corporate education in the year 2000 will focus on creating a learning environment where modular, multisensory instructional modules will be distributed on demand to employees. The focus of this corporate education and training 10 years from now will be on learning under the control of the employee rather than in a corporate classroom where the employee "goes to get trained."

What does learning under the control of the employee mean? It means that instruction will be provided in bite-sized modules instead of formal courses. It also means that more courses will be automated using on-line documentation systems. Finally, and probably most significantly, it ultimately means that more corporate training will be distributed to employees (using either technology or self-guided learning workbooks) rather than under the central control of management. The final outcome to this will be employees who have the freedom to initiate the types of learning experiences they need to achieve improvements in their jobs.

When executives like Barry Arnett look into the future, even the words to describe corporate education are new. This new vocabulary of corporate education includes such attributes as:

Modular. Meaning addressing a single skill rather than a course addressing multiple skills.

Multisensory. Stimulating sight, sound, and touch in a variety of innovative ways.

Portable. Moving easily from home to office.

Transferable. Moving across languages and cultures.

Interruptible. Having the ability to stop and start easily.[10]

While this may all sound like utopia, it is not. As all jobs within the corporation become more complex and require a higher level of skill, the skill mix and knowledge required of employees will be in a continual state of flux. So, companies must experiment with ways to make learning increasingly controlled by the learner. This means in effect learning which is modular, multisensory, portable, transferable, and interruptible. But how? The common thread among companies profiled here is to experiment with making learning occur on the job and in the context of a real work assignment.

Companies are experimenting with new ways for employees to learn using alternative learning technologies: technology-based methods operated by the learner. The list of these technologies runs the gamut from computer-based training, multimedia (i.e., a combination of computer-based training with full motion video, audio, animation, and graphics), interactive video, distance learning (providing one-way video and two-way audio communication between an educator and a learner) and electronic performance support systems, which integrate information, instruction, and system support to provide whatever is necessary to generate improved job performance. It is this last one—the electronic performance support system—on which many companies are pinning their hopes for the future.

As defined by IBM in their book, *A Vision of IBM Human Resource Performance in the Year 2000*, an electronic performance support system is:

. . . a system that enhances employee and organizational performance and learning with a minimum of human intervention. The components of the system are integrated at the employee's work site and correspond to the job that the employee is working on, thereby integrating it with the actual work environment. The system consists of several components including, but not limited to, interactive training, databases, and expert systems."[11]

Specific case studies of how companies are actually using electronic performance support systems are given in Gloria Gery's book, *Electronic Performance Support Systems* (Boston: Weingarten, 1991). But for our purposes here, an interesting question arises: Is an electronic performance support system training or simply a job aid? As defined by Gery, it's really a combination of both, with the goal of increasing an employee's performance on the job. The use of hybrids of training/job aids is increasing because workers are being called upon to have an increasing amount of knowledge in order to satisfactorily perform their jobs. And with jobs becoming complex and requiring workers to call upon vast banks of information, the distinctions between education, training, and job aids are becoming blurred, less obvious, and virtually indistinguishable. Performance aids, which supply Just-in-Time information or instruction to help employees perform an action, often fill the same need as training: to improve the employee's performance on the job. As learning has become intertwined with actually performing one's job, job aids are becoming a critical alternative to traditional training.

The concept of Just-in-Time learning is borrowed from the Just-in-Time inventory concept, a method of inventory control used in many flexible organizations. The theory behind Just-in-Time inventory is that in order to reduce waste and cost and increase productivity, companies often carry less inventory—often one or two days of inventory. When applied to learning, Just-in-Time implies that performance will be increased if learning happens as close to the time workers need new knowledge as possible.

Just-in-Time learning has become increasingly important as the shelf life of much knowledge presently held by employees has become shorter. In fact, Mick Mortlock, training manager at Intel University, has said that, "The average shelf life of knowledge for a software engineer—that is the amount of time before his store of knowledge becomes obsolete—is about two-and-one-half years, an electrical engineer about five years, and a mechanical engineer about seven years."

The shortened shelf life of knowledge has put pressure on training professionals to develop innovative ways to make learning happen at an employee's moment of need. One company that is heavily involved in experimenting with multiple delivery methods to distribute "just-in-time" learning is Sun Microsystems. Through Sun U, its corporate university launched in 1990, Sun Microsystems is creating a range of "portable learning programs." As Peter Smith, the director of Sun U sees it, the future of corporate training rests with an organization's ability to strategically examine how to best utilize various technologies to solve training needs. This means instead of "falling in love with technology," training practitioners at companies such as Sun Microsystems and Intel are first determining the optimal delivery mode for each training need before they rush out to set a date of when and where to convert existing training programs into portable learning programs using alternative technologies.

Fidelity Investments' Just-in-Time Performance Aids for Customer Service Reps

Fidelity Investments, through its Retail Training Services group, provides an interesting example of how technology is used to solve a training need for Fidelity's customer service reps. In the past, Fidelity Investments trained customer service reps in a traditional fashion to achieve its goal of exceptional customer service. New reps learned about Fidelity Investments products and the how-tos of customer service through classroom instruction and printed materials.

The explosive growth of Fidelity's product base in the late 80s created a need for the company to reexamine its training approach. With its mutual funds alone now totaling 170 different fund types, the company was selling more products than any individual rep could be expected to learn and remember in detail. Yet Fidelity still needed its reps to be able to respond to customer requests for information and service promptly, courteously, and accurately, without having to flip through thick manuals or transfer the customer's call elsewhere within the organization.

Fidelity's solution was to develop a computer-based job aid that enables the rep to handle virtually any customer inquiry or transaction. The aid provides factual financial information to answer various customer requests such as a fund's end-of-day balance, how to redeem shares, and the address of the nearest Fidelity Investment Center. It also prompts the rep throughout the script to provide a high level of service. For example, if a customer asks for the address of a Fidelity branch, the rep's screen will not only supply the address, but also prompt the rep to ask the customer if he needs travel directions, will supply them, and will also supply the hours of operation for the branch office.

What's interesting about this computer-based performance aid is the way it anticipates the customer's every question (down to the hours of operation of a center he or she wants to visit) and prompts the rep with the answers. As a result, the Fidelity customer service rep is able to learn how to deliver exceptional customer service, by exceeding each customer's expectations. This is something every organization with a far-flung network of customer contact workers is striving for. The rep actually learns this standard of service excellence through using this computer-based performance aid. Each time a Fidelity customer asks a question, the job aid provides answers which exceed the customer's original question. What Fidelity Investments ultimately hopes for is that the rep will internalize this behavior and exceed customer expectations in other aspects of his or her job.

Indeed, an ingredient in the success of Fidelity's solution is the careful analysis behind it. To develop this computer-based performance aid, Fidelity used the same sophisticated market research techniques it employs to test new financial products. The program not only incorporates research into every question customers ask, it has also been tested at Fidelity's Consumer Laboratory, the same place new financial products and services are tested with consumers. Before introducing the system, Fidelity had its customer service reps use the system in a series of simulated exercises to ensure that they could navigate through the system easily while answering a customer's inquiry. The payoff for Fidelity: Reps are able to perform their jobs while exceeding customer expectations for service and without spending big chunks of time off the job in traditional training.

TRANSFER OF LEARNING

As we have seen in this chapter, the focus of experimentation within Corporate Quality Universities is on helping employees learn, rather than just sending them to scheduled one-time training events. Another subject of new focus is the area of knowledge transfer. In other words, companies are grappling with the question of how to ensure that employees transfer learning back to their jobs.

One of the traditional assumptions associated with training has held that what happens back on the job is out of the control of the trainer. This assumption implies that further knowledge and skill development on the employee's part is the supervisor's responsibility. But according to many directors of Corporate Quality Universities, nothing can be further from reality.

Companies increasingly believe they must work in partnership with employees, provide them with the tools to transfer learning back to the workplace, and work with them to ensure that they use these tools on an ongoing basis. Let's look at how one Corporate Quality University—Sprint's University of Excellence^{SM}— approaches this issue. At the University of Excellence^{SM}, each course includes a Before-During-After (BDA) exercise for both the participant and the manager. This means that *before* each participant begins a training program, both the participant and manager receive guidelines for what to expect from the course and how to prepare for it, then *during* the course the participant and manager are prompted for what skills and tools to practice, and finally, *after* the course, several follow-on activities are suggested for both the participant and the manager.

Figure 5–3 shows the BDA for Sprint's Leadership Link course. Notice just how detailed the guidelines are for both the participants and the manager, so each specifically knows what is expected in transferring learning back to the workplace.

The Leadership Link course is Sprint's basic first-line management course taken by all Sprint supervisors within one year of their appointment as supervisors. The course covers the roles and responsibilities of being a frontline leader within Sprint's organization.

Judy Simmons, curriculum manager at Sprint's University of Excellence^{SM}, believes the BDA for this course has been instru-

FIGURE 5–3

Facilitative Leadership Link Course Training Support Guidelines at Sprint University of Excellence[SM]

Manager	Participant
Before	*Before*
• Familiarize yourself with course content by reading course objectives.	• Familiarize yourself with course content by reading course objectives.
• Explain to participant why she or he was selected to attend training.	• Clear your calendar of all responsibilities during training.
• Be available for precourse discussion with participant.	• Discuss precourse issues with your manager.
During	*During*
• Develop opportunities for participant to use new behaviors immediately on the job.	• Determine how you will apply the knowledge, tools, and skills of the Leadership Link course to your work environment.
• Plan ways to reinforce participant's use of new skill behaviors.	• Practice the skills that will enable you to perform confidently in your work environment.
• Arrange for participant to share learning with others in department when she or he returns from workshop.	• Get feedback from other participants on your performance of the new skills.
After	*After*
• Be available for postcourse discussion with participant.	• Arrange a postcourse discussion with your manager.
• Communicate your role in supporting the transfer of skills.	• Take the necessary actions to transfer skills to your job, (i.e., implement action plan created in course).
• Set follow-up date to meet again and discuss progress of skill transfer.	• Follow up with your learning partner to discuss challenges of implementing new skills on the job.

Courtesy of Sprint's University of Excellence[SM] 1992.

mental in helping Sprint's first-line managers transfer the skills they learn in class (i.e., supervisory skills as well as active listening skills) to their new jobs as supervisors. "The goal of BDA is to standardize postcourse learning so it is consistent among participants," says Simmons. One of the concepts embedded in the BDA, which has been quite successful for Sprint in achieving this transfer of learning, is that of a learning partner. Sprint's University of Excellence^{SM} encourages participants in all courses to choose a learning partner. This learning partner is a classmate, usually from another department, who meets regularly with the participant in the month following the course to discuss ways to transfer learning back from the class to the job. This type of knowledge networking is becoming a critically important component for transfering learning back to the job.

INFORMAL LEARNING

One of the most difficult jobs companies face is to institutionalize a spirit of continuous learning. Ideally, companies want employees to learn not only the skills of a particular job, but also good learning habits so they can eventually exploit every opportunity to learn new skills and new roles informally on the job.

This spirit of continuous learning has been identified as one of the keys to building a competitive advantage. Michael Rothschild reinforces this thought in his recent book, *Bionomics: The Inevitability of Capitalism.*

> Gaining an efficiency advantage is really just accumulating experience faster than one's competitors and this is turning out to be the key to an organization's long-term growth and survival. Therefore, if a firm can somehow accelerate its own learning, its competitive position will ultimately improve.[12]

The goal is to move beyond the paradigm of a formal learning experience—whether delivered in the classroom, on a computer, on a television screen, or through a job aid—to the area of informal learning.

Informal learning, as defined by Victoria Marsick and Karen Watkins in their book, *Informal and Incidental Learning in the Workplace*, is "experience-based, nonroutine, and tacit learning so that each experience adds to a person's knowledge base."[13]

In other words, informal learning includes such things as meeting with peers in one's own department as well as other departments, observing co-workers, visiting plants to watch how products are made, learning from one's mistakes, learning about a competitor's products and services, and other unstructured ways of acquiring learning in the course of doing one's job. Informal learning occurs whenever a senior technician walks over to help a junior technician who hits a snag on some project. It occurs constantly in the normal interactions between supervisors and subordinates, and in the normal give and take among peers.

In fact, the whole concept of informal learning becomes more important as the shelf life of knowledge required for many jobs becomes shorter and shorter. How can companies promote this informal networking of knowledge among peers? Perhaps the best example of an innovative approach to creating an environment where informal learning thrives is Corning's orientation process for managers known as the SMARTProcess (an acronym standing for Self-learning, Motivation, Awareness, Responsibility, and Technical Competence).

Essentially, the SMARTProcess is a guided self-discovery method of learning which encourages employees to "get smart about the company" by talking with and observing co-workers and department heads at work. The process recognizes that informal knowledge networking is an invaluable way to help new employees learn about their jobs and the organization as a whole.

During the SMARTProcess, new employees receive a workbook which essentially asks employees to develop a comprehensive understanding of the total organization and, specifically, how they fit into this big picture.

While the SMARTProcess provides employees with the framework to learn about the company, it's up to each individual employee to conduct interviews with peers, department heads, plant managers, and seasoned experts within the company to discover the answers to such questions posed in the SMARTProcess workbook as:

- What is the mission of the company? List and describe the company values and how *you* can live the values in your job.[14]
- Diagram your organization showing the names of each player, their key areas of responsibility, and the types of changes which have occurred within this department during the last six months.

After new employees have completed this workbook (it usually takes about three months), they are scheduled for a one-and-one-half-hour discussion with a group of peers and their SMART-Process coordinator to discuss what they learned during this orientation process. It's here that new employees give important feedback on how they went about the process of knowledge networking and what suggestions they have to improve this process. Finally, after successfully sharing their knowledge about the company with co-workers and managers, they are certified in their assimilation to the company. But clearly, the ultimate goal is to have employees continue learning informally about how the company "really works" and share their best practices with co-workers. This whole area of informal learning as a discrete method of learning is beginning to take on a growing importance within companies. As jobs and opportunities change with greater speed, the need for employees to continually learn new information, knowledge, and skills will increase. Formal training, whether conducted in a classroom or even on a computer or video screen, can assist with some of this training. But much learning should happen informally, through an active participation on the part of the employee toward exploiting the learning potential in each daily situation. What this translates to is a growing need for more companies to develop self-guided learning tools that teach employees how to learn from their experiences with co-workers, supervisors, and department heads.

In their role as learning laboratories, Corporate Quality Universities are getting an important message across to employees: that they are committed to experimenting with new ways for employees to learn—in a formal classroom, at their worksite working on real problems, and informally networking with peers. Building a culture of continuous learning is at the heart of what each Corporate Quality University profiled here aspires to do within its respective organization.

The next two chapters examine continuous learning on another level—the collective learning of the entire organization. Chapter 6 looks at how various companies collectively learn by forging partnerships with suppliers, customers, and educational institutions, all geared to improve the competitiveness of the organization in the global marketplace. Chapter 7 examines how recognition programs have been elevated to a business practice so that the entire organization collectively learns the best practices of each individual employee.

The goal of all of these learning experiments is nothing short of institutionalizing a spirit of continuous lifelong learning throughout the entire organization.

Chapter Six

Outreach: Forging Partnerships with Suppliers, Customers, and Schools

WHY PARTNER? IMPROVED COMPETITIVENESS

Intense global competition is causing a profound reconfiguring of the marketplace. To give a concrete example illustrating the intensity of this competition, the U.S. Council on Competitiveness reported last year that America's lead had evaporated in one third of the new technologies it had dominated only 10 years ago.

Essentially, this competition falls into two categories: tangible and intangible. *Tangible competition* refers to direct competition among products and services, that is, how the features and benefits of one product compare to those of another. *Intangible competition* has more to do with the quality of the process, that is, the ability of a company to manage an entire system—of which suppliers, customers, consumers, employees, and even educational institutions are a vital part. As more products are perceived to be at parity by customers, a phenomenon known in the automotive industry as *product convergence*, there is increasingly less room for companies to compete on tangible grounds. The only remaining and viable way for a firm to differentiate itself from its rivals is through a focus on intangibles, that is, the quality of the human systems and processes behind its products and services.

This new goal of carving out competitive advantage through a focus on human systems, rather than through relatively easier-to-achieve product or service enhancements, requires a fundamental change in a company's way of thinking. Companies can no longer think of themselves as self-contained entities, but more and more as parts of systems whose links consist of the organization's relationships with suppliers, customers, and even the educational institutions which supply them with new hires. A company's efforts to improve the quality of its service and the quality of its people must take into consideration the entire system, not just the individual, isolated components. This may mean taking the initiative to develop training for the employees of customers; it may mean looking at the company's suppliers as partners rather than adversaries; and it may also mean reaching out to local community colleges to build alliances with them so they eventually supply the company with people who have the skills, knowledge, and competencies needed both now and in the future.

In other words, the ability to enter into and sustain partnerships is coming to the fore as a key aspect of competitiveness. The ingredients that make for successful partnerships mirror those present in a good marriage: a willingness to participate wholeheartedly, mutual trust, understanding, open communication, respect, and a commitment to continuously improve.

A number of Corporate Quality Universities are proving a natural and effective locus for building just the sort of array of partnerships with suppliers, customers, customers' sales forces, and schools necessary to improve overall competitiveness. The idea of a company building partnerships with those parties with whom it deals in order to seek improvements in quality and productivity is really not new at all. Japanese companies routinely develop interlocking partnerships with suppliers, a process known in Japan as *kiretsu*. And U.S. companies often work together informally with preferred suppliers and customers. What is new is that American companies interviewed for this book have, in effect, formalized what naturally happens when a company and its suppliers and customers work together successfully on an informal basis. They find that joining with members of their systems in a quest for improvement within the Corporate Quality University framework can lend to their relationships the kind of emphasis, energy, and purpose that distinguishes an authentic partnership.

The Corporate Quality University provides an effective vehicle for encouraging such relationships because it gives companies a way to involve targeted outsiders in a sustained joint pursuit of quality improvement and continuous learning.

But there's another reason companies are entering into these partnerships, that is, to have the entire employee/customer/supply chain collectively learn the company's quality vision and, importantly, the types of skills, knowledge, and competencies all the links in the chain must have to live out the quality vision. The companies profiled in this book are increasingly engaging in a dialogue with their product suppliers and the universities that supply them with new recruits each year, to share the specific skills and competencies the company requires from its supply chain. Companies believe this type of collective learning is vitally important to sustain the company's competitive advantage in this decade and the next.

The impetus behind partnering with employees, suppliers, and customers is the need to ensure that each link in the employee/customer/supply chain understands the company's quality vision and all join hands and intellects in a common purpose: achieving customer satisfaction. This may lead to eventually developing mutual strategic and tactical goals and even coauthorship of patents and processes. Figure 6–1 shows the various linkages between a company and its customers, product suppliers, and educational suppliers. Increasingly, quality-driven companies such as Motorola, Intel, and Saturn Corporation, to name just a few of the companies profiled here, are recognizing that they have to impact this entire system to ultimately deliver their quality vision to the end-user and to effectively leverage their resources.

PARTNERING WITH EMPLOYEES

Workplace changes of the past 20 years have redefined the relationships between employers and employees. In past decades, employees took the subordinate role, giving their obedience and loyalty to a paternalistic corporation in return for pay and job security. As organizations become flatter and as the marketplace becomes more uncertain, the whole notion of job security has been replaced with career security. Now, astute employees realize

FIGURE 6–1
The Supplier/Customer Partnership Chain

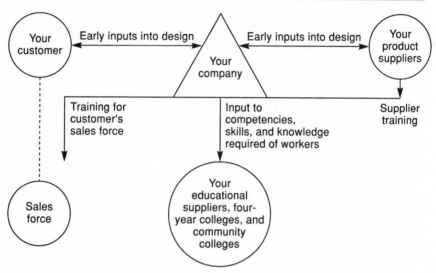

Courtesy of Quality Dynamics, Inc.

they must learn and practice a set of workplace competencies that their employers need to be successful in the global marketplace. Employers are reinforcing this notion of career security by designing processes and systems so employees take responsibility for learning and practicing the employer's CORE competencies. Some employers are going one step further in not only outlining a set of discrete formal and informal learning activities needed to master the company's CORE competencies, but also tying completion of these activities to the employee's compensation. So, together, the employer and the employee spell out an individual employee's learning goals and the corresponding rewards (i.e., increased compensation and/or promotion) for achieving these goals.

This employer/employee partnership takes the form of an agreement whereby the company provides opportunities to the employee to build career skills, and in turn the employee commits to learning and mastering those skills which lead to improved productivity for the organization. Two companies in very different businesses, Saturn Corporation and Arthur Andersen, provide interesting examples of employer/employee partnering.

Saturn Associates Enter into Partnership Agreements to Enhance Their Professional Development

Approximately three years before the first production workers were hired at Saturn Corporation, managers were busy at work developing the components of the Saturn "learning culture." As a result of their careful planning and articulation of Saturn's position regarding training, this learning culture flourishes today. As stated by Gary High, Saturn's manager of human resources, at the 1992 American Society for Training and Development Conference and Exposition, this learning culture can be defined as one where:

> Every employee has his or her own training and development plan.
>
> Training has a demonstrable impact on job performance.
>
> Training is an investment rather than a cost.
>
> Training is driven by the needs of the organization.
>
> A high percentage of Saturn's own employees are involved in providing training.[1]

Central to Saturn's learning culture is the partnership Saturn builds with each individual employee, leading to higher and higher levels of team and professional competence. This partnership is formalized in an agreement known as the individual training plan. It's in this plan that Saturn employees and their supervisors outline the specific training and development activities that each employee will undertake in a given year. These activities may range from taking a formal training class, teaching a training class, cross-training a team member, reading a book, completing a computer-based training program, or attending a seminar. Once the employee successfully completes this combination of formal and informal learning activities, it represents approximately 5 percent of the employee's work time, translating into 12 to 13 days per year or approximately 100 hours of learning.

Importantly, this partnership stresses employee professional development so that each Saturn employee learns a new skill or a new role to improve his or her performance on the job, not merely to complete a required number of training hours.

The Saturn employee partnership is representative of a new model for training—one where the emphasis is on broad professional development rather than narrow skill acquisition. This partnership agreement with Saturn employees does something else—it links Saturn's commitment to training to the employee compensation system. According to the partnership agreement, 5 percent of each Saturn employee's base compensation is at risk each quarter, pending meeting his or her training and development goals outlined in the individual training plan. Tim Epps, vice president of people systems at Saturn, comments on the benefit of this compensation system when he says, "Doing the right training in the right way at the right time really can leverage the company's ability to build more cars and in the end increase everyone's salary level."[2]

But linking the attainment of training goals to one's compensation may at first blush sound rather stern. However, according to Saturn's Gary High, it has helped motivate employees to achieve higher levels of performance by taking the ambiguity out of one's job. Saturn employees know that in order to receive the remaining 5 percent of their base salary, they must live up to the goals in their individual training plans and complete a combination of various formal and informal learning and development activities. Saturn's use of an incentive-based professional development plan reflects the company's belief that success at Saturn is dependent upon all employees making a commitment to lifelong learning.

Arthur Andersen's Consultants Enter into the Major/Minor/Masters & Continuing Education Program

Arthur Andersen's strong commitment to training won the firm the ASTD's 1992 award for excellence in workplace education. (Previous recipients of this award have included Federal Express, Xerox, Motorola, Ford, and Dayton-Hudson.) One of the recent

FIGURE 6–2
Arthur Andersen's Major/Minor/Master & Continuing Education Program

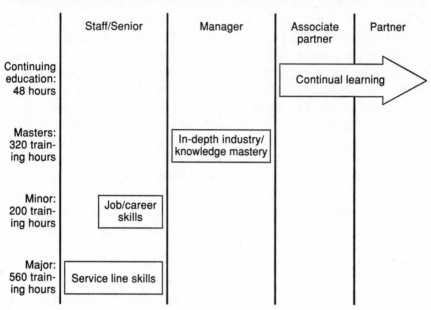

Courtesy of Arthur Andersen.

innovations—as of 1990—within Andersen Consulting, the consulting arm of the firm, is a training model known as the Major/Minor/Masters & Continuing Education Program (MMM&CE). Essentially, this program refers to a process that all Andersen consultants—from entry level through partner—undergo to acquire an appropriate group of skills tied to their specific levels within the organization. For example, at each level of an Andersen consultant's career, there is a corresponding curriculum of formal training courses and informal learning activities that must be completed before the consultant can move on to the next level—be it senior, manager, associate partner, or partner. This program is shown in Figure 6–2.

According to Larry Silvey, a partner in the professional education division, the combination of a formal curriculum along with a required number of training hours at each level of the

MMM&CE program was developed to ensure the quality of Andersen consultants. As Silvey sees it, "Our consultants are our most important asset. We decided to formalize a process which would train these consultants in how to bring all of the areas of expertise of our firm together to service clients."

The primary difference between the MMM&CE and the previous training model used by Andersen Consulting is its emphasis on ensuring the professional development of each consultant by tying achievement of training goals to an individual's job promotion. MMM&CE specifically spells out a mix of formal training classes, multimedia training programs, job assignments, and informal knowledge networking with peers that must happen before a consultant can be promoted to the next level at the firm.

MMM&CE works similarly to a traditional university. In a university, a student picks a major and then supplements this major with in-depth knowledge in a minor: another discipline. At Andersen Consulting, employees are hired into a particular service line of business (either Strategic Services, Systems Integration, Change Management, or Business Process Management). This service line is their "major" and they must complete a total of 560 training hours over a period of 5 to 6 years and demonstrate competency before they move on to the next level, that of senior. Once the consultant is promoted to senior, he or she enters into the "minor" program where the requirement is 200 training hours and the consultant participates in industry-specific training (usually meeting a specific practice need in his or her office), as well as management development-type training. Next, when the consultant is promoted to manager, he or she enters the "masters" program where the requirement is 320 training hours leading to the acquisition of deeply specialized skills and knowledge in the issues and business challenges surrounding a particular industry (i.e., financial services, telecommunications, or health care). Finally, having demonstrated competencies at the masters level, the consultant can be promoted to associate partner and now enters the "continuing education" part of the program, fulfilling 48 hours of continuing education annually at the partnership level.

Sound tough? The MMM&CE program, which ties the completion of training to job promotion, is Andersen Consulting's way of ensuring that their 11,657 consultants have the requisite skills, knowledge, and competencies needed to optimally service clients. Silvey describes what he sees as the end benefit of the MMM&CE program: "Our clients want deep expertise of a team of professionals proposing business solutions, rather than one person providing answers to the immediate problem at hand." This partnership between the firm and its employees seeks to build broad professional development for each consultant rather than for him or her to simply acquire a smorgasbord of discrete skills. And much like Saturn, the heart of the program is the contract between the employer and the employee which outlines the specific skills, knowledge, and competencies needed to move up the career ladder. As employees fulfill their end of the contract, they in turn ensure their employability in the marketplace.

PARTNERING WITH SUPPLIERS

The partnership-building mindset can also enhance the way in which an organization manages its suppliers. The old-style relationship between companies and suppliers was characterized by arm's-length dealings and little involvement. American companies have realized that this adversarial relationship with suppliers has hindered them as they have watched Japanese companies create a competitive edge through a series of alliances with their suppliers and customers. Now, more and more companies, especially those that compete directly with Japanese firms such as Motorola and Intel, are forging long-term alliances with suppliers and working with them to ensure that both sides embrace the same set of quality practices. Often, this requires supplier training.

The Semiconductor Industry Provides an Example of Partnership Building

The semiconductor industry provides an interesting example of an industry which, under the gun of intense global competition, was forced to reinvent itself by adopting the principles of total quality and, in the process, forming strong partnership bonds with suppliers and customers. The event that forced this change was the loss of business due to foreign competition. As of the mid-1980s, the American semiconductor industry led the world in innovation and the introduction of new products. Now, eight years later, many links in the supply chain are dominated by foreign companies. In fact, 62 U.S. equipment and material companies have disappeared since 1990. Some companies have failed, others have merged, but nearly half were acquired by foreign interests.[3]

The American semiconductor industry fought back with the creation of SEMATECH, a consortium of 14 semiconductor firms which aims to restore U.S. leadership in semiconductor-making equipment. Together, these companies comprise about 80 percent of the semiconductor business in the United States. SEMATECH, which is funded jointly by member firms and the U.S. Department of Defense, is described in its 1991 annual report as an "experiment in generic, precompetitive cooperation."[4] The participating companies share precompetitive research and technology, the individual expertise of their employees (225 member-company assignees have rotations at SEMATECH headquarters in Texas), and a desire and commitment to make continuous improvements to products, processes, and service, as well as to lower the total cost of ownership.

From indications, SEMATECH is beginning to accomplish its goal. The *New York Times*, in its October 5, 1992, issue, reported that SEMATECH has been credited with helping to reverse the decline in market share of U.S. semiconductor equipment makers. According to the *New York Times* reporter, the U.S. share of the $20 billion market for semiconductor manufacturing equipment climbed from 38 percent in 1990 to 41 percent in 1991.[5]

The 14 semiconductor firms, including Motorola, Intel, Hewlett-Packard, and IBM, to name just a few, have identified partnership building as nothing less than a survival skill. The organization has set for itself the twin goals of heightening members' awareness of the importance of partnering and providing training in the specific skills involved in building productive long-term alliances with customers and suppliers. As Michael Oswald, SEMATECH's manager of partnership training, says, "SEMATECH's mission is to be the lightning rod within the semiconductor industry: to wake up member companies as well as their equipment and material suppliers to the need to build relationships that are viable in the long term."

As SEMATECH well recognizes, an organization's ability to partner usually requires a fundamental, organizationwide shift in attitudes and behaviors. The biggest challenge for the organization often lies in putting aside a deeply ingrained guardedness toward outsiders in favor of adopting a more cooperative posture. To help its members make this transition, SEMATECH has developed a series of training seminars entitled "Partnering for Total Quality."

Offered to the member companies' employees, "Partnering for Total Quality" shows them how to think about suppliers and customers in a new and enlightened way. It begins with a self-assessment quiz designed to help trainees assess how well their organization's culture fosters partnering and to build partnering awareness inside the company by promoting constructive dialogue among departments. This quiz, which can be useful to all companies in thinking about building their relationships with customers and suppliers, was developed using the seven Malcolm Baldrige criteria as a framework. It is shown in Figure 6–3.

SEMATECH uses this quiz in their Partnering for Total Quality seminar. The quiz helps participants assess the attitudes and behaviors used within their company before they learn the how-to's of partnering, such as how to launch a program to train suppliers and customers in quality principles and, notably, how to evaluate and choose the right suppliers for long-term alliances, one of the most difficult challenges of partnering. SEMATECH's approach to partnering is a valuable lesson for all companies as they try to build relationships with the significant others in their customer/supply chain. So go ahead and take the same first step SEMATECH's members take and see how your company scores in fostering a spirit of partnership.

Motorola's Partnership with Suppliers

One company which uses supplier training as a launching pad for building long-term business partnerships is Motorola. Motorola University created the supplier program, called Partnership For

FIGURE 6–3
Partnering Awareness Self-Assessment Quiz*

Scoring
1—Not at all
2—To a small extent
3—To a moderate extent
4—To a great extent
5—To a very great extent

1. Leadership
With regard to supplier relations, our senior management leadership:
A. Supports total cost decision making and nonadversarial negotiations. _____
B. Has established mutually beneficial, open communications based on trust as our mode of operation. _____
C. Has designated a senior individual (champion) responsible for communicating these Partnering values to every employee and to ensure that an effective supplier partnership program is in place. _____
                                                          Subtotal 1 _____

2. Customer Involvement and Satisfaction
Our organization:
A. Actively participates in key customer meetings to understand requirements, expectations and long-term technical and business strategies. _____
B. Follows up with customers to determine customer satisfaction and to gain information for improvement. _____
C. Has empowered customer-contact employees to resolve problems promptly and to take extraordinary measures, when appropriate, to provide effective and timely service. _____
                                                          Subtotal 2 _____

3. Strategic Quality Planning
Regarding our planning cycle, our organization:
A. Thoroughly understands our supply chain's ability to meet the quality requirements in the time-frame required at a cost that will permit long-term financial viability. _____
B. Participates in customer meetings to understand and prioritize activities for continuous improvement. _____
C. Works with our supply chain to ensure that they have the education, training, technology, human resources, and capital to meet future requirements. _____
                                                          Subtotal 3 _____

FIGURE 6–3
(continued)

---

4. Human Resource Utilization

With regard to employee/customer/supply chain interactions, our organization:

A. Encourages employee accountability for ethical and responsible business practices based on mutual trust and respect through individual training, objectives setting, and performance evaluations. _____

B. Encourages the creation of cross-functional teams within the organization that mutually define goals, requirements, dependencies, and expectations, and then supportively work with the supply chain. _____

C. Establishes clear definitions of responsibility, supports decision-making authority at the lowest practical level, to encourage rapid responsiveness to customers, suppliers, and intracompany inquiries. _____

Subtotal 4 _____

5. Quality Assurance of Products and Services

Our organization:

A. Has systems for measuring quality and variability through adequately, documented joint assessment and valuation with suppliers. _____

B. Has communicated the quality methods and correlates those methods with our supply chain. _____

C. Encourages information and data sharing with meaningful, frequent, and timely feedback of problems and successes. _____

Subtotal 5 _____

6. Information and Analysis

Our organization maintains a quality and information database that:

A. Includes information about customer requirements; internal operations and processes; safety, health, and other regulatory considerations; benchmark data; supplier quality results; and other processes that ensure validity of information, standardization, and timely access throughout the organization. _____

B. Is shared between customer and supplier to provide definitive information for improved performance, to assist in developing joint value analysis decisions, and to mutually determine Total-Cost-of-Ownership. _____

C. Provides access to customer/supplier technology roadmaps and to long-term planning information. _____

Subtotal 6 _____

FIGURE 6–3
(continued)

7.   Quality Results
Our organization:
A.   Has supplier quality and certification programs in place that reward continuously improved performance.   ____
B.   Participates in joint customer/supplier value analysis discussions for product improvements and reduction of TotalCost-of-Ownership.   ____
C.   Participates in mutually supported customer/supplier yield improvement programs.   ____

Subtotal 7   ____

Summary	Subtotals
1. Leadership	____
2. Customer Involvement and Satisfaction	____
3. Strategic Quality Planning	____
4. Human Resource Utilization	____
5. Quality Assurance of Products and Services	____
6. Information and Analysis	____
7. Quality Results	____
Total Points	____

Evaluation of Results

Review points by category to quickly highlight areas for improvement. Scores of less than 9 points per category indicate the need for immediate improvement efforts. A score of 12 points per category indicates that factors are in place that will allow your organization to compete effectively in the marketplace. A score of 13 to 15 points per category indicates than an attitude of continuous improvement is in place that will promote long-term success.

This self-assessment quiz is part of the SEMATECH Partnering for Total Quality Program designed to provide the semiconductor industry infrastructure with the tools necessary to implement Total Quality.

(concluded)

Growth, as early as 1982. According to Paul Brault, manager of supplier/customer training at Motorola University, the Partnership For Growth Program focuses on three objectives: (1) to improve communications between Motorola and its suppliers, (2) to improve the business performance, and (3) to share mutual growth opportunities.

The premise behind the Partnership For Growth Program is to share with selected Motorola customers and suppliers the lessons Motorola has learned in continuous performance improvement. Essentially, the Partnership For Growth Program includes having customers and suppliers complete four core courses that Motorola internal employees also undergo. These include "Understanding Six Sigma," "Manufacturing Cycle Management," "Introduction to Techniques for Quality Improvement," and "Design for Manufacturability." As a group, these courses bring select Motorola customers and suppliers together to learn the same things Motorolans learn: how to achieve Motorola's vision for quality, reliability, cycle-time reduction, and profit.

The Partnership For Growth program allows customers and suppliers the flexibility of either attending courses at their own locations, attending Motorola University, or even licensing courses from Motorola to conduct on-site. By the end of 1991, about 6,000 suppliers and customers participated in about 125,000 hours of training, generating roughly $2.3 million dollars in revenues for Motorola. This represented a 35 percent increase over the 1990 participation in this program.[6]

But over and above the revenues generated by the program (this is essentially priced on a break-even basis), the Partnership For Growth program has brought bigger benefits. It has accomplished a mindset shift in Motorola employees' perceptions of suppliers and customers—from guarded associates to business partners.

The training for Motorola suppliers has not been voluntary. Motorola requires that preferred suppliers must participate in this training in order to maintain their preferred-supplier status. Nonetheless, the response from suppliers who participate in this training has changed from annoyance to receptiveness. "Initially, our suppliers balked when we mandated this training as well as the requirement for all suppliers to apply for the Malcolm Baldrige Award. But now, many suppliers see the end benefits," adds Brault. The primary benefit for suppliers has been that, as a group, they have begun to better understand Motorola's culture of continuous learning and have built this into their operations. This, in turn, has brought improvements in their productivity levels while meeting Motorola's goals for quality.

As a result of the creation and success of its Partnership For Growth program, Motorola earned *Purchasing* magazine's 1991 Medal of Excellence. The award recognized Motorola for its effectiveness in making continual improvements in its own processes as well as those of its suppliers. The specific achievements that led to Motorola's winning this award were impressive indeed. They included developing the Partnership For Growth program to train both customers and suppliers, conduct on-site quality audits of all preferred suppliers, and, finally, drive down the sheer number of suppliers. For example, the communications group at Motorola has pared the number of suppliers from 4,200 to 1,155. Why has paring the number of suppliers become an objective? Motorola now works with a select group of suppliers who share the company's vision of quality and are better able to meet their requirements for continuous improvement.

With its supplier training program at Motorola University up and running, Motorola has been able to move on to the next level and focus on building partnerships with preferred suppliers and getting them into the design process at an earlier stage. Brault adds that, "Many quality problems really boil down to specification issues and that's why Motorola created the Partnership For Growth program to, in essence, search out the best-in-class suppliers, train them, and then work with them in the early design phases of a project to make continuous improvements in quality, service, and, last but not least, price."

An example of Motorola's next-stage partnership building efforts is its engineering exchange program, whereby engineers from various suppliers literally take up residence at a Motorola plant. The objective of this program, along with scores of other early supplier development programs, is to involve suppliers early enough that they can be proactive in assisting Motorola with ideas for new products or processes, rather than be reactive to product design specifications. The program had its first trial run in 1990, when a resident engineer from Continental Circuits spent a couple of weeks getting acquainted with product development processes at Motorola's plant in Plantation, Florida. This program has since won a citation from *Purchasing* magazine as a "perfect example" of early supplier involvement.

The Next Goal of Supplier Partnering: Supplier Training Consortiums

If training suppliers has led to building long-term business part-nerships with suppliers, what is the next level of partnership building going to be? Motorola University, once again, has taken the lead in creating a Supplier Training Consortium, which in-cludes Motorola, DEC (who is both a supplier and a customer), Xerox, and SEMATECH. This Supplier Training Consortium, formed in 1990, is intended to be a clearinghouse for information about supplier training. Another of its goals is to establish cross-certification requirements so that a supplier who completes one company's supplier training program is certified by this Consor-tium and the supplier's training is recognized by the member companies.

The ultimate vision of Supplier Training Consortiums is to de-velop a supplier base that understands member companies' qual-ity visions and is fully prepared to meet both the current and evolving industry needs. But how does a company deliver these supplier training programs? The approach taken by the Supplier Training Consortium is to build a network of Supplier Training Centers™ (STC™) across the country using community colleges as the distribution point for supplier training programs. Commu-nity colleges are used instead of state or private four-year univer-sities because their charter requires them to respond to the needs of local businesses. Using the community colleges as the distri-bution point serves another function as well: having the supplier training programs become college accredited. While college ac-creditation of supplier training programs was not the initial goal of the Supplier Training Consortium, it appears to be the direc-tion for future supplier training programs.

The lessons of the semiconductor industry, where quality prac-tices have been in place for a decade, illustrate the importance of taking a systems view of training, where the goal is not just to provide training, but to learn how to build alliances with key members of a company's customer/supply chain. Increasingly, Corporate Quality Universities are becoming the nerve center in offering customers and suppliers the opportunity to participate in forums to learn how to create a work environment where everyone continuously strives for improvements. The old emphasis of Corporate Universities on building subject matter expertise has given way to a new focus—one where Corporate Quality Universities help the members of their employee/customer/supply chain learn how to do business in a changing workplace, where there are fewer boundaries and more communication between all the links in the chain. But a word of caution, which may seem obvious, should be noted here. Before companies rush out to open their doors and courses to suppliers and customers, they must give careful thought to what they want to achieve and which courses and/or training programs are suitable for outsiders. The companies profiled here have spent time to clearly spell out their objectives and develop a specific catalog of courses targeted to outside suppliers and customers.

PARTNERING WITH CUSTOMERS

The progressive companies profiled here have also developed training under the university umbrella for their customers, the client companies who sell their products. Initially, many customer training programs started as a way to train a customer in how to use the company's products. But, over time, the concept of customer training has broadened to include training customers in how to run more successful and profitable businesses. What better way to increase customer loyalty than by helping customers build more profitable business operations?

Dana Corporation's Customer Training

A company with a long-standing tradition of training customers is Dana Corporation, a $5 billion company which is the third largest automotive parts manufacturer in the world. In fact, Dana's emphasis on customer training dates back to 1941, when the company launched the Doctor of Motors program, a correspondence course, still in operation today, for automotive technicians to update their skills in automotive repair. At the completion of the correspondence course, each automotive technician receives a Doctor of Motors® emblem to proudly wear on his jacket, signaling to customers that he has participated in formal continuing education.

Over time, this emphasis on training customers evolved into a week-long, hands-on customer training program at the Dana Customer Training Center in Ottawa Lake, Michigan. It's here that automotive technicians learn not only how to install, operate, and repair Dana's products, but also how to run a more-successful auto repair shop. While the automotive technicians pay a nominal registration fee of about $150 to enroll in these programs (this fee is more to ensure their commitment than to recoup the costs of training development and delivery), they have never been more enthusiastic in their attendance. During 1992, attendance reached 5,000 customers.

Dana's commitment to providing customers with training has to be understood in the context of the company's philosophy of providing exceptional training and development to its own employees. Dana Corporation was profiled in the book *In Search of Excellence* as a shining example of a company that has a strong people orientation, one which believes fervently in the importance of treating employees as the company's most critical asset. In fact, in the company's 1991 annual report, ongoing education for Dana employees is highlighted as vitally important to the company's continued success. Dana's belief in education led to the creation of Dana University in 1969, which is dedicated to the continuous self-improvement of every Dana employee.

Through its Doctor of Motors® program and its hands-on customer training at the Dana Customer Training Center, Dana extends this commitment to providing exceptional training to its customer constituency. Gary Corrigan, director of Dana's customer training services, believes training customers will continue to grow in overall importance as companies discover this to be a powerful marketing tool to differentiate the company's products and build long-term alliances with customers. Corrigan says, "The core of our customer training program is built around training customers to be more successful in their businesses, certifying them in various skills and then recognizing them for their achievements." Corrigan believes that what makes customer training so powerful as a marketing tool is the high level of involvement that naturally happens between the company and its customer during the course of the training. This benefit is best summed up in a quote that Corrigan has spread throughout the Dana Customer Training Center, from wall posters to inserts in brochures. The quote, which dates back to Confucius, goes like this:

Tell me, I'll forget. Show me, I may remember. But involve me, and I'll understand.

The primary reason Dana focuses its efforts on training its customers is the increasing sophistication of cars. Automotive technicians are now required to know a vast amount of information on how to repair today's sophisticated cars. For example, in 1980, the professional manuals on automotive repair totaled 30,000 pages. Then, in 1990, these manuals grew to more than 90,000 pages. It is estimated that as cars continue to use sophisticated computers and increase in complexity, these automotive manuals, in the year 2000, will run 275,000 pages.

How do Dana's customers, the repair shops, react to this training? According to Corrigan's results from a recent phone survey, 90 percent of the students have recommended the program to a co-worker. This word-of-mouth has promoted Dana's customer training to other customers. There are other ways that Dana knows the customer training programs are working. For example, Dana executives estimate that more equipment and parts are sold because of the customer training programs. When the repair shop knows more about how to run a business, and when its technicians are both more adept at repairing cars and more knowledgeable about Dana, its capabilities and product line, the business performs better and can buy more from Dana.

But Dana's customer training has produced a side benefit that other companies profiled in the book have noticed as well: reduced employee turnover. According to Dana's Corrigan, "We have been able to break down the myth that once employees are trained, they leave for a better job elsewhere." Corrigan says he has done telephone surveys of customers who have completed Dana's Doctor of Motors® program and hands-on training program. He has found that, one year after training, automotive technicians were not only still on the job, they were satisfied workers. Training, as Saturn, Xerox, Motorola, and scores of other companies have found, reduces the ambiguity associated with a job and helps a worker feel more satisfied on the job and less likely to change to another job.

And, let's face it, as far as Dana Corporation is concerned, reduced employee turnover at their customers' sites is good for their businesses. When a repair shop can keep a top technician, this means that repair jobs will most likely get done right. And this will probably translate into customers who are also satisfied and continue doing business with the shop. Corrigan sums up his case for customer training in saying, "We have estimated that a 5 percent increase in customer retention at our customer's repair shop can mean as much as a 25 percent increase in profit to them." So, it's no wonder that Dana's customers have become a word-of-mouth sales force for Dana customer training.

What's on the horizon for Dana's customer training program? The next order of business is to develop alliances with community colleges and vocational schools around the country so they can become the distribution point for additional Dana customer training programs. Dana is also looking to more extensive usage of satellite technology to broadcast customer training to the more than 300,000 locations around the country that repair cars. Corrigan's goal is nothing short of training customers at their moment of need.

Xerox Document University
Institute of Customer Education

Xerox, long noted for its history of training excellence, first launched a centralized education facility in 1971 to provide superior training to internal employees, and over time, this training was extended to its customers. As stated in the 1993 Xerox Document University catalog, the goal of the facility was:

> to be a place where Xerox people (employees, current customers, and potential customers) come together to learn about the company's varied document-processing technologies, products, and how to better meet the management challenges of the future.

There are three major schools of learning within Xerox Document University (XDU), Executive Education, Professional Development, and Advanced Customer Training. Of these three, Advanced Customer Training (ACT) has been in existence for over ten years and has proven highly effective in generating satisfied customers for Xerox. For example, Xerox ACT has trained over 8,500 customers since its inception. These customers learn how to have maximum uptime for their equipment, while acquiring skills in copy quality enhancement and application usage. Over time, the graduates of Xerox ACT become resident experts on Xerox products, and often help Xerox by minimizing or even eliminating many unnecessary service calls on the equipment. The real benefit of this training, however, has been in the area of customer loyalty. Xerox-trained customers have strong feelings of customer relations, and truly feel like an integral part of the Xerox team. As Gary Aslin, director of Xerox Document University and a former sales executive says, "The best sales person a Xerox sales manager can have is a well-trained customer."

Within the last two years, Aslin has begun to focus on building the Xerox Institute of Customer Education to provide broadly based executive and professional development training to customers, in addition to advanced customer training. The rationale here is simply to help Xerox customers become more successful in their businesses. While there are still many course offerings for Xerox customers in how to maintain equipment and understand the technology of the "document," the fastest growth area is in developing courses in executive presentation skills, sales training, quality management tools, diversity awareness, and management skills for frontline workers. What Xerox is attempting here is to leverage its tradition of training excellence in building a profitable business in training customers.

A New Target for Training— the Customer's Sales Force

For some companies, another valuable way to partner with customers is to train the customer's sales force. Companies are taking this initiative for a number of compelling reasons. First, they are always looking for ways to build closer bonds with their customer companies. By providing training to their sales forces, they are really offering customers a competitive edge in selling their product to the end-user. But, additionally, training a customer's sales force can give a company an opportunity to get closer to understanding the needs of the end-user and ultimately use this input in the development of new products. Finally, the total quality movement has prompted many corporations to look at their people as a vitally important asset and source of differentiation. So training a customer's sales force can become an important leverage point in a company's employee/customer/supply chain.

However, companies providing this training to customers' sales forces are concerned that once the customer sales personnel benefit from training, they will abruptly leave and go sell for the competition. As mentioned earlier, the follow-up research done by four companies who have extensive efforts in place to train their customer's salespeople—Ford Motor Company, Hart Schaffner & Marx, The Iams Company (a $300 million privately held company in the premium pet food market), and Dana Corporation—indicate that customers' employees who are trained tend to stay on the job. The explanation: Training reduces job ambiguity, a major reason why people quit their jobs. When employees do not know what is expected of them, they are far more likely to leave than when expectations are clear and employees feel they have the skills to do the job. So, providing training for the customer's sales force increases its professionalism and this, in turn, creates greater satisfaction and stability among workers.

Ford Motor Company, Hart Schaffner & Marx, and The Iams Company are examples of companies in quite diverse industries that have developed their customer training programs within a university framework. They are presented below as illustrations of three distinct and innovative approaches to customer sales force training.

Ford Heavy Truck University targets training at the dealer team. Ford Heavy Truck University may have no ivy walls, no ancient literature classes, and certainly no bricks and mortar, but it is dedicated to continuous learning and development of its students—the Ford dealer team. Ford Heavy Truck University consists of a network of classrooms across the country where Ford Heavy Truck dealer principals, sales managers, and sales staff learn specialized product knowledge, consultative selling skills, and customer service skills. Jeff Kahn, director of Ford Heavy Truck University, explains Ford's motivation behind launching Ford Heavy Truck University when he says, "As more products are viewed by consumers to be at parity, the most viable way to add value to a product is through the people on the selling floor."

Ford Heavy Truck University provides a classic case of how a company goes about applying the principles outlined in Chapter 2 to training. Prior to the launch of Ford Heavy Truck University, training focused on technical and product knowledge skills. Then, in the mid-80s, Ford Heavy Truck commissioned a needs analysis to understand what type of training was required and needed by various segments of its work force, including the dealers, the dealers' employees, Ford management, and Ford sales managers in the field. The results of this research pointed to the need to view training as a long-term business strategy, as well as an opportunity to build numerous partnerships with the dealers and even the dealers' customers in order to develop the best-trained people in the industry.

With the launch of Ford Heavy Truck University in April 1988, a comprehensive and integrated training program was developed to ensure that the Ford Heavy Truck dealer team had the right mix of skills needed to sell Ford Heavy Trucks. What's more, the training for these dealers was not solely focused on product and technical skills as training had been in the past. Now, Ford Heavy Truck University developed courses on Ford culture and values, its commitment to quality, benefit selling, competitive product knowledge, interpersonal skills, and, importantly, how to apply the results of Ford customer satisfaction studies to selling Ford Heavy Trucks.

This curriculum was developed as part of a systematized effort to deliver a consistent message of Ford quality across various levels, functions, and segments. This common language, delivered to both the frontline dealer's sales force, sales managers, and the parts and service personnel, was the critical link missing from previous training programs.

Ford Heavy Truck University carries out the traditional university theme in several ways: it offers a course catalog, a senior ring, and even certification levels, which resemble college standings, to graduates. Each level—associate, senior, and master—

requires dealers to successfully perform specific competencies. The emphasis is not just on the college-style accoutrements, but on the professional development of each trainee so he or she achieves higher levels of performance on the job.

Certification levels were designed for a couple of reasons. First, Ford managers believed that by packaging the training into certification levels, with the demonstration of competencies at each level and corresponding recognition of these competencies, the training at the University would be linked to the corporation's strategic business needs. Second, since the training at Ford Heavy Truck University is eligible for continuing education credits at Northwood Institute (a Michigan-based university granting a degree in automotive marketing), trainees had to be able to demonstrate measurable levels of proficiency to be granted continuing education credits.

Finally, to keep the Ford Heavy Truck University on track, Ford managers created a board of regents, again building on its university theme. The goal of the board of regents is to ensure that the training offered meets the needs of Ford, the dealer organization, and, importantly, the participants themselves. At FHTU, the Board of Regents is composed of dealer principals, Ford managers, and a mix of certified, senior-, and master-level associates, who give feedback on how to continually improve the design, delivery, and evaluation of the training to better meet trainees' needs on the job.

What's next for Ford Heavy Truck University? The entire program is planned now to extend to the dealers' parts and servicing departments, since this has been a critical, but often overlooked, area in terms of training. "Often, our customer satisfaction is as dependent upon the after-sales support as the initial sales effort," adds Kahn of Ford Heavy Truck University.

While Ford Heavy Truck University is primarily directed to the sales force of Ford dealers, its purpose is much like that of any other Corporate Quality University outlined so far in the book: to be a vehicle for continuous learning in support of a company's business objectives.

Hart Schaffner & Marx creates a retail university for the sales forces of its customers. Why would a manufacturer of expensive men's suits set up a university for the retail sales forces of its customers? Ken Hoffman, president and chief executive officer of Hart Schaffner & Marx, says the impetus was simple. "We wanted to get closer to the end-user (i.e., the suit buyer), and, in the process, provide our customers—the retailers—with much-needed professional training."

In February 1990, HSMU opened its doors to 275 students from 30 states across the United States. Located above one of the Hart Schaffner & Marx factories in Chicago, HSMU is designed to teach retailers—from managers to salespeople and alterations personnel—the science of selling men's suits: specifically, suits made by Hart Schaffner & Marx. This training is free to all retail accounts who carry Hart, Schaffner & Marx suits; those who do not must pay a small tuition fee per course. However, this tuition fee can often be offset by scholarships from suppliers to Hart Schaffner & Marx (i.e., the companies who supply them with buttons, fabric, and even sewing machines), so many retailers pay only for the travel expense associated with sending their salespeople to the course.

In fact, one of the innovations in creating HSMU was the support it generated from numerous suppliers. HSMU got off the ground when Jerry Marxhausen, executive vice president of Hart Schaffner & Marx, created an endowment fund and requested that suppliers to Hart Schaffner & Marx, such as Burlington Industries, Apparel Machinery & Supply Co., and even some Italian companies who supply fabric, donate money to start up a training organization for their customers' sales forces. The response was overwhelming. These suppliers contributed about one third of the start-up costs, totaling roughly $350,000.[7]

The overriding goal set for HSMU by Hart, Schaffner & Marx is to create and expand a loyal customer base. HSMU does this by not only teaching the retail salespeople how a Hart Schaffner & Marx suit is made (this is where a lot of the training for retail sales associates was formerly targeted), but also how to sell the suits to their customers. The retail salespeople at HSMU learn a set of sales skills "that any hard-driving IBM salesperson knows," such as how to handle objections, close the sale, and maintain relationships with clients. Peter Huston, director of HSMU, has created a curriculum for selling suits that covers the subject in its finest detail. Students study diagrams illustrating how to physically approach a customer in order to open a sales dialogue and

even practice mock telephone scripts in prospecting for customers. HSMU believes that if they can teach their customers'
sales forces to be more successful at selling suits, over time this
will translate to greater sales volume for Hart Schaffner & Marx.
The curriculum as it was originally developed is shown in Figure 6–4.

In the past two years of its operation, Huston, director of
HSMU, has been tracking the results of HSMU. So far, surveys
show greater job satisfaction among the retail associates who attended HSMU (in line with research results from Dana Corporation on their training programs for its customers' sales forces) and
greater customer loyalty among the retailers. But has this increased sales of Hart Schaffner & Marx suits? HSMU's Huston
hedges in answering this one, saying only that retailers need assistance in tracking the isolated impact of HSMU on sales.

**The Iams Company trains customers to be more success-
ful running their businesses.** The Iams Company, started in
1946, is the fruit of Paul Iams's determination to create the highest quality pet food on the market at that time. Prior to Paul Iams'
venture into the pet food business in 1946, many pet owners prepared their pets' diets in their own kitchens, while many others
used canned pet food. The Iams Company virtually created the
premium dry dog food market with the manufacture of Iams dog
food in 1950.

Since then, The Iams Company, a $300 million privately held
company, has become the market-share leader in the premium
pet food market and, in the process, has developed a strong commitment and belief that training its employees as well as its customers is an essential part of the success of the company. This
emphasis within The Iams Company on continuous training and
self-development is carried out by Iams University, often referred
to as the "Motorola University" of small companies. Iams University, a network of classes across the country, provides training to
select members of the Iams business channel, such as distributors, pet stores, veterinarians, and breeders.

The objective of training offered by Iams University is not only
to train customers in animal nutrition and well-being, and the

FIGURE 6–4
The HSMU Curriculum

Store Management	Business Plan	Product
Image	Customer Retention	Sales Skills
Clientele Building	Fitting Skills	Service Skills

Business Plan	*Image*
• How to create a plan. • Focus on behavior. • How to use, monitor, and measure goals.	• Looking the part. • Visual display. • Floor planning.

Product	*Service Skills*
• Construction. • Piece goods. • Features vs. benefits. • Custom box. • Direction and trends.	• A service perspective. • Types of service. • Communication skills. • Personal attention ideas.

Sales Skills	*Store Management*
• Effective greeting. • Determine needs. • Professional presentation. • Handling objections and questions. • Multiple selling. • Customer profiles.	• Steps to a service culture. • Management styles and personalities. • Motivating others. • Planning and goals. • Profit impact of market strategy.

Fitting Skills	*Clientele Building*
• Proper tools and etiquette. • How to measure. • Relationship of model and body type. • Technical instruction.	• How-to system. • Maximize the phone. • Prospecting.

Courtesy of Hart, Schaffner & Marx University.

Iams product line, but also to train them in such areas as sales, business management, customer service, and personnel policy matters. Since many of Iams' customers are small pet store businesses or one-person veterinarian practices, this training and self-development coursework is viewed as a one-of-a-kind benefit with high professional value. The Iams University training is as highly prized in the pet store business as Hart Schaffner & Marx University's training is among suit salespeople.

Two Iams programs stand out as being exemplary, one training pet store owners in how to operate a more successful business and the other developing leadership and marketing skills among Iams distributors (i.e., those who distribute the Iams product line to pet stores, garden shops, veterinarians, and others). The first program is a software program entitled, "How To Make More Pet Store Profits," offered to pet store owners for the modest fee of $100. This one-day course simulates what it's like to run a pet store and takes training participants through exercises in budgeting, advertising, merchandising, inventory, and, importantly, developing pricing strategies. According to Jack Tootson, the director of Iams University, the program has been enormously helpful in building professional management skills for pet store owners who, as small business owners, need to broaden their skills in order to run a more successful operation.

However, Tootson is finding that while these seminars provide pet store owners with many tips in how to run a more successful business, they must be creatively marketed to generate attendance. Since many pet stores are small "mom-and-pop" businesses, taking a day to "go get trained" appears on the surface to be a luxury. Tootson is trying innovative ways to offer continuing education programs on-site, as well as setting up the seminars at trade shows to make participation as convenient and as time efficient as possible.

The second program, entitled the Iams Distributor Leadership Institute, is a two-day seminar meeting each quarter, bringing distributors together with The Iams Company senior managers and outside business consultants to share ideas for building a more successful distributorship. During the two days, distributors learn about trends in the pet food business, the goals and vision for The Iams Company, and, importantly, the best practices of companies in similar lines of business.

In addition to these one-time training events, Iams University has also developed a catalog of continuing education books and video/audio tapes, known as F.I.L.E., which stands for Free Information for Learning and Education. This catalog, offered free to all Iams customers, recommends self-paced learning courses, books, seminars, and conferences which might be helpful to the continuing learning needs of Iams customers. These customers can then borrow these books and tapes for up to 30 days. Interestingly, the topics include both professional development, such as time management, negotiation, and listening, and personal development areas of financial planning, psychology, and dealing with divorce. While the F.I.L.E. is only a couple of years old, it has been very successful with customers as a quick, cost-free, and convenient way to continuously learn.

The Iams Company customer programs offered through Iams University is an innovative example of how a company with $300 million in sales is reaching out to train its employees and keep customers and stakeholders. What better way to ensure a company's own continued success?

PARTNERING WITH COLLEGES AND UNIVERSITIES

Another type of partnership seen more and more frequently is that between industry and institutions of higher learning. The interplay between companies and academic institutions, both vocational or technical colleges and traditional colleges and universities, is becoming more frequent and more purposeful than in the past, as both focus on how to prepare their respective constituencies for working in a competitive, rapidly evolving work environment.

Corporate Quality Universities have become the focal point for efforts by schools and companies to carry on the sort of dialogue that makes collaborative efforts possible. Partnerships with academic institutions are taking a variety of forms, ranging from college accreditation of Corporate Quality University courses to joint design of school curricula for specific disciplines and degrees. This section examines several specific examples.

College Accreditation of Corporate Training Programs

The means through which companies have traditionally supported and encouraged employees' continuing education outside the company is through the practice of tuition assistance. While tuition assistance provides strong incentives for employees to continue with their education, it doesn't contain much of a mechanism to guarantee either the company or the employee that the resulting learning will match the set of skills, knowledge, and competencies needed to be successful in the company.

Companies are slowly realizing that they need to do more to prepare workers in the skills needed for the future, and this realization is giving rise to innovative alliances with local colleges. Dr. James Van Dyke, associate dean of Rio Salado Community College (one of the community colleges which has built a strong alliance with both American Express and America West Airlines), believes companies who rely solely on tuition reimbursement for employee education will fall short of their goal of a prepared work force. Instead the concept of "customized education" will gradually replace straight tuition reimbursement among quality-driven companies.

This concept of customized education refers to the alliances corporations make with community colleges and some four-year institutions to build a customized training curriculum for specific job categories. These customized training programs are eligible for college accreditation while also meeting the requirements for workplace competencies outlined by the corporation.

Companies have found that the ability to offer training which is eligible for college credits offers benefits for both the employee and the company. For many employees, such training is often their first exposure to college-level work. As Deb Robbins, manager of American Express Quality University[SM], says, "We hope that if employees get college credit for training programs they complete, they will be more motivated to further their educations and pursue two- or four-year degree programs as deemed appropriate to their jobs." In addition, the companies who offer training eligible for college credit are often viewed by prospective employees as more desirable places to work. But the real motivator is deeper than that and well put by Robbins: "A recent employee survey contained some hard indications of the disparity in education levels between our frontline workers and our managers. We believe that by providing training that is eligible for college credit, we can close this gap and hopefully promote more frontline workers who have real customer contact into management positions."

American Express Quality University[SM] **training program leads to an associate degree in customer service.** The partnership between American Express Quality University and Rio Salado Community College is one example of customized education. American Express Quality University[SM] believes that delivering exceptional customer service involves a discrete set of skills in using the phone, handling customer interactions both orally and in writing, and demonstrating problem-solving skills. In addition, the customer service representative must also be familiar with the American Express quality vision and know how to apply the principles underlying this vision to his or her job. A partnership in building a degree program to meet these needs seemed to be the perfect solution. "We actively sought an educational partner who understood our mission, was flexible in wanting to work with industry, and also had the desire to create a professional program in customer service," says Deb Robbins. After a careful analysis of several local community colleges as well as four-year state universities, American Express found just such a partner: Rio Salado Community College, a two-year "college without walls" near Phoenix, Arizona. One of the reasons Rio Salado was chosen to be the educational partner to American Express was the college's track record in building a flexible, customized curriculum for America West Airlines, another local business in the Phoenix area.

The partnership between American Express Quality University[SM] and Rio Salado Community College resulted in the creation of an associate degree in applied science in Customer Service,

FIGURE 6–5

Program—American Express Quality University[SM]
Rio Salado Community College

Degree: Associate of Applied Science Degree in Customer Service
Total Number of Credits: 64 Credits

Required courses	16 Credits

Total Customer Service
Principles of Quality Service
Interpersonal Communication
Conflict Resolution
Business Communication
Human Relations In Business

Electives	14 Credits

American Express Quality University courses have been evaluated and up to 20 individual courses have been packaged together into modules suitable for direct substitution as electives in this program. Rio Salado Community College is willing to accept up to 14 credits as electives.

General education core	34 Credits

Includes such courses as Freshman English, Math, Humanities, Natural Sciences, Social Sciences, and Critical Reading (using customer problems to solve case studies).

Courtesy of American Express Quality University[SM].

the first degree designed to develop professional skills in aspiring customer service workers. The types of courses which make up this degree program are shown in Figure 6–5. Essentially, the purpose of the program is to train students in a set of professional skills deemed critical to delivering exceptional customer service by both American Express and Rio Salado Community College. The program is open to anyone—whether he or she is an American Express employee or not—who wants to make a career in customer service. Certainly, one of the benefits of the program for American Express employees is that the courses offered by American Express Quality University[SM] have been evaluated by Rio Salado Community College and up to 20 individual training courses are eligible as electives for college accreditation in the associate degree program in Customer Service.

Since these courses vary in length, they were ultimately packaged into modules in order to be eligible for college credit. The basic formula used by Rio Salado Community College to evaluate American Express courses for college credit eligibility is one companies should be familiar with if they pursue this goal. In the case of the American Express/Rio Salado partnership, it included an evaluation of four aspects of American Express Quality University^{SM} training programs.

- The content area of each course. This must focus on college-level material.
- The length of time of each course. The formula: one credit is granted for 13.3 hours of classroom time. Courses taken using alternate delivery technologies are also examined and an appropriate adjustment is made.
- How each course measures the competencies acquired. The course design should take into account some certification of competencies students will be required to demonstrate at the end of the course.
- Who teaches the course. In some states, Arizona being one, the course must be taught by an individual who is certified to be a community college instructor. Essentially, this means that those teaching the course must have five years of demonstrated expertise and experience in the content area and have taken a course in community college certification procedures. Finally, the associate of applied science degree program in Customer Service was designed by American Express and Rio Salado Community College to recognize the growing trend in alternative delivery of training. American Express coursework taken in various forms of delivery (e.g., correspondence, audio, video, computer, and distance learning) are eligible for college credit provided, of course, there is a measure of the skills and performance of the student. In effect, this allows American Express employees anywhere in the world to complete the degree regardless of their location.

Industry/College Partnerships on the Rise

If making corporate training programs eligible for college credit is such a good idea, why isn't it more prevalent among corporations? According to Dr. Lance Davis, director of PONSI at the American Council for Education, "Companies have traditionally been resistant to having outside organizations evaluate their learning objectives, grading systems, and documentation of student performance." This resistance appears to be lessening, though, as more companies create employee training programs which have measurable competencies as an output of their courses.

Companies have been working with organizations such as the Program on Noncollegiate Sponsored Instruction known as (PONSI), for the last 20 years. PONSI is the brainchild of the American Council on Education (aka ACE), a Washington, D.C.-based nonprofit group that lobbies on educational issues and represents a majority of the country's colleges and universities. ACE has evaluated courses conducted by the military since 1945. In 1974, ACE expanded its role to also cover evaluating corporate training programs and recommend appropriate ones for college credit. PONSI evaluated some 200 corporate training programs in 1992 alone, in such areas as robotics, restaurant operations, and bank management. For example, the entire two-week program in advanced restaurant management at McDonald's Hamburger University is eligible for two semester hours of undergraduate college credit.

But the drawback of going through PONSI's process is the fact that it offers no guarantee that the company's corporate training programs will actually result in transferrable college credits. PONSI only recommends that a specific corporate training program be eligible for college credit; it cannot grant the credit itself. The ultimate responsibility for obtaining credit rests with the individual employee, who must approach a particular college and request that the PONSI recommendation be honored in his or her program of study.

Among the 30 companies interviewed for this book, there is evidence of increasing interest in building industry/college partnerships. In some cases, there's a desire to obtain college credit for corporate training programs, but the greater motivation is to ensure that the college teaches the types of skills and knowledge the company needs to be successful in the marketplace.

Working with colleges to develop these joint industry/college programs, howerver, involves working through a number of obstacles. The colleges themselves have been slow to adapt their policies and procedures to forge these corporate partnerships. As Dr. Jim Van Dyke of Rio Salado Community College says, "Colleges and business organizations speak in two very different languages. Colleges need to be much more flexible in building customized education programs for industry." In addition, there's another obstacle affecting college/industry alliances—the trend toward short instructional learning modules, delivered on demand to individual learners. The Rio Salado Community College/American Express alliance takes this trend into consideration when it grants credit for coursework taken through alternate forms of delivery.

As colleges and industries continue to work together, the goal should be one of building customized curriculums linked to a career path within an organization. College accreditation of corporate training programs is simply the means to this broader and more critical objective. Customized educational programs like the American Express Quality University^{SM} associate of applied science degree in Customer Service blend the organization's training programs with core courses at Rio Salado Community College. In the end, the program leads not only to a college degree, but to a higher-skill and higher-wage job for the employee. This is precisely what these joint industry/college programs are attempting to do: bridge the gap in the technical level of jobs that Secretary of Labor Robert Reich believes is so sorely lacking in Ameria.

Colleges and Universities Are Viewed As Educational Suppliers to Companies

College accreditation of corporate training programs is one form of company/university partnership. Another is to build a strategic linkage between a company and a college in order to promote a broad and in-depth sharing of knowledge and technologies among the student body who may one day become future employees.

To get an idea of the scope of change to the industry/school relationship this type of partnering represents, think of the limited range of such relationships in the past. In the old days, interface between schools and industry was largely confined to one activity: recruiting graduates. Managing a company's graduate recruiting function used to be a lot like managing any other

supplier. Traditionally, a company would give its list of requirements (e.g., grade point average, involvement in extracurricular
activities, and leadership capabilities) to designated colleges and
universities and then wait as the schools scurried feverishly to
round up an array of suitable graduates. Dialogue between corporations and colleges would be minimal, and the entire interaction was a relatively formal, distant, once-a-year affair.

Times have changed. That arm's-length, lopsided relationship
between a company and the colleges and universities from which
it recruits, where one side makes all the demands and the other
gropes to meet them, has given way to a proactive partnering in
which each side is now concerned with making sure the requirements of tomorrow's workplace are met. Motorola, through Motorola University, has once again taken the lead in recognizing
the importance of building these academic partnerships. These
partnerships serve several purposes highly valuable to the corporation: to identify opportunities for staff rotation and student
internships, to exchange course materials, to acquire new technologies and research information related to training, and, importantly, to work with universities worldwide to ensure that
they understand the competencies the company requires of its
current and future employees.

Motorola University is at the forefront of building these types
of educational partnerships. Motorola University's vision as it re-
lates to building these educational partnerships is stated in its
1991 year-end report as:

> Motorola University seeks to form strategic partnerships with insti-
> tutions of higher learning globally in order to gain access to educa-
> tional and research sources that bring distinctive competencies in
> new technologies, program design, development and delivery or ac-
> creditation, and to influence their curriculum development to meet
> the skills and knowledge needs of all workers.[8]

Initially, Motorola executives thought that forming a network
of global relationships with universities around the world would
simply be an ideal way to distribute Motorola supplier training
programs, translate course materials into various languages, and,
over time, gain college accreditation of Motorola University training programs by colleges abroad. In a number of cases, this was

initially the case. For example, Asia Pacific International University delivers Motorola University supplier training courses, and 12 Motorola University courses on quality, manufacturing, and management are eligible for credit in the undergraduate program at Asia Pacific International University. Soon, however, this goal was expanded to include developing joint technical courses. But, over time, the ultimate goal has been to develop complementary talents and a pooling of resources for a more strategic and creative outcome. Motorola hopes these alliances will enable it to share Motorola's "customer satisfaction" culture within these international educational institutions of higher learning and establish Motorola as an employer of choice within those countries.

Motorola's long-term goal is to establish a significant university partnership in every region where Motorola has a major population or a major corporate presence. The reason for creating these partnerships goes back to the charge of Motorola University, to be a catalyst for continuous improvement and lifelong learning. As Bill Wiggenhorn says in his 1991 year-end message to Motorola University management, "We can no longer operate in single islands of achievement. We must build interlocking bridges that support the sharing of knowledge and technology."[9] During the past few years, Motorola University has met this goal by forging academic partnerships with 15 universities in areas around the world where Motorola has a major corporate presence.

The University Challenge

Perhaps one of Motorola's most significant recent achievements in building academic partnerships is the creation of the University Challenge. The University Challenge is the brainchild of Bob Galvin, chairman and CEO of Motorola. The University Challenge brings companies and universities together in a joint effort to promote the integration of quality management practices and the teaching of quality principles at the university. Galvin conceived this effort out of a conviction that both businesses and academia have a shared responsibility to learn about, teach, and practice quality. Galvin had felt academia was only paying lip service to the quality movement and was slow to either teach it or integrate it into their curricula. Furthermore, he felt that America's global competitiveness could be improved only when academia participated fully in the quality movement. So he presented academia with a challenge: learn how to implement quality and then do it, with the assistance of select business partners.

Under this program, up to 100 business and engineering professors from selected universities attend a week-long symposium held at Motorola University. There, they receive training in how to integrate the principles of quality into their business and engineering curricula and into the administrative processes running their universities. These professors are sponsored by the five participating companies: Motorola, IBM, Milliken, Proctor & Gamble, and Xerox. From an initial application of 27 universities, 8 were ultimately chosen to participate in the University Challenge. These include Purdue University, Carnegie Mellon, Georgia Tech, the University of Wisconsin, MIT, Rochester Institute of Technology, University of North Carolina, and Tuskegee University. Interestingly, the criteria used to select these eight universities was modeled after the Malcolm Baldrige Award, specifically, zeroing in on an university's ability to plan, implement, and integrate quality principles into the organization.

The University Challenge has come to be looked upon as a model for what will increasingly be more prevalent partnerships between businesses and universities. As structured, the University Challenge has benefits for both the universities and the sponsoring companies. University personnel receive in-depth expert training in such quality principles and methods as responsiveness to customers, cycle-time reduction, and the use of cross-functional teams. At the same time, the sponsoring companies are able to communicate to these universities the types of skills, knowledge, and competencies they are seeking in new hires. Earl Conway, former manager of quality for Proctor & Gamble, one of the sponsoring companies, says, "We view the University Challenge as a pilot project. If it's successful, we believe more companies will enter into these types of partnerships with academia, in order to ensure that their incoming graduate pool possesses the competencies needed for the future."

Beyond these immediate benefits, however, the University Challenge has more far-reaching implications. It is hoped that the universities who participate in these programs will begin to take a more customer-focused view of educating students for entry into the business world. The University Challenge provides universities with valuable input from their customers so they can ultimately teach students the skills businesses require of new hires.

Educational Institutions Are Making Headway in Applying Quality Principles

There are a number of universities and community colleges already making progress in meeting the needs of local businesses. Two case studies, Fox Valley Technical College and Southern Methodist University, are outlined below to show some of the programs in place within the academic community that are designed to align their institutions with changing business demands and preferences. These case studies can be helpful as models for additional business/university partnerships in the making.

Companies often wonder, "Should I be working with a community college or a four-year institution" in building partnerships with academia? The answer to this question is not a simple one and, as in any business decision, it depends upon the company's objectives and needs. Community colleges have, as their charters, to be responsive to the needs of local businesses in their communities. To this end, a number, including Fox Valley, have been successful in developing outreach programs to train and retrain local businesses in quality principles. Also, because they are smaller, community colleges can more easily experiment with integrating quality principles into their systems. Four-year state and private universities, generally, are more research-oriented and have focused their efforts on revising their MBA and engineering curricula, not necessarily reaching out to meet the needs of local businesses.

Fox Valley and its Academy for Quality.   Fox Valley Technical College in Appleton, Wisconsin, is an example of a community college that has taken the lead in implementing quality principles internally and working with local businesses to ensure that the skills and knowledge it teaches are what are expected in the marketplace. In fact, Fox Valley Technical College's (FVTC) Quality Academy has been referred to as the "Motorola University" of community colleges. That's because FVTC implemented a quality model across the entire college and, in the process, redefined itself to better respond to the needs of its customers (i.e., the businesses who hire its students). After doing this, FVTC decided to go one step further and establish the FVTC Academy for Quality in Education. Director Calley Zilinsky says, "The Academy for Quality has been set up as an outreach program to provide training for other colleges and universities as well as employees in local companies in how to apply the quality concepts and tools to an academic setting."

Fox Valley has made substantial progress in both integrating quality across the organization and in revising its curriculum to include quality topics. On the first score, Fox Valley faculty actively explored with local businesses the type of competencies students should have in a particular field of study. Then the faculty revised the curriculum accordingly.

This focus of aligning the curriculum to be responsive to business needs is certainly a new way of thinking for colleges. In a sense, the colleges in partnership with local businesses are trying to encourage the faculty to view teaching as any other quality process and to experiment with ways to improve the process by designing a curriculum which meets the needs of local businesses.

Southern Methodist University builds its graduate business curriculum based upon competencies needed by local businesses. Some graduate schools of business have been listening to the voice of change. At the insistence of the companies who hire the graduates of these schools, they have started to revise their curricula. One graduate business school in particular, Southern Methodist University, in Dallas, Texas, has begun to include training in soft skills (i.e., listening and presentation skills) along with traditional business training. How did this happen? It was at the insistence of a task force of executives from prominent local employers, such as J. C. Penny, American Airlines, Frito-Lay, and Xerox. This task force was formed to advise SMU faculty on developing a new curriculum to train business students in the competencies they required from new hires.

The task force eventually led to the formation of a Business Leadership Center, where new courses have been developed in coaching, presentation techniques, and listening. But, in addition to this, SMU has taken a tack similar to that of companies with Corporate Quality Universities. They now insist that students must demonstrate competencies in both hard and soft skills before graduation. This shift has in turn altered the requirements for incoming students to the SMU graduate School of Business. Now, not only must students meet the academic requirement of having achieved a score of 650 or higher on the GMAT (Graduate Management Admissions Test), they must also demonstrate proficiencies in business writing, listening, and presentation skills. In 1991, the first year of operation for the Business Leadership Center, incoming students met the 650 GMAT requirement, but only 35 percent met adequate proficiency levels in soft skills. SMU's new requirements and courses are evidence of a spreading recognition that tomorrow's employees will need a good foundation of interpersonal skills, as well as business skills, to succeed.

PARTNERING WITH K–12 SCHOOL SYSTEMS
Motorola's Multilevel School Partnership Model

The emphasis on partnership building has not stopped with suppliers, customers, and universities. Motorola, for example, has made a commitment to building partnerships with select K–12 school districts. In the words of Gary Tooker, president and chief operating officer, Motorola wants to become a more responsible customer of the K–12 educational system. In a specially prepared booklet written by Motorola and distributed to the household of every Motorola employee in the United States (that's over 100,000 households), Motorola's Gary Tooker describes the reason Motorola has become intent on building partnerships with local elementary school educators:

It is now more apparent than ever that the continued success of Motorola depends upon our ability to hire and retain a world-class work force in America. Our employees must be bright, flexible, able to interact with their associates in participative and problem-solving teams, and be capable of continuous learning as our workplace changes.[10]

This world-class work force is supplied by the current K–12 educational system. It is this system that Motorola University has targeted to develop multilevel partnerships as a way to vastly increase the quality of education in the K–12 systems where Motorola has a market presence. Figure 6–6 is the systems model that Motorola University is using to develop these multilevel partnerships to ensure that the graduates of the school system in targeted districts have the required competencies needed for success within Motorola.

This educational model recognizes that the greatest opportunity for change in the elementary schools is at the policy and systems level. Companies have previously responded to the crisis in the educational system with piecemeal measures, that is, by providing special services (e.g., equipment donations) or classroom enrichment opportunities, such as bringing business leaders into the classroom or even adopting an entire graduating high school class. But these resources have not attacked the problem at the systems level, where real change can be made. This systems intervention used by Motorola University involves a two-year commitment from Motorola through which it brings together a network of local businesses, educators in school districts, representatives from local colleges, community leaders, and parents to recommend how to improve the quality of teaching and the quality of education.

As of 1992, Motorola University, under the direction of Ed Bales, Motorola's director of education, external systems (Bales is essentially Motorola's point person for K–12 education), has targeted 17 school districts in Illinois and two school districts in Massachusetts, areas where Motorola has a substantial corporate presence. These will be pilots for developing and implementing an approach known around Motorola as District Learning Leadership teams, Motorola's attempt to create organizational change at the school district level. The objective is to continuously im-

FIGURE 6–6
Motorola University Multilevel Educational Partnership Model

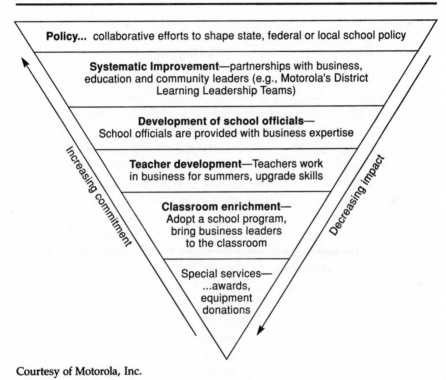

Courtesy of Motorola, Inc.

prove the curriculum within these school districts, how the curriculum is delivered, and, finally and importantly, how well students are learning the identified competencies.

The goal of the partnerships Motorola is developing with the K–12 school systems is to align the school district's curriculum with the skills and knowledge required by local business leaders and colleges; in essence, to create world-class mindware. It's this *mindware* that Motorola, as well as other companies profiled here, believe will increasingly determine a company's competitive advantage in the 21st century. While Motorola University is providing the leadership and manpower for this effort, it ultimately hopes to create hundreds of thousands of learning experiments within various school districts by encouraging superintendents, principals, teachers, and students to use new and expansive patterns of thinking and learning in the classroom.

The Kyrene De La Mirada School: A Break-the-Mold Elementary School

La Mirada means "the view" in Spanish. This is the name of a new K–5 school currently in the process of development. What's interesting about this school is that it will be the result of a collaboration between the Kyrene elementary school district in Phoenix, Arizona, and Intel Corporation. This collaboration started in 1991 when the Kyrene school district asked Intel to buy three acres of land in order to build a new K–5 elementary school. Intel executives took this opportunity to step back and ask themselves how they could better work with schools in communities where Intel was a prominent employer. Their response to the request from the Kyrene school board was to donate the three acres of land on the condition that Intel Corporation and the Kyrene school district engage in a partnership to design a Break-the-Mold school. "Our vision of a Break-the-Mold school," says John Swain, Intel's public affairs manager, "is to prove new teaching methods, develop new curricula, and start turning out better graduates."[11]

This Break-the-Mold school plans to incorporate a number of new approaches, including running the school under an Intel/Kyrene management review committee and a community-based steering committee, as well as utilizing constant feedback from Intel as to the types of skills, knowledge, and competencies Intel will require of workers in the 21st century, when today's incoming students to La Mirada will graduate from high school and join the labor force.

So how did Intel determine the types of skills, knowledge, and competencies necessary for the 21st century? For starters, Intel, in collaboration with the Kyrene school district, Arthur Andersen Consulting, and a group representing parents, students, and community leaders, organized a seminar they called a Visioning Conference. Essentially, this conference brought together a mix of people from the educational, corporate, and community worlds to create a vision of what the La Mirada school should ideally teach its students to prepare them for jobs in the 21st century.

Interestingly, the list of competencies coming out of this Visioning Conference are strikingly similar to the types of CORE workplace competencies that the Corporate Quality Universities profiled in this book currently teach employees, customers, and suppliers. They include knowing how to learn, being able to build alliances, work in teams, know how to think critically, and, above all, develop a spirit of continuous improvement and life-long learning. Figure 6–7 highlights the types of skills needed for a La Mirada graduate in the year 2005.

Intel hopes that La Mirada will provide a model for partnerships between companies and schools for others to follow. Scheduled to open its doors in September 1993, La Mirada, and the vision it embodies, will be monitored by business leaders and educators across the United States.

Partnership building is quickly becoming a critical competency for progressive companies in the 90s. This chapter surveyed some of the more interesting and innovative partnerships now underway between companies and their employees, customers, suppliers, and the universities and school systems who educate their future work forces. This practice will fundamentally alter the way business is conducted now and in the future. Increasingly, at the customer-focused companies profiled here—companies such as Saturn, Xerox, Arthur Andersen, Motorola, Intel, and Ford—the emphasis is on building partnerships with each link in the employee/customer/supply chain. These partnerships are forming for two critical reasons: to improve the company's competitiveness and to help all members of the employee/customer/supply chain collectively learn and put into practice the company's CORE workplace competencies.

The Corporate Quality University has become the focal point for building a vast array of these alliances which, in many cases, start out as training programs and seminars but, over time, grow and deepen into long-term business partnerships.

What do companies ultimately hope to attain from their efforts at partnership building? The goal, quite simply, is to have a continuous learning mentality run full circle in the employee/customer/supply chain.

FIGURE 6–7
La Mirada Graduate in the Year 2005

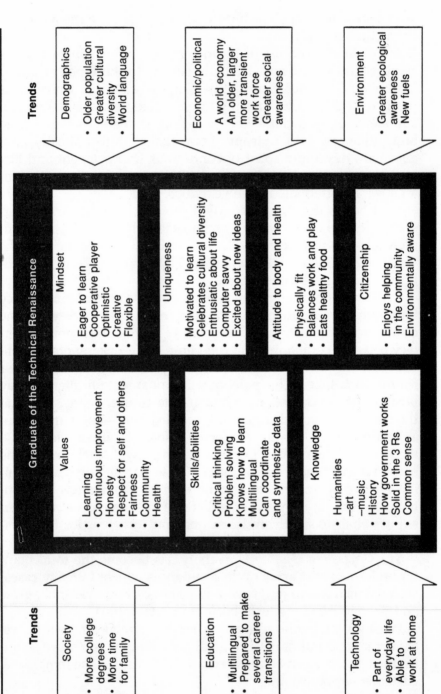

Trends

Demographics
- Older population
- Greater cultural diversity
- World language

Economic/political
- A world economy
- An older, larger more transient work force
- Greater social awareness

Environment
- Greater ecological awareness
- New fuels

Graduate of the Technical Renaissance

Mindset
- Eager to learn
- Cooperative player
- Optimistic
- Creative
- Flexible

Uniqueness
- Motivated to learn
- Celebrates cultural diversity
- Enthusiatic about life
- Computer savvy
- Excited about new ideas

Attitude to body and health
- Physically fit
- Balances work and play
- Eats healthy food

Citizenship
- Enjoys helping in the community
- Environmentally aware

Values
- Learning
- Continuous improvement
- Honesty
- Respect for self and others
- Fairness
- Community
- Health

Skills/abilities
- Critical thinking
- Problem solving
- Knows how to learn
- Multilingual
- Can coordinate and synthesize data

Knowledge
- Humanities
  - art
  - music
- History
- How government works
- Solid in the 3 Rs
- Common sense

Trends

Society
- More college degrees
- More time for family

Education
- Multilingual
- Prepared to make several career transitions

Technology
- Part of everyday life
- Able to work at home

Courtesy of Intel Corporation.

Chapter Seven

The Power of Recognition: Reinforcing Learning

A NEW SCIENCE: A SYSTEM FOR RECOGNITION

While nearly all managers and companies understand that recognition presents a way to keep employee morale high and accomplish goals, many use it less effectively than they might as a tool to reinforce learning. Why? On the level of the individual manager, some dismiss recognition as a "pat on the back," a mere gesture. Others think money is the only reward that really counts. And still others simply don't know how to give recognition in a productive manner. On the level of the company, official recognition measures, such as promotions, are often too sporadic or too highly competitive to bring forth the work forcewide, day-to-day individual commitment necessary to produce the successful behavior change that is the goal of training.

But consistent recognition of the individual employee's accomplishments can propel the employee to get involved and excited about work and, above all, *want* to continue learning every day on the job. Max DePree, in his book, *Leadership Is an Art*, poses a question every manager should ask: "What is it that most of us really want from work? We probably want to find the most effective, most productive, and most rewarding way of working together. We also would like to have a job that meets our personal needs for belonging, for contributing, for meaningful work, and for the opportunity to grow on the job. But perhaps most important of all, we'd like someone to say 'Thank You.' "[1]

Companies which have developed the type of world-class training we've been discussing are taking careful heed of this last point. One of their chief concerns is the classic training dilemma: How do you reinforce training so that it translates into lasting improvements in individual performance and collective learning for the organization? A number of companies interviewed for this book report finding an answer in a practice which seems simple and obvious, but is proving among the most potent of reinforcement tools: recognition.

Recognition is a powerful motivator because it satisfies our need for approval and acceptance. People will go to extraordinary lengths to win the approbation of their peers and superiors. For some people, recognition is a more meaningful reward than financial gain.

Realizing this, companies such as Corning, Texaco, and Xerox are taking steps to improve the use of recognition organization-wide. They are applying the same systematic, focused approach to recognition that they have applied to the training process itself. In other words, these companies are becoming scientific about recognition. This involves several separate measures:

- Companies are identifying recognition as a key business skill and a powerful tool for reinforcing learning and performance.
- They are providing training in how to give recognition.
- They are providing structured ways for recognition to be given, both formally and informally.
- They are looking at recognition as a key quality imperative on a level with Corporate Quality University training and employee empowerment.

These companies are first making a distinction between the simple recognition program revolving around an event, such as an annual awards banquet, to an entire recognition system where recognition is deployed on a consistent and ongoing basis to sustain employee learning. While virtually all companies that are quality driven have well-established reward programs honoring the heroic and exemplary deed of a few individuals, now an increasing number of companies are beginning to institute a recognition system that reaches more employees, more often. This

FIGURE 7–1
Recognition Shifts from an Event to a System

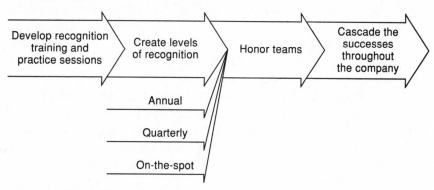

Courtesy of Quality Dynamics, Inc.

system starts with training employees in how to effectively use recognition to increase productivity and ends with devising creative and innovative ways to cascade both individual and team successes down and across the organization. This systems approach to recognition no longer limits the recognition to a handful of corporate stars for thinking of big breakthrough ideas. Instead, the goal has become to recognize each and every employee for his or her contribution and in this way sustain the message of training for the entire work force. Figure 7–1 shows this systematic approach to giving recognition.

This systems view of recognition is based on the idea that there are advantages to spreading recognition beyond the monthly, quarterly, and annual rewards to a select few. While these programs are still important and in wide use today, they are being redefined to stress the opportunity to exalt the best practices of employees, rather than just have the CEO award a corporate plaque. The goal of this systems view of recognition is to use the process of recognition as a business tool which, if used correctly and regularly, can result in increased employee productivity. Companies like Xerox, Corning, and Texaco, who use recognition systematically, largely do so to sustain and nurture the many ways employees learn in formal classrooms and informally on the job.

The key to this systems approach to recognition starts with training employees in the how-to's of recognition. Often, this "recognition training" happens within the core curriculum of the Corporate Quality University. (Texaco's recognition training will be examined in depth in the following pages.) Next, while companies with recognition systems still incorporate the annual or monthly corporate awards honoring employees and teams, these awards are now being redefined as more than just celebrations. Instead, they are becoming an integral way for employees across the organization to share their best practices. In addition, these annual and quarterly recognition programs are now being supplemented with on-the-spot recognition programs, where an employee who catches a co-worker going the extra mile can recognize that individual's efforts. Finally, this systems approach to recognition ends when companies create innovative internal communication vehicles for employees to connect with one another and cascade their successes across the entire organization. The net result of viewing recognition as a system, rather than as a one-time event or a series of infrequent programs, is to ultimately motivate everyone within the organization to continue learning and apply this learning to optimize his or her performance on the job.

Texaco's Training in Recognition

Texaco is an example of a company that has redefined this paradigm of recognition. According to Tom McMullen, the director of Texaco Quality Institute, Texaco now considers recognition a business practice having the power to reinforce business priorities. Once Texaco designated recognition as a skill to learn and then practice on the job, McMullen went on to create a training program to instruct all managers in the importance of recognition and how to deliver recognition to produce maximum productivity gains.

McMullen admits that thinking about recognition in this way is clearly a new mindset for the company. Jim Kinnear, president and CEO of Texaco, stresses the importance of delivering recognition when he says, "It's a tough world out there, with a lot of competition. The winners all have the self-confidence and determination to stay in there and prevail. Giving well-deserved recognition in an appropriate way builds self-confidence and self-esteem in our work force."[2]

When you think about recognition in this way, you realize it can be a more challenging skill to develop than even a technical skill, which can be learned and then executed in a standardized way on the job. Recognition, on the other hand, represents an interesting paradox. On the one hand, effective recognition has to be convincing, specific, timely, and well planned, yet at the same time it should be spontaneous and genuine.

STARQuality Recognition, Texaco's recognition training program, was created to fill a need addressed by employees in the 1990 Texaco Vision and Values Survey. In this survey, about 40 percent of the Texaco employees said they did not feel recognized for making quality improvements on the job and, what's more, about 35 percent of the employees said they did not feel important to the organization. Specifically, these employees wanted their managers to recognize their improvement efforts. As one Texaco employee says in the STARQuality Recognition video, "When I am recognized for a job well done, it makes me feel all charged up to get up the next day and see what else I can do for the company".

Texaco went on to design the STARQuality Recognition training program, a seminar to train Texaco employees in the how-to's of recognition. The seminar starts off with a videotape in which Texaco's president, Jim Kinnear, shares how it feels to be recognized for a job well done. In the beginning of the tape, Kinnear reveals how important it was to him to have his boss recognize that he was doing a good job when he was working halfway around the world. Other employees come forward and tell about feeling "excited, surprised, and generally good" about themselves when a manager takes the time to recognize an achievement. The employees appearing in the videotape also describe attempts at recognition that may have been well-intentioned, but turned into disasters. They point out how recognition that is poorly delivered or poorly timed leaves them feeling "stupid, awkward, and undeserving" of the recognition, especially when it's given so long after an accomplishment that it is no longer meaningful.

Texaco makes the how-to's of giving recognition easy to remember by giving each letter of the word STAR a meaning associated with recognition. For example:

S—Specific. State precisely what effort, improvement, or achievement is being praised.

T—Timely. Time the honor closely to the achievement recognized.

A—Admiring. Express your admiration . . . tell the individual or team that you are personally impressed and why.

R—Relevant. Point out how the achievement contributes to the group vision, goals, and bottom line. Remember, everyone wants to believe that he or she truly makes a difference.[3]

Following the STARQuality Recognition training program, each employee is given a laminated business card defining the specific how-to's of recognition. The idea here is that recognition is a skill which requires practice on the job.

The STARQuality Recognition training video and development session has been instrumental in developing the critical skill of giving effective recognition within all levels of employees at Texaco. It's a skill that will be increasingly important as employees work together in teams to solve problems and improve processes. As the ability of team members to work together as a cohesive whole becomes increasingly critical, recognizing the contributions of each individual employee to the group effort will, in the end, help build stronger teams.

Creating Levels of Recognition

Companies who are experimenting in this area are expanding their recognition efforts beyond the once-a-year event celebrating heroic performance. Their goal is to integrate recognition much more closely into employees' daily jobs, so that learning and good performance are constantly reinforced. A number of firms are doing this by creating levels of recognition. This approach provides a way to meaningfully honor both small day-to-day accomplishments and the major feats and achievements they produce. While the annual awards banquet still has its place, it is now often embedded within a recognition system which includes an annual award, a series of quarterly awards, frequent on-the-spot recognition, and a means of cascading recognition-worthy successes throughout the organization (see Figure 7–1). Janet McLaughlin, director of education and training at Corning Incorporated, believes it is the power of an entire recognition system which ultimately motivates employees and reinforces learning on a day-to-day continuing basis.

For example, at Corning, managers frequently give out instant recognition cards. These cards, the size of a business card, are a spontaneous way for managers to say thank you. On one side of the card, managers can write a small note thanking an employee for a specific accomplishment, like staying late to finish a special assignment. On the back of the card, the employee can choose from a number of instant recognition awards, like a bouquet of flowers, a pound of chocolate fudge, or two tickets to a local sporting event, all of which have a cash value of about $10. Managers at Corning have the discretion to hand out literally hundreds of these instant recognition cards in a year. McLaughlin gives out about 10 of them during the course of a week. "My direct reports are pleasantly surprised by my responsiveness to their efforts" says McLaughlin.

At Corning, this instant recognition program is provided for in each division's budget. The manager has the prerogative to either hand out one of these instant recognition cards or, if the accomplishment merits a more significant acknowledgment, he or she can write a check on the spot honoring the employee with a Corning division cash award.

This drive to recognize employees on the spot is not limited to large companies like Corning. Computer Management Development Service (CMDS), a $5-million-a-year, privately held company providing administrative software for colleges and universities, has only 60 employees, yet the company fervently believes in the power of on-the-spot recognition. Two years ago, it instituted a recognition program making use of coupons. Under this program, a book of 12 recognition coupons, each worth the equivalent of $5.00, is given to employees at the beginning of each year. When a CMDS employee (called, once again, an associate) catches a co-worker going that extra mile, he or she is encouraged to give that person a recognition coupon. The procedure for awarding these recognition coupons to co-workers is a simple one. The CMDS associate presenting the recognition coupon must write the date and reason for giving the recognition coupon and then sign his or her name to the coupon. The CMDS recognition coupons are used like the old Green Stamps were. CMDS associates can either redeem a coupon for a small award—like admission to a local movie theater—or save up a number of coupons and use them for a larger award, such as a dinner for two at a local restaurant.

While the coupons are part of a larger recognition system which includes both monthly awards and a large annual award given by CMDS management, they serve a very distinct purpose. The idea behind them is to provide opportunities for peer recognition among co-workers in the normal course of a work day, not necessarily for thinking of a breakthrough idea. For example, CMDS associates are awarded recognition coupons for helping a co-worker with a computer equipment problem or doing an especially fine job in giving a demonstration to a client. The idea here is to encourage recognition of the many small achievements people do in their jobs and then share this information company-wide, so the entire organization collectively learns the accomplishments of individual employees. And, as with Corning's instant recognition cards, each coupon comes with an award. However, the emphasis is not on the size of the financial reward, but on the process of "catching a co-worker going an extra mile" on the job.

These on-the-spot recognition vehicles are more than ways to delight employees. They have been conceived as a means to propel employees to greater achievements through immediate, positive feedback for jobs well done. With these instant recognition awards, employees do not have to wait six to nine months to receive a big prize from the chairman. Instead, these recognition awards are instant and, importantly, in many cases, they are given by peers to each other. What both Corning and CMDS hope for is that the immediate nature of the recognition will boost productivity by motivating employees to carry their positive feelings back to the job and become more creative and involved in their work, share more ideas with co-workers, and, in the process, build stronger work teams. While both companies' recognition systems provide for monthly and annual awards, representatives from both Corning and CMDS believe it's this spontaneous recognition which ultimately leads to building employee motivation and self-esteem on a continuous basis.

This emphasis on creating a systems approach to recognition deployed on a consistent and ongoing basis also helps increase employee satisfaction. A corporation's ability to ensure that employees are satisfied in their jobs is moving to the forefront of corporate issues. For example, in the 1992 Xerox corporate priorities, the need to have satisfied employees is right behind the number one priority of achieving total customer satisfaction (above the priority of increasing market share and return on assets). Companies are realizing that, over time, they will see increased competition for well-trained employees. As this competition intensifies over the coming decade, employees will demand a satisfying work environment or work elsewhere. So, gradually, companies are waking up to the fact that happy, satisfied workers who feel recognized for their accomplishments in their jobs on a consistent basis are more inclined to produce high-quality products and deliver superior service than unhappy, frustrated ones. Devising systems and processes to ensure employee satisfaction has become an important precursor to achieving total customer satisfaction. Reflecting this renewed dedication to employee satisfaction, companies such as Corning, Texaco, Xerox, and even CMDS, a 12-year-old company, are creating models of recognition systems that improve employee satisfaction and increase productivity.

Honor the Team, as Well as the Individual

The traditional formula for corporate success has focused on the individual as the ultimate source of innovation and competitive strength. Accordingly, quality programs based on this traditional model have sought to encourage innovation and improvements at the level of the individual. As companies have flattened their organization structures and as participative management has become more widespread, however, it is increasingly the team that is seen as the primary unit of corporate performance. Further, more and more companies are coming to appreciate the potential of the team to produce gains and improvements greater than what individuals working alone can achieve. As a result, recognition is increasingly being used as a tool to support team performance, as well as individual excellence.

Peter Senge captures the spirit of teams working together when he writes:

> When you ask people about what it is like to be part of a great team, what is most striking is the meaningfulness of the experience. People talk about being part of something larger than themselves, of being connected, of being generative. It becomes quite clear that, for many, their experiences as part of a truly great team stand out as singular periods of life lived to the fullest. Some spend the rest of their lives looking for ways to recapture that spirit.[4]

Motorola has a recognition program in place which encourages employee teams to try to reach this level of all-out performance and excitement. The program is known as the Motorola Total Customer Satisfaction Team Competition. It is an extensive effort to honor the extraordinary accomplishments of teams and share these best practices corporatewide.

Motorola's Total Customer Satisfaction Team Competition.

"At Motorola, total customer satisfaction is more than a corporate vision. It is a commitment by employees who are working together to make the vision a reality."[5]

Cross-functional, problem-solving teams have become one of the most important innovations in the last decade. To recognize the accomplishments of cross-functional teams, Motorola created a team problem-solving showcase, known as the Total Customer Satisfaction Team Competition. During the competition, teams made up of employees at all levels from around the world demonstrate how members join forces to solve a problem or improve a process. "Our total customer satisfaction teams are by far our largest and most effective means of sharing our corporate successes on a global basis," says Brenda Sumberg, director of quality for Motorola University.

But why a competition, why not just an award recognizing the accomplishments of some of Motorola's most productive teams?

Sumberg, who was one of the judges in the 1991 competition, believes the competitive aspect of the recognition really propels employees to achieve new levels of teamwork and enthusiasm. The competition has become known as an in-house quality Olympics at Motorola. It simulates the real Olympics with timed presentations and a certain value placed upon showmanship.

The idea for the Total Customer Satisfaction Team Competition arose as a result of a visit to Japan by Motorola's top brass. In 1989, several Motorola senior executives visited Motorola operations in Japan, Malaysia, and Singapore. There, they observed Motorola compete in the Japanese National Productivity-Raising Competitions. In fact, all companies with operations in those countries are eligible to compete in this competition. So impressed were the visiting Motorola executives by the event that they implemented the competition concept within Motorola on their return. "I have never seen something take hold so fast; within a very short amount of time, a process was put into place to launch our own total customer satisfaction teams," adds Brenda Sumberg.

The process Motorola designed for the Total Customer Satisfaction Team Competition was deliberately modeled on that used in Japan, Malaysia, and Singapore. "We did not want to go too far afield from the process our people were already following in Asia, in case they wanted to compete in both Asia and within Motorola," says Gene Simpson, vice president and director of participatory management programs at Motorola. Essentially, teams of employees are formed, many of which are cross-functional, to solve a problem or improve a product or process. These teams work in one of five areas: Total Cycle Time, Participative Management, Profit Improvement, Six Sigma Quality, and Product/Manufacturing Leadership.

While company meetings where teams come together to share experiences are common in industry, only Motorola has gone so far as to organize a worldwide event that ends with the company's top managers acting as judges. In designing this event, Motorola held to a couple of requirements. First, Motorola was intent on having one competition, with no differentiation of levels or functional categories. Simpson adds, "We wanted to emphasize the process and make the logistics as simple as possible."

Second, Motorola made sure that the teams considered as finalists in the competition demonstrated extraordinary achievements. For example, the 3,000 worldwide teams which formed to participate in the 1991 competition were gradually winnowed down to only 22 finalists who competed in the final Total Customer Satisfaction Team Competition in Schaumburg, Illinois.

Simpson recalls, "I frequently get calls from Motorolans who are looking for the rules on how to form a team. I tell them all the same thing—you go figure it out by yourself. There are no rules for forming these teams, no contest bureaucracy." Instead, the teams form in any number of ways—from a spontaneous suggestion by a group of employees who already are in contact with each other, to a manager's request that a group form to address a particular issue. Perhaps it's this lack of rules that allows the participants the freedom to be creative, have some fun, and, along the way, solve workplace problems and suggest ways to improve a process.

The 3,000 teams of employees who entered in 1991 represented approximately 30,000 employees, or roughly 35 percent of the Motorola work force. The teams participated in local and regional competitions and eventually were funneled down to 22 finalists. "It's important to remember that these teams build upon a 20-year foundation in participative management along with a massive investment in training at Motorola University," says Motorola's Simpson.

At the finals, finalist teams are given 12 minutes to present their winning case to a 14-member panel consisting of Motorola senior executives and distinguished customers. They use an eclectic blend of comedy and drama to show how team members work together to come up with a new process that enhances quality. Interestingly, one of the requirements of the final competition is that each team member must have a role in the final presentation. This helps to physically show how the team spirit and camaraderie among all members results in achieving the impressive results.

In addition, the competition, in and of itself, becomes a near-spiritual experience for both participants and judges. George Fisher, Motorola's chairman and chief executive, has called the Total Customer Satisfaction Team Competition, "a collage of the power of the team process." Brenda Sumberg, director of quality, adds, "As a judge, I saw tears in the eyes of other judges as well as individual team members. These presentations show in the most dramatic way imaginable how these outstanding teams of Motorolans pursue the quality vision in their day-to-day jobs."

Simpson, who is also the master of ceremonies for the final competition, believes the team competition is successful for two reasons. First, the team presentations tell powerful stories of team excellence in anticipating and exceeding customer needs— stories that are inspiring to the entire Motorola work force. Second, the show biz aspect makes the team competition fun to enter for the individual employees, fun to watch for the judges, and memorable for the rest of the employee population.

Simpson adds, "Because finalist teams have to put together what amounts to a 12-minute theatrical production, recapping how they defined their problem and then went about solving it, they end up being quite entertaining." In fact, even the team names are entertaining. For example, there were the Wippersnappers, derived from Work in Progress and the BEAP Goes On, referring to the Back End Automated Process for testing Motorola's Bravo pagers at one of Motorola's plants. This entertainment factor really captures the imagination of the rest of the employee population. Soon, everyone's buzzing about who won the competition and how they did it. It doesn't take long before nearly all employees get caught up in the event and are curious about the details of the specific ways winning teams put quality principles into practice on the job. The team competition really brings the spirit of quality to life, makes it fun and entertaining, and, in the process, motivates employees to wonder, "How can I implement the winning solutions in my department?"

The 22 teams who made it to the finals in Motorola's team competition in 1991 were from eight countries—Japan, France, Israel, Scotland, the Philippines, Malaysia, Taiwan, and four teams from the United States. They were scored on a number of criteria, including teamwork, analysis techniques, remedies, results, institutionalization, and the overall quality of their 12-minute presentation. Figure 7–2 shows the score card used by the Motorola judges to determine the winners. Using these criteria, in 1991, 8 gold medals and 14 silver medals (all the teams who made it to

FIGURE 7–2

Motorola Inc.
Corporate T.C.S. Team Competition Scoring Form

Organization: _____

Team Name: _____

Date: _____

Key Initiative: Total Cycle Time   Six Sigma Quality   Participative Management

Profit Improvement   Product/Mfg. Leadership

Category	Criteria	Score 0 to 10	Weight	Weighted Score
Teamwork	• Appropriate team structure and membership. • Participation by all members. • Understanding and use of group dynamics.		1	
Project selection criteria	• Criteria and methodology evident in selection. • Identification of customer and his needs. • Clear and aggressive goals established.		1	
Analysis techniques	• Appropriate analytical techniques are used. • Customer's needs are considered. • Growth in team's knowledge and skill with tools.		2	
Remedies	• Alternatives explored, implementations thorough. • Containment versus root cause prevention is clear. • Enhancements or improvements were made. • Innovation in the remedies or implementation.		2	

Category	Criteria	Weight
Results	• Results reflect goals and difficulty of project. • Ancillary effects identified and evaluated. • Results verified and documented.	2
Institutionalization	• Improvements sustainable and permanent. • Improvements have application in other areas. • Grasp of concept of continuous improvement.	1
Presentation	• Clear, concise, follows the process. • Skillful, appropriate use of presentation aids.	1

Weighted Score

Deductions (−1 point for each min. > 12)

Total Team Score

Time (minutes)

Judge

Comments

the final competition received either a gold or a silver medal) were awarded to teams for their outstanding implementation of quality processes and practices in their departments. About half of the finalist teams worked on manufacturing problems and the other half worked on customer service problems. These ranged from improving the cycle time on the factory floor to processing sales orders faster. The future goal for the competition is to have more teams working on direct customer issues and problems.

What's the award for the 8 gold and 14 silver finalists? Interestingly, the award is primarily recognition from one's peers. While a plaque is given to both the gold and silver finalists (in fact, the plaque is identical for both categories of winners), Motorola executives such as Simpson and Sumberg believe the most important award is not tangible; rather, it is peer recognition for a job well done.

While the Total Customer Satisfaction Team Competition is designed to honor winners, the real value of the competition is the collective learning that takes place among the thousands of Motorolans who work together to put quality theory into practice. Simpson adds that "The real goal of Motorola's team competition is to assist the corporation in furthering its participative management practices." The Ronamakers, one of the 1991 Gold Medal winners of Motorola's Total Customer Satisfaction Team Competition, present a good example of a high-performing work team in action.

The Ronamakers—1991 Gold Medal Winners

Who are the Ronamakers, you might ask, some rock group held over from the 60s? Motorola's Total Customer Satisfaction Team Competition is such a special event; it's impossible to grasp just how extraordinary it is without a real example, the Ronamakers.

The Ronamakers are a cross-functional team consisting of 14 individuals from the automotive and industrial electronics group spanning manufacturing facilities in the United States and Europe. Since each team invents a persona to exemplify its corporate mission, the Ronamakers chose a name to suggest their goal—Increasing Return On Net Assets. The team was charged with increasing inventory turns from the then-current levels of 7.9 turns to double-digit levels, while maintaining flexibility in meeting the changing demands of customers.

At the final presentation of the Total Customer Satisfaction Team Competition, the Ronamakers began their presentation saying that they try to live up to their motto, "One good turn deserves another." This set the stage for an entertaining explanation of how a worldwide, cross-functional team set out to improve inventory management and, in the course of one year, saved Motorola $2.3 million. How did they portray this savings? Do you think they used sophisticated data processing technology to produce a four-color chart? Well, if that's what you think, you should see the Ronamaker's videotape of their winning presentation. In it, the Ronamakers are shown presenting a gift-wrapped, life-size package to Bob Galvin. In it is a three-foot check made out to Motorola for $2.3 million. While each presentation is humorous, fun, and entertaining, when you watch the videotape of each final presentation, you begin to understand Brenda Sumberg's comment about the emotional impact of the event. The high of working with a truly great team and watching them in action is an unforgettable experience for everyone and a lasting way the entire organization collectively learns about each employee's achievements.

The Ronamakers ended up with a gold medal. "But more important than winning," says one of the team participants in the tape, "is the feeling of increased communication and understanding between all of my team members from around the world."

The Intel Quality Award. If Motorola's Total Customer Satisfaction Team Competition is modeled after the Olympics, then the Intel Quality Award is Intel's version of the Oscars. In a suspense-packed convention center closely following on the heels of the Academy Awards, Intel bestows recognition on up to three organizations within the company. But instead of a parade of Hollywood stars proclaiming, "And the winner is. . . . ," Craig Barrett, Intel's chief operating officer, quietly opens the sealed envelope to announce the winners of the Intel Quality Award.

According to Barrett, the Intel Quality Award serves a number of purposes. "We can all improve through self-analysis and some friendly competition," he says. "The Intel Quality Award promotes both. Because it is based on the Intel values, any improvement brought about by the award should automatically result in better corporate performance in serving shareholders, customers, and employees."[6] In addition, Barrett adds that public recognition of those groups doing the best job of improving their performance in line with Intel values inspires others to strive for continuous improvement. This ability to help the entire organization collectively learn is at the heart of the Intel Quality Award.

The Intel Quality Award was created in 1991 to recognize and reward groups within Intel that demonstrate improvements in performance and adherence to Intel's values at the highest level. While Intel already had several recognition awards for individual achievement and small-group accomplishments, the Intel Quality Award gave Intel managers the opportunity to recognize entire business organizations who demonstrate truly outstanding performance.

The Intel Quality Award does more than recognize a business organization's outstanding performance; it also requires each participating organization to undergo self-assessment against the Malcolm Baldrige criteria. This self-assessment begins with managers participating in an eight-hour internal assessment course given at Intel University, which trains them in the how-to's of the rigorous assessment process. (In fact, this course is deemed so important that it has recently been developed into a self-study guide so Intel managers can quickly and easily learn how to assess their own organizations.) Then, assuming that the individual business organization reaches a minimum score of 500 points out of a possible 1,000 points scored on the Baldrige, then, and only then, can applicants go to the next step, which involves a detailed assessment of the strengths and weaknesses of their performance compared to Intel's six values: results orientation, risk taking, discipline, customer satisfaction, quality, and a great place to work. Intel's translation of the 1,000 points on the Malcolm Baldrige to 500 points needed for the Intel Quality Award is shown in Figure 7–3.

Why does an organization need to achieve only 500 out of 1,000 points? Dave Hall, Intel's former director of quality technology and one of the judges of the Intel Quality Award, provides some insight into this issue. "We purposely created a minimum self-assessment score of 500 points because we wanted to encourage as many organizations as possible to go through the self-assessment process. We also tried to eliminate the paperwork associated with the Malcolm Baldrige Award by asking those business organizations who are applying for the award to keep their oral presentations to one hour and their written presentations to no more than 10 typed pages. In essence, our intent is for business organizations to learn about their strengths and weaknesses, rather than to create a 'dry-run' of the Malcolm Baldrige application process."

The approach taken at Intel differs sharply from that of most companies who use the Baldrige criteria for self-assessment. Many of these companies create internal infrastructures of volunteer examiners to rate and score each department against the criteria set out in the Baldrige application. This core group of volunteers becomes, in essence, the "internal experts" within the corporation. Instead, Intel's intent is to train all managers, rather than just a core group, in the how-to's of performing self-assessments within their departments. Dave Hall, Intel's former Director of Quality Technology, adds, "We decided it was critical for all our managers, not just a select few, to use the Malcolm Baldrige process as an opportunity to step back, look at the systems and processes already in place, and ask themselves, How can these be improved."

Intel's treasury department, a 1991 winner of the Intel Quality Award, is an interesting example of how a nonmanufacturing department of Intel successfully used quality tools and techniques to win the 1991 Intel Quality Award (see page 290).

FIGURE 7–3
Intel Internal Assessment Scoring Summary

Group or Organization: _____ XDS _____   Date: _____ APRIL 1991 _____

Category (1991 Guidelines)	Points	% Score	Points Awarded	COMMENTS:
1.0 *Leadership*	100		60.50	
1.1 Senior executive leadership	40	50	20.00	
1.2 Quality values	15	70	10.50	
1.3 Management for quality	25	80	20.00	
1.4 Public responsibility	20	50	10.00	
2.0 *Information and Analysis*	70		40.00	
2.1 Scope and management of quality data and information	20	70	14.00	
2.2 Competitive comparisons and benchmarking	30	40	12.00	
2.3 Analysis of quality data and information	20	70	14.00	
3.0 *Strategic Quality Planning*	60		30.00	
3.1 Strategic quality planning process	35	50	17.50	
3.2 Quality goals and plans	25	50	12.50	
4.0 *Human Resource Utilization*	150		72.50	
4.1 Human resource management	20	40	8.00	
4.2 Employee involvement	40	40	16.00	
4.3 Quality education and training	40	40	16.00	
4.4 Employee recognition and performance measurement	25	70	17.50	
4.5 Employee well-being and morale	25	60	15.00	

5.0 *Quality Assurance of Products and Service*	140	73.50
5.1 Design and introduction of quality products and services	35	50	17.50
5.2 Process quality control	20	70	14.00
5.3 Continuous improvement of processes	20	50	10.00
5.4 Quality assessment	15	40	6.00
5.5 Documentation	10	60	6.00
5.6 Business process and support service quality	20	30	6.00
5.7 Supplier quality	20	70	14.00
6.0 *Quality Results*	180		102.00
6.1 Product and service quality results	90	60	54.00
6.2 Business process, operational, and support service quality results	50	40	20.00
6.3 Supplier quality results	40	70	28.00
7.0 *Customer Satisfaction*	300		123.00
7.1 Determining customer requirements and expectations	30	30	9.00
7.2 Customer relationship management	50	40	20.00
7.3 Customer service standards	20	40	8.00
7.4 Commitment to customers	15	50	7.50
7.5 Complaint resolution for quality improvement	25	50	12.50
7.6 Determining customer satisfaction	20	50	10.00
7.7 Customer satisfaction results	70	40	28.00
7.8 Customer satisfaction comparison	70	40	28.00
Grand Total	1,000		501.50

Courtesy of Intel Corporation.

Intel's Treasury Department
A 1991 Winner of the Intel Quality Award

Intel's treasury department was one of the three business groups that won the 1991 Intel Quality Award. A small organization with 90 employees worldwide, the department is recognized as a model administrative area which has adapted the quality principles used by manufacturing to the business of managing Intel's finances. Over the past five years, Intel's treasury department has been responsible for speeding up money collection from customers and enhancing the return on investments. In fact, the treasury department at Intel has been recognized as a leader in the banking and investment industry for its long-standing history of being innovative in developing investment techniques and making money for the corporation.

Intel's treasury department was one of the winners of the 1991 Intel Quality Award, in part for its ability to take risks which produced substantial results for Intel. For example, the treasury department was able to increase the corporation's net income from $31 million in 86 to $142 million in 90. One of the many tools they used to produce this result was to incorporate state-of-the-art information systems to execute many financial transactions.

One of the challenges of the application process for the treasury department was to apply the Malcolm Baldrige criteria to an administrative area of the company. While the treasury department had a reputation for fixing problems very quickly, it had not developed a process to actually benchmark response times. Now, after having gone through a self-assessment process that goes along with applying for the Intel Quality Award, Intel's treasury department has been able to measure the maturing of their quality approaches and processes. In fact, as a result of the comprehensive review process inherent in the Malcolm Baldrige criteria, the treasury department has been able to identify strengths and weaknesses throughout every aspect of the business.

The experience of the treasury department shows that the Intel Quality Award does more than honor teams for their accomplishments. By linking self-assessment with team recognition, the Intel Quality Award is more than an award, it's a tool to facilitate group learning.

Cascading Employee Successes throughout the Organization

The final element in the recognition system illustrated in Figure 7–1 is the ability of the organization to cascade employee successes down and across the company. Why is this so critical?

Let's suppose one of your business units solves a problem which improves customer service or reduces costs significantly. It's also an approach that can be helpful to other business units— if only they knew about it. But there's no telling whether or not your business units *will* hear about it because, right now, the only way such news gets around is through word-of-mouth or the occasional newsletter article. In fact, there's even a possibility that some business units are off trying to solve the exact same problem and are completely in the dark that a better way has been put into practice. To reduce this likelihood, companies need to create ways to spread best practices throughout the organization. You've heard the old saying, "Success breeds success." Well, companies are now spending time, money, and resources to develop ways to capture the successful efforts of individuals and teams and replicate these successes whenever and wherever possible.

Basically, companies are experimenting with any way they can think of to make heroes of employees who take initiative and live the quality vision in their day-to-day jobs. Cascading these successes has become the new mantra for companies intent upon building a world-class work force. While training employees to develop new practices and processes in their work environment is, of course, critically important, companies are realizing that something must happen after the training to keep the spirit of innovation and improvement alive. Specifically, employees must share with one another their best practices. In other words, creating ways for employees to network with one another has become an important continuation of training and learning. The reason for this increased emphasis on sharing the successes is primarily due to changes happening in the workplace. Employees simply cannot wait for formal training programs to learn about better ways to do their jobs. They must learn from each other and experiment with integrating this learning into their departments.

While many companies routinely spread the word about in-house successes through traditional internal communication vehicles, such as the company newsletter and the in-house magazine, such measures are often not enough to motivate employees to ask themselves, "How can I experiment with these techniques in my department?" While in the past, the traditional in-house video or company newsletter might have been adequate to pass along information on employees' achievements, now the focus is not so much on just passing on information, but encouraging employees to have dialogues with each other so that the successes and lessons learned are spread throughout the company. The challenge, in other words, is to create opportunities for employees to network with each other.

This increased emphasis on networking the successes is really redefining the paradigm of internal communications within the company. Internal communications vehicles must go beyond transmitting information to becoming the catalyst to make things happen. Communications vehicles must be developed to encourage employees to intelligently network with each other and exchange best practices that can be adapted to their areas. Four examples are provided below, from Allstate's Log Book, Motorola's Yearbook, KPMG Peat Marwick Sharing Rally, to Xerox Teamwork Day, which show the range of possibilities companies are experimenting with in cascading employee successes throughout the organization.

The Allstate Log Book. Allstate first introduced Customer Focused Quality to the corporation in 1989. Everyone knew a critical component of the quality process was awareness and recognition. So, the first communications vehicles introduced were brochures and posters announcing the importance of Allstate Customer Focused Quality. But in order to convince the skeptics who thought quality was another fad, hopefully soon to die off, the Allstate internal communications department decided that what they really needed to do was to show Allstate quality in action, with employees using quality tools and techniques in their everyday jobs.

As Lesley Haley, project manager for Allstate awareness and recognition, says, "You have to show people that quality works. You cannot expect them to just read a brochure or poster and understand the true benefits of the quality process." With that vision in mind, the Allstate internal communications department created a video of five outstanding examples of quality in action. So far, this sounds rather routine. But, in addition to the video, Allstate created an accompanying book they call the Log Book. The Log Book is just what it sounds like: a book giving employees a simple format to "log in" a brief synopsis of their particular best practices along with their names and telephone numbers so others can contact them about how to spread best practices to other departments or regions of the country. Interestingly, the Log Book was intentionally designed to be loosely bound so pages could be easily copied, distributed, and shared companywide. So, rather than create an elaborate hardbound brochure, the Allstate team recognized what they really needed was a book that would "travel well—from one employee to another."

Essentially, the Log Book is really a framework to help Allstate employees network with one another. According to Allstate's Haley, "The concept of the Log Book has gone over like gangbusters." Haley admits that, sometimes, employees need a little help connecting with one another to spread their individual successes throughout the company. The Log Book is really Allstate's way of teaching employees how to network with co-workers around the country. So far, these Log Books have been sent to each Allstate vice president and corporate manager, with very positive feedback on the continued need to develop these types of creative vehicles for internal communication.

The Motorola Yearbook. As Gene Simpson, vice president and director of participative management programs at Motorola, says, "A lot of our time and energy is now spent on how to make the glow last longer." At Motorola, this means developing creative forms of internal communication which allow employees the greatest opportunity to network their successes.

Motorola has learned that just including an employee's name and phone number in the company newsletter, or even on an electronic database, is often not enough to motivate employees who are sometimes halfway around the world to pick up the phone and start a dialogue with another employee. The key, then, is to design and implement nontraditional techniques to encourage employee networking. One that is now on the drawing board at Motorola, under the auspices of Gene Simpson's area, is the creation of a yearbook for the team members who were awarded gold and silver honors in Motorola's Total Customer Satisfaction Team Competition.

Since the Motorola Yearbook isn't out yet, it is impossible to comment on its impact within the corporation. But the very concept of creating a yearbook of top performers, complete with an employee's picture and some biographical data, such as length of service with the company and a brief description of his or her contribution, certainly sounds like fun. Let's face it, the concept of a yearbook brings back memories of high school sweethearts, winning football teams, and shared intimacies with friends. What's more inviting—looking up someone in a yearbook of top performers or accessing similar information in an electronic database? While employees may *say* they understand the value and power in networking best practices, many approach the task of networking with some trepidation. What the Motorola yearbook does is help employees overcome their initial resistance by creating an enjoyable and entertaining vehicle, one they associate with "the good times," and, importantly, one that is easy to use.

KPMG Peat Marwick Sharing Rally. Remember your high school or college football rally? Well, KPMG Peat Marwick built upon this concept to create, in 1991, the KPMG Peat Marwick Sharing Rally. Jon Madonna, chairman of KPMG Peat Marwick, describes the purpose of this sharing rally in a letter welcoming all participants:

> As participants in KPMG Peat Marwick's first Sharing Rally, you have the opportunity to share your ideas, your successes, and to work together as a team to identify and fine-tune key programs necessary to the firm's continuous improvement initiative.[7]

KPMG Peat Marwick's Sharing Rally is organized twice a year for representatives of the firm's Quality Service Councils. These councils are made up of various levels of employees within a local office who act as "architects" of their office's quality process. They routinely receive input from clients and in turn, recommend ways of delivering better service to clients.

The primary challenge faced by these 82 representatives is captured by Vince Cannella, KPMG Peat Marwick's partner in charge of quality and managing partner of the St. Louis office, when he says, "What we ideally want is to have a spirit of continuous improvement run through the blood of the firm. We believe one way to accomplish this is to orchestrate opportunities for Quality Service Council representatives to communicate with one another."

The Sharing Rally is KPMG Peat Marwick's answer to this challenge. It brings these 82 Quality Service Council representatives together every six months to ensure that they share their best practices in serving clients, help co-workers think of ways to deliver better service to their local clients, and build excitement for the process of continuous improvement. According to Cannella, "We want these representatives to have a forum to discuss better ways to service clients throughout the firm."

Xerox Teamwork Day. Perhaps the oldest and best-known company forum for cascading the successes throughout the organization is Xerox's Teamwork Day. Every fall, employees at Xerox Corporation sponsor a major event which celebrates teams who have made improvements using quality tools and processes. Teams representing every department within the company participate and share their successes with co-workers, customers, vendors, and other special guests.

Teamwork Day at Xerox grows bigger and bigger each year. For example, in 1991, over 20,000 attendees gathered in three locations—Rochester, Los Angeles, and Dallas—with satellite link-ups connecting the presentations and speeches at these three cities to over 60 Xerox field locations.

Xerox's Teamwork Day Vision. Xerox Teamwork Day serves several purposes, according to Sandy Frieday, human resource specialist for Xerox.[8] First, it is an excellent way for teams to share information about the quality processes being used, how they are applied, and their results to date. The second benefit of Teamwork Day is that it is an outstanding way to recognize teams of employees who have achieved truly outstanding results for the corporation. In fact, the event has become like a huge festival, with balloons, over 100 booths, and interactive displays at each location, all arranged to enable employee teams to demonstrate how they have used training in problem-solving and quality improvement practices to achieve customer satisfaction and better business results. Finally, the most important benefit of Xerox Teamwork Day is the opportunity to network the successes of Xerox employees around the world and, in the process, increase the collective learning of the entire organization.

The successes that Xerox employees share are quite specific and serve as a learning tool for others in the corporation. For example, the 1991 Xerox Teamwork Day recognized the outstanding accomplishments of seven Xerox teams from around the world. The types of accomplishments the teams share range from implementing a new work process to developing improvements in customer survey techniques. The following are just some examples of the types of team successes honored during Xerox Teamwork Day in 1991.

- The Ohmagari Hanabi Circle from Fuji Xerox was honored because of their success in decreasing the number of paper jams due to the use of recycled paper. This team's actions resulted in increased customer satisfaction and a substantial increase in revenue from paper sales.
- The Event Marketing Team from Rochester, New York, presented how to plan, execute, and measure product trade show events in a cost-effective manner. This team was responsible for developing a process for planning and implementing a trade event which required a minimal amount of resources while exceeding the number of sales leads generated as a result of the event.
- Task '94 Team from McLean, Virginia, presented a unique approach to improving customer satisfaction by implementing a survey process to better understand the perception of Xerox among key customers and then plan how to increase

satisfaction. The results showed that out of 18 major accounts, 15 accounts showed significant improvement in
Customer Satisfaction ratings.[9]

Xerox's Teamwork Day has become an idea that, in the words
of one Xerox customer, "many companies have shamelessly sto-
len." In fact, Xerox has received so many benchmarking calls that
they have prepared a how-to document, entitled "Summary of
Teamwork Day Planning," for companies who want to understand how to plan and implement a Teamwork Sharing Day. The
document covers everything from how to set up a design committee to a monthly checklist of what the chairperson of the event
should do to organize a similar event within their company.

This document does not leave any detail in planning the event
to chance. For example, the document even covers how employees should set up these booths, what type of leave-behind brochures employees should prepare, and even how to convey in
one sentence the major achievement of the team members.

John Kelsch, Xerox's director of quality, sums up the power of
Xerox Teamwork Day when he says, "What we are after is to have
the entire organization collectively learn the best practices of individual teams in solving problems and achieving customer
satisfaction."

Xerox employees who attend Teamwork Day get an opportunity to see for themselves Xerox's dedication to continuous improvement and customer satisfaction with living examples from
Xerox employees around the world.

The Key Is Connectivity

The examples from Allstate Insurance, Motorola, KPMG Peat
Marwick, and Xerox point to a common thrust: to move the organization beyond being simply aware of the need for continuous
improvement—a point many companies have reached—to creating an active networking culture in which individual improvements and innovations are shared and spread as a matter of
course. In other words, just as the emphasis in training
has shifted from periodic doses of instruction to continuous lifelong learning, the emphasis in recognition has correspondingly

moved from celebrating isolated successes to reinforcing successes as they happen and driving them throughout the organization with the help of recognition systems. The most visionary
systems—such as those at Xerox and Motorola—link recognition
to networking. Here, recognition is used not only to reinforce
good work but as a way to get employees talking together about
their successes and ideas, so that the best ideas can take hold
throughout the organization.

A well-thought-out recognition system is becoming an increasingly important factor in a company's participative management
process. Companies are realizing that in order for their workers
to participate more actively in designing and improving work
processes, they must be recognized for their best practices, then
given the opportunity to network these best practices throughout
the organization.

Essentially, the recognition system outlined in this chapter
points to a paradigm shift in how companies think about the role
of their internal communications. Where company newsletters
were once adequate to pass along information about the company, now the goal is to capture the many great ideas that
employees generate on a daily basis and spread these ideas
throughout the organization, so the entire organization collectively learns and benefits from each individual employee's
best practice.

What distinguishes the approaches taken by companies such
as Allstate Insurance, Motorola, Intel, Corning, KPMG Peat Marwick, and Xerox is that recognition has been elevated to a business practice, rather than just a motivational tool, to keep the
"employee juices running." When employees understand the
power of recognition as a business practice, it can be integrated
into each individual employee's way of thinking and acting. The
goal is then to promote connectivity between employee groups,
departments, and divisions so that a company's best practices are
cascaded throughout the organization.

Chapter Eight

Ten Lessons in Building a World-Class Work Force

A global marketplace, increased competition, and a continuing reorganization of work are the new realities facing today's organizations and their employees. To compete, nothing short of world-class performance will do. The limited demands on workers to know only one narrow repetitive job no longer apply. Now, workers from the factory floor to the customer service hotline must think and act for themselves. For more and more companies, the choice is growing increasingly stark: go for world-class performance or be left behind.

Corporate Quality Universities represent an attempt to meet this challenge. As a group, they have come to represent an expanded vision of training which provides all employees with a foundation in the organization's quality vision, values, and culture. As this book has shown, the companies who have established Corporate Quality Universities have fundamentally altered their thinking about who should be trained in corporate America and what they should be trained in. Continuous learning; a heightened focus on broad skills and, importantly, "human soft skills"; knowing how to build partnerships with suppliers, customers, and schools; hiring smart; and training employees in how to recognize the achievements of co-workers are the emerging dimensions of state-of-the-art corporate training as it is being redefined at the companies profiled in this book.

The advanced and highly developed model for training represented by Corporate Quality Universities provides a valuable blueprint for companies of all sizes interested in enhancing their own corporate training programs. As we enter the 21st century, the skills of the work force will be fundamental to each

FIGURE 8–1
Paradigm Shift of a Corporate University

Training:	Learning:
• Building/campus.	• Corporate process.
• Audience: Internal employees; largely professional managers.	• Audience: All employees, customers, product suppliers, and educational suppliers.
• Goal: Upgrade technical skills.	• Goal: Build CORE workplace competencies.
• Methodology: Learning by listening.	• Methodology: Learning by doing, networking, and role modeling.
• Management initiated.	• Employee initiated.
• A one-time event.	• A lifelong learning process.

Courtesy of Quality Dynamics, Inc.

company's competitiveness. All companies, regardless of their size, will need to develop strategies for promoting continuous learning in the workplace in order to successfully compete in the global marketplace. The lessons learned from the 30 companies profiled here, if acted upon, can enhance any corporate training program, whether grand or modest in scale. This chapter looks at 10 specific lessons for improving work force competitiveness through training.

These 10 lessons reflect a central belief: A company's work force is its primary resource for creating value. Work force-based competitive advantage is proving more enduring than technology-based competitiveness, which quickly slips away as new technologies become equally accessible to companies on a global basis. Work force excellence, however, is the unique result of a company's hiring and training practices; it creates an advantage that cannot easily be duplicated and can always be renewed and improved.

This book has examined how the Corporate Quality University has been put to use by several dozen companies to provide continual learning for all workers. In essence, this heightened focus on continuous learning has shifted the paradigm of corporate education. As Figure 8–1 shows, the focus of training is no longer on a one-time event taking place in a formal classroom. Rather, the emphasis now is on providing employees with a process for continuously learning on the job. What's more, the target audience has been expanded from internal employees—largely professional managers—to all levels of employees, as well as customers, suppliers, and educational institutions. In other words, companies are striving to increase their total human capital in order to attract and maintain highly trained workers.

THE TEN LESSONS IN BUILDING A WORLD-CLASS WORK FORCE

1. Tie the goals of training to the strategic needs of the organization. As we have seen, training at Corporate Quality Universities is more than just passing along information or building generic business skills. The most effective programs tie training to the organization's strategic business requirements and, importantly, maintain the organization's core competence in every field and at every level. In an article in *Fortune* magazine, Thomas Stewart described CORE competence as "the sum of everything everybody in the company knows that gives the company a competitive edge in the marketplace."[1]

The CORE curricula at such Corporate Quality Universities as Disney University, the Walton Institute, and General Electric Management Development Institute do just this. The university training specifically zeroes in on the skills, knowledge, and competencies that define the uniqueness of each company. For example, Disney University has been instrumental in training all levels of employees to deliver the Disney magic of quality service and entertainment. This combination of vision and training is what enables Disney to make its outdoor parks the entertainment extravaganzas that they are. Similarly, the Walton Institute teaches Wal-Mart associates specifically how to deliver the exceptional level of customer service that Wal-Mart is associated with in the retail industry. Compare this to many retail store training efforts which primarily focus on teaching store managers the basics of merchandising and inventory management. Finally, the granddaddy of corporate universities, General Electric Management Development Institute, has successfully transported many training programs and processes—specifically Workouts—to various GE divisions as a way to promote GE's culture of speed, simplicity, and self-confidence in the workplace.

Having successfully aligned training with their CORE competence, some companies make sure training stays on track by establishing a board of directors and various councils made up of line business managers from various disciplines (i.e., sales, manufacturing, engineering) who function similarly to a corporate board of directors. These boards and councils advise, counsel, and review the overall direction of training to ensure that it promotes the company's strategic vision. While these boards and councils at each Corporate Quality University differ in their composition, their function is to lend an informed, objective perspective to ensure that the training offered under the Corporate Quality University umbrella is strategy-driven.

2. Provide all levels of employees with opportunities for lifelong learning.   The idea that employees are a firm's most important asset is most in evidence at companies that employ large numbers of "knowledge workers," such as accountants, business consultants, lawyers, software programmers, and engineers. Gradually, though, more and more companies are viewing all workers—not just professional managers—as knowledge workers. Today, almost all types of work—from shop floor employment to clerical employment and middle management—is being redesigned so workers are empowered to take more responsibility. Workers at various levels are expected to have a broad set of skills that were previously required only of supervisors and managers.

The companies profiled in this book are firmly committed to treating their workers as their most important asset. They are demonstrating this commitment by providing continuous training and retraining opportunities for *all* levels of employees, offered in many cases through their Corporate Quality Universities. By doing so, they help to make learning a habitual activity for employees, instead of an occasional event.

By focusing on continuous learning rather than conducting one-time training events, these companies are essentially forging a new psychological contract with employees. In effect, many of the companies profiled here are promising to develop the skill levels of their work forces and in turn promise employees lifetime employability.

As we've seen, some of them have gone so far as to formalize their promise in policy. Corning, Intel, and Saturn Corporation guarantee to all workers that 5 percent of their work time will be devoted to ongoing training and development activities over the course of their entire work life at the company.

Such enlightened measures can lead to win-win situations for both companies and employees. While training boosts worker productivity and general employability, it makes companies more competitive as employers. Increasingly, what will set companies apart from the rest will be their commitment to develop and improve the skill levels of their employees.

3. Require workers to be accountable for learning new skills.   One of the important contributions of many Corporate Quality Universities has been to encourage the creation of an annual individual training and development plan as a vehicle to help employees be accountable for learning new skills. These plans are quite specific. They lead each employee to higher and higher levels of both professional and team performance. They are reviewed regularly to respond to the evolving needs of the workplace and the marketplace and ensure that the *right* employees participate in the *right* training and learning activities at the *right* time.

The pace of change requires that employees take a proactive stance toward education and training. This means that each and every employee should have a clearly articulated education and development plan outlining the combination of formal and informal learning activities he or she will complete and a timetable for completing them.

The Individual Development Plan serves a number of purposes. First, as its name implies, there are many ways for employees to develop themselves. This might include taking a formal training course, completing a self-paced workbook, or even being an instructor in a training class. In addition, these plans zero in on the sequence of learning so employees learn what they need to know just before they are likely to apply it in a current position. For example, at IBM, an employee's individual development plan may recommend that an employee complete a series of instructional modules in a specific sequence before applying the skills learned in those modules to software development. This emphasis on planning the sequence of learning has been instrumental in increasing productivity. Thirdly, these plans instill in each employee a commitment to self-management. Since change in the workplace is so fast, employees cannot rely on their supervisors or their human resources managers to manage their career development. Instead, they must be responsible for their own self-development. Based on the principle that "what gets measured, gets done," these plans have become an important tool to help employees examine their needs, plan their professional and personal development, and then track their performance against the goals laid out in the plan.

Finally, these plans ultimately hold each employee accountable for achieving his or her training goals. As the examples from Saturn and Arthur Andersen show, achievement of one's training goals are being closely tied to one's compensation and career path.

This accountability to learn ultimately benefits both the individual employee and the corporation: The employee adds to his or her skill level while the corporation develops the highly skilled work force needed to succeed in the global marketplace.

4. Extend training beyond the internal employees to key members of the customer/supply chain. The companies profiled here, such as Motorola, Intel, Xerox, and The Iams Company, all make heavy investments in training their work forces (most invest between 3 and 5 percent of their payroll on training), but they do something else as well. They extend their training throughout their entire customer and supply chains. It's no longer enough to just have well-trained employees. To succeed, companies must also develop partnerships with a core group of suppliers and customers so they work in concert to assist companies in achieving their quality vision in the marketplace.

Companies are realizing that their success is dependent to a large extent upon the success of a select group of suppliers and customers. The companies profiled in this book are shouldering the responsibility of improving their total human capital by providing training to the company's entire business network, that is, their employees, customers, suppliers, and, importantly, the schools whose graduates will someday enter their work forces. This emphasis on training all the members of a company's business system is redefining the nature and scope of training. Training is directed to all these members of a company's business chain in a way that is much broader and more relevant than in the past. Companies no longer simply train customers in how to use their products or services. Instead, today's customer training programs are more closely geared to helping customers run their businesses successfully. For example, Dana Customer Training Center and Ford Heavy Truck University, cited in Chapter 6, offer courses to help improve the business performance of their customers, such as how to generate repeat business (Dana's program) and consultative selling skills (taught at Ford).

Another twist on customer training is that smaller companies are doing it too. Customer training used to be the domain of the giants. Now, firms such as Computer Management Development Services (CMDS), a $5 million software company, and Iams, a $300-million-plus maker of premium pet food, are reaching out to their customers by offering training through their respective Corporate Quality Universities. Both companies are using the educational infrastructure of the Corporate University to forge closer links with customers. They are discovering that being able to offer this kind of benefit helps differentiate them from competitors.

But perhaps the most innovative efforts in extending this passion for training throughout the company's customer supply chain are those that involve reaching out to schools. Motorola is just one example of a company that, through such efforts as the University Challenge and District Learning Leadership teams, detailed in Chapter 6, is attempting to cultivate a commitment to quality in schools and thereby promote a highly qualified student force. As more companies compete on the intangibles of service and the quality of their people, having everyone in their customer/supply chain collectively learn the company's quality vision has become crucial to an organization's success. It's this type of redefinition of training—specifically, as a way to export the company's core competence throughout the business chain—that makes the companies profiled in this book truly leaders in building a world-class work force.

5. Hire smart so training can have the greatest impact on productivity. In the past, many human resource specialists believed that training was the key to mastery of virtually any skill. But as workplace skill requirements have expanded, this is no longer universally true. Many skills required of workers today assume they also have a broad set of human traits, such as persistence and initiative. For example, workers can be trained in the various steps to solve a business problem, but unless they also possess judgment, initiative, and perseverance, they will have difficulty following the problem-solving steps to a successful conclusion. Training, therefore, must be considered only one aspect of a process which also includes smart hiring. In other words, for training to have its fullest impact on productivity, companies must "hire smart" to ensure that productivity gains will occur from training.

Increasingly, the interview process is focusing not only on assessing the hard skills implied by the achievements on each employee's resume, but also on determining in a scientific fashion whether or not the prospective new hire has such key human traits as initiative and drive. It is widely held by human resource directors at the companies profiled in this book that these traits will be critical for employee success in flatter organizations where responsibility and authority are moved down the corporate hierarchy.

A number of companies, including Motorola, Corning, and Saturn Corporation, have been successful in designing what they call a *performance-based interview*. In a performance-based interview, the interviewer asks prospective employees to describe situations and actions in which he or she has successfully demonstrated the specific human traits the company is looking for in its work force.

For example, Motorola's Quality for Hire program, described in Chapter 3, reflects how much time and attention to detail Motorola is putting forth in identifying cellular manufacturing operators for Motorola's Arlington Heights plant who have the human traits the company needs. At this plant, prospective employees are asked to give specific examples during the interview process of how they demonstrated initiative or persistence in previous jobs or school programs.

Saturn Corporation not only incorporates the performance-based interview into its hiring process, but also requires prospective employees to undertake a simulation of what it will be like to work on the Saturn assembly line. This two-hour production simulation essentially has prospective employees both build a product and meet with teammates to recommend improvements.

The lesson from these companies is a simple one: Know what you're looking for in prospective new employees and then screen all applicants (factory workers as well as managers) to ensure they have the mix of hard skills and human traits you need to be successful in the marketplace.

6. Consider new employee orientation a strategic process, rather than a one-time event.   Orientation programs used to last about one hour and covered such mundane topics as working hours, pay periods, vacation schedules, insurance, and health benefits. Today, many Corporate Quality Universities include programs and courses to orient the new employee to the vision, values, and big picture of the company, not just the policies and procedures for entering and exiting. This new model of orientation has elements similar to Japanese orientation practices. Under this model orientation is a gradual process, rather than a one-time event.

For example, in many Japanese companies, the orientation process is usually viewed as an opportunity to inculcate the new employee to the organization's culture, values, traditions, and philosophy, often based on the thoughts of the original founder. At a number of American companies profiled in the book, the intent of orientation is similar, that is, to have the employee bond with the company.

The reasons for the increased emphasis on orientation in the curricula of Corporate Quality Universities are twofold. First, American companies are recognizing the high cost associated with employee turnover—especially since 50 percent of new hires leave within the first seven months. So, companies realize they can no longer leave the important job of communicating their strengths and competitive advantage to chance. Several companies are using their Corporate Quality Universities (such as American Express Quality University[SM], MBNA America Customer College, and First of America Quality Service University) to train employees in the organization's vision, values, culture, philosophy, and, importantly, how the company differentiates itself from competitors. The goal is to have new hires firmly grounded in the company's philosophy and quality vision as soon as they start their jobs.

The second reason for the growing emphasis on orientation is the recognition that employees bump shoulders with prospective and current customers on a daily basis. The company wants to ensure that employees are effective as representatives of the company. Therefore, orientation programs designed as a strategic process help to ensure that all new hires develop a firm foundation in the company's values, culture, traditions, and philosophy of customer service, as well as bond with the company and its quality vision. Orientation then becomes a vehicle for building corporate citizenship among new employees. If we believe that employees will treat customers the way they themselves are treated, then creating a carefully scripted process for new employee orientation becomes the company's way of building customer satisfaction.

Delivery of these orientation programs has also gone through a paradigm shift. In the past, instructors delivered the overview of the company in a traditional lecture format; now these orientation programs often involve the principles of active learning and use "home-grown managers" as instructors.

For example, Intel often has one of its ESMs—executive staff members—serve as the instructor and deliver the message about the company's culture, vision, values, philosophy, and, importantly, the specific behaviors associated with success at Intel. Corning's approach epitomizes active learning. Guided by a workbook, new employees gain knowledge about the company through a series of structured learning activities. The workbook leads them through a step-by-step, information-gathering mission in which they must meet face-to-face with key personnel representing various departments, customers, and suppliers, to ask questions, learn about the business of each, and record what they have learned. On completion of the workbook, they are then certified as having successfully completed Corning's orientation program.

So, regardless of a company's specific orientation program, the growing trend among those profiled in this book has been to view orientation as the foundation for employee empowerment rather than a one-hour policies and procedures discussion.

7. Design a CORE curriculum to stress the three Cs— Corporate Citizenship, Contextual Framework, and CORE Competencies. The curricula at Corporate Quality Universities are significantly unlike those of the corporate university commonplace a decade ago and these dissimilarities are a direct result of what's happening in the workplace. As noted throughout this book, to be successful in the workplace, one needs broad skills. Jobs today require employees to solve problems, think creatively, listen to co-workers and customers, negotiate, and, above all, know how to learn. This skill set was previously required only of managers and supervisors.

Now, as companies adapt total quality practices and drive decision making down the organization, more and more employees must think and act like managers. This has led Corporate Quality Universities to develop broad curricula stressing the three Cs:

Building corporate citizens
Providing a contextual reference
Developing competencies

Building Corporate Citizens

As outlined in Chapter 4, a purpose of training is to develop corporate citizens who are knowledgeable about the history, culture, traditions, and values of the company. The goal here is to engender a strong feeling of attachment and connectedness to the company similar to what citizens feel for their city or country. Companies want employees to identify with the firm and to live the corporate mission in their day-to-day jobs.

Providing Contextual Reference

The second C is contextual reference, which refers to a well-informed understanding of the company's big picture and its products and services in the context of what competitors are offering in the marketplace and the best practices of the industry as a whole. Numerous programs and initiatives are cropping up at Corporate Quality Universities to train employees in the features and benefits of their own company's products, as well as how they stack up against competitors' products and services. The goal is for all employees to be able to clearly communicate the company's strengths to both current and prospective employees.

Developing Workplace Competencies

The final C refers to building the company's CORE competencies. This involves training employees in the specific competencies the corporation has deemed critical to its long-term success. A number of companies intent upon building a world-class work force are distinctive for having spent extensive time, money, and resources conducting research and benchmarking studies to target and define the set of CORE competencies required in employees to maintain overall competitiveness.

Just to give you an idea of how extensive this research can be, Corning's Needs Analysis Study, which was instrumental in defining Corning's Competencies for Excellence (outlined in Figure 3–1), involved completing interviews with over 240 top performers within Corning as well as several hundred leaders from other leading-edge companies. The data comprised over 10,000 pages of transcripts from individual interviews, focus group sessions, and telephone interviews with both domestic and international leaders.

Several generic workplace competencies have emerged from the research conducted at the various companies profiled in this book. They are outlined and defined in detail in Chapter 4, but they are worth mentioning again to stress the types of competencies the workplace of the future will demand of more and more employees. As you look down this list, you will recognize many competencies normally associated with excellent leaders. As we've noted, the workplace is demanding more employees to have this managerial skill set.

CORE Workplace Competencies

Learning skills. Knowing how to continually develop and master new skills and new roles.

Basic three Rs. Having a command of reading, writing, and math to handle increased decision making on the frontline.

Interpersonal skills. Knowing how to listen, communicate, and cooperate with other people in a work situation.

Creative thinking and problem solving. Knowing how to identify problems and see the connections between the solution discovered and possible approaches to the next problem.

Leadership and visioning. Having a vision for one's work team or department that fits into the corporate mission and goals.

Self-development. The ability to manage one's own career by identifying the skills and knowledge one needs to be valuable in the workplace and working to acquire them.

While these competencies were once associated primarily with managers, they are quickly becoming part of an empowered worker's tool kit in the 21st century. And with 80 percent of the people who will be working in the year 2000 already on the job, the responsibility for providing ongoing opportunities to learn will fall to the businesses. Those businesses that thrive will be those that organize themselves for learning and then capitalize on what they've learned.

8. Experiment with ways for individual employees and teams to learn—both inside and outside the classroom. The Corporate Quality University has become a testing ground for experimenting with new ways for employees to learn new skills and new roles within the organization. The traditional classroom format in which the trainer does most of the talking is being supplemented with more innovative techniques. Corporate Quality Universities are experimenting with ways to encourage employees to learn by doing. Experiential learning exercises and company-specific case studies are two examples of new training activities in which the trainee, not the instructor, takes the principal role. Here, trainees may be in a classroom, but instead of passively listening to an instructor, they are actively working on real-world problems and opportunities and practicing how to solve them to the customer's satisfaction.

Chapter 5 presents a number of examples of these experiential learning exercises and case studies. The idea behind this active learning is to provide employees with an opportunity to practice the skills necessary for success in customer-driven organizations before using them on the job. Instead of memorizing a set of instructions for what a quality customer interaction should be, employees who go through these real-world experiences, practice how to solve a customer problem, identify a business opportunity, or lead a team to improved performance. Then, these employees more easily transfer their successful behaviors back to their jobs.

General Electric's Workouts (as profiled in Chapter 5) take the concept of active learning one step further by creating opportunities for teams of employees to become involved and excited about making suggestions for improvements. Essentially, these Workouts bring together GE employees with their managers to work out real problems and issues and propose solutions. The point of Workouts is to have employees learn together how to improve their work and give them an opportunity to have their recommendations listened to and acted upon. What these experiments in active learning hope to prove is that a satisfied work force is also a more productive work force.

9. Sustain the message of training with a system of employee recognition. So far, no one has to be convinced about the value of the training programs offered at these Corporate Quality Universities. But how have companies gone on to sustain the message of training? Effective employee recognition has become an increasingly important element in building a world-class work force. Once an employee is trained to solve problems and deliver the company's quality vision, the next critical step pursued by a number of companies is to reinforce training through a systematic approach to recognition. This systems view of recognition holds that when recognition is deployed in a consistent way across the work force and is seen as a business practice, rather than a one-time event, the message of training can be reinforced throughout the organization. This broader approach to recognition in place at companies such as Corning and Texaco underscores the importance of delivering recognition in the *right* way and at the *right* time. The goal of this systems view of recognition is to use recognition as a tool to significantly impact business productivity and propel employees across the organization to greater achievements in the future.

One of the striking lessons companies have learned is that many employees may not know *how* to recognize each other's achievements. So this systems view of recognition starts with training in—of all things—the how-to's of effective recognition. Training in recognition is finding its way into the curricula of these universities and showing up alongside courses in listening, communicating, and problem solving.

But this emphasis on recognition does not stop with understanding and practicing how to effectively deliver recognition to a peer, teammate, or subordinate. Recognition training is often supplemented by a companywide system which recognizes individual and team accomplishments, on-the-spot, monthly, quarterly, and yearly so an employee's or team's achievements are honored publicly before the rest of the organization. The goal here is to celebrate what the organization wants to see more of and to consider the recognition system as an integral way for employees to learn best practices in the workplace.

10. Cascade employee successes throughout the company. The final and most important step in building a world-class work force is to cascade individual employee successes down and across the organization. Employees who have participated in training and have succeeded in redefining and enhancing their jobs must be encouraged to connect with other employees and share their successes.

This is perhaps one of the greatest challenges faced by American managers: to create an environment that shares knowledge and collective learning. Just as money under the mattress benefits no one, individual successes are poorly used if allowed to be hidden from the organization. Rather, they must be moved out of an individual employee's department and spread to other departments so all employees can use an individual's best practices to improve their work. Turning the talents and achievements of each employee into an asset available to all employees is the goal a growing number of American companies are after.

The words of Taiichi Ohno, the father of the Toyota production system, are especially relevant here. He was fond of saying that success comes not from the system, but from the spirit that supports the system.[2] Finding ways to create this spirit and spread best practices throughout the organization is a difficult challenge indeed. The course most often chosen for spreading best practices is simply to publicize them through newsletters, company-sponsored magazines, and libraries of best practices. But many companies are realizing that simply reading about someone else's success won't necessarily inspire the reader to replicate it himself or herself. For best practices to really take across the organization, employees must actively connect and cooperate in an attempt to learn from one another. Companies are working hard to create innovative ways to make these constructive connections happen.

Some of the efforts at creating this connection profiled in the book, such as Motorola's Yearbook, Allstate's Log Book, KPMG Peat Marwick's Sharing Rallies, and Xerox Teamwork Day, are all targeted to accomplish the same goal: to cascade individual best practices throughout the entire organization. Spreading the collective learning can then have the greatest impact on sustaining the message of training and raising the productivity of the work force.

These 10 lessons are ones any company—of any size—can benefit from, whether or not they organize their training and retraining around the structure of a Corporate Quality University. The 10 lessons outlined here reinforce how important it is to design an entire system to build a world-class work force. This system starts with smart hiring and orientation, then goes on to provide every link in the company's employee/customer/supply chain with opportunities for lifelong learning and, finally, ends with recognizing and cascading employees successes down and across the organization. It's this entire system—rather than any one part of it—which can best prepare workers for the competitive realities of the 21st century.

The handful of trendsetting companies profiled in this book who are investing heavily in training their workers serves as a useful model for organizations which aspire to world-class performance. When seen in light of the fact that, according to the American Society for Training and Development, only 11 percent of workers receive any training at all from their employers, the achievements of these companies are even more impressive.[3] Clearly, a challenging road lies ahead for U.S. corporations, and their efforts to redefine training in progress at Corporate Quality Universities is helping to light the way. The ability of the companies profiled here to create a world-class work force lies in their realization that training and development constitute continuous lifelong endeavors for the corporation, the individual employees within it, and key members of the corporation's customer/supply chain.

Afterword

As we enter the 21st century, the skills of the work force will be fundamental to each company's competitiveness. The American companies profiled here will become models for scores of other companies—both large and small—to study when experimenting with how to best cultivate and exploit their human capital. One of the strongest themes to emerge from this book is the recognition that training must be redefined from a one-time event, targeted to one's internal employees, to a process of lifelong learning, encompassing a company's customer/supply chain, as well as their internal employees.

But will increasing a company's training expenditures across select members of their business system produce increases in productivity? It's becoming clear from the company case studies reported in this book that the model companies do, in fact, spend heavily on training, about 3 to 4 percent of their payroll. They have also made inroads in redefining their work environments so employees have an opportunity to use their newly acquired skills in problem solving and team building to make improvements in their jobs.

Investments in training alone will not produce the type of productivity increases we, as a country, are striving for. Instead, it is the combination of investing in training and experimenting with a myriad of ways to encourage employees to learn as they work that distinguishes the approaches taken by these companies and makes them models for scores of other companies. One of the greatest lessons to be learned from the companies highlighted in this book is that survival in the 21st century requires not only a better trained work force, but also a high-performance work environment where all workers have a conceptual grasp of their work, fix problems as they arise, and are committed to look for ways to improve their work. In addition to redesigning the work environment, the companies profiled here have recognized an often overlooked fact of life: promoting a culture of lifelong learning implies that employees *want* to learn and feel a sense of urgency that continuous learning is needed for survival in the marketplace. After all, training is not like medicine, where all one has to do is take two pills and wait to get better in the morning. Instead, everyone in the work force must clearly see the need to broaden their skills and become involved in their jobs so they continuously look for a better way of working. How are companies instilling a passion for learning within their employee population? The companies profiled here are forging a new psychological contract with employees—one which acknowledges the importance of lifelong learning and spells out both the company's and the individual employee's responsibility to develop "lifetime employability." With the old notion of lifetime employment having gone by the board, companies will now have to offer workers regular opportunities to add to their marketable skills and credentials to ensure each employee's lifetime employability.

Successful firms—those who will be prominent players in the 21st century—must do more than commit to training their work force. The truly dominant players understand the need to organize themselves as learning systems, where every part of the system—hiring, training, and recognition of employees—promotes both individual and collective learning. A key component of this learning system will be the degree to which companies make this learning system "accessible" to all the stakeholders in the organization. This means investing not only in training programs but also in technologies, tools (i.e., self-guided learning workbooks) and best practices forums where employees learn while they work.

As companies vie for a shrinking number of skilled workers throughout the 1990s, the ability to offer all levels of employees opportunities to continuously learn new skills and participate in the decisions which affect them will not only become necessary to building a successful firm, but will be a crucial factor in attracting and maintaining a first-class work force. The companies profiled here will be joined by a growing list of both public and private organizations who recognize that human capital is by far the most precious form of capital there is.

Appendix

YOUR NETWORKING GUIDE TO THIRTY CORPORATE QUALITY UNIVERSITIES

Your company may be interested in understanding the best practices of companies who are committed to building a world-class work force. The following is a list of 30 companies who share a common goal: They all look at training as a process of lifelong learning rather than a place to "go get trained." This list of 30 companies is not meant to be a comprehensive one encompassing every company with a Corporate Quality University possessing this philosophy of lifelong learning. It is, however, a list of companies providing exemplary ongoing learning opportunities for internal employees and, in many cases, key members of the company's customer/supply chain. Increasingly, these companies will be studied by scores of others as training become *the* critical tool to building a world-class work force.

Amdahl University
Amdahl Corporation
1250 East Arques Avenue
Sunnyvale, California 94088

American Express Quality University^{SM}
American Express Travel Related Services Division
20022 North 31st Avenue
Phoenix, Arizona

Apple University
Apple Computer, Inc.
20525 Mariani Avenue
Cupertino, California

Arthur Andersen Center for Professional Development
Arthur Andersen & Co. SC
1405 North Fifth Avenue
St. Charles, Illinois 60174-1264

Banc One College
Banc One Corporation
100 Broad Street
Columbus, Ohio 43215

Bristol-Myers Squibb Pharmaceutical College
Bristol-Myers Squibb Company
P.O. Box 4000
Princeton, New Jersey 08543

CMDS Team University
Computer Management and Development Services
P.O. Box 1184
Harrisonburg, Virginia 22801

Corning Education and Training Center
Corning Incorporated
Corning, New York 14831

Dana Customer Training Center
Dana Corporation
8000 Yankee Road
Ottawa Lake, Michigan 49267

Disney University
The Walt Disney Company
P.O. Box 10,000
Lake Buena Vista, Florida 32830-1000

Federal Express Leadership Institute
Federal Express Corporation
3035 Directors Row
Memphis, Tennessee 38131

Fidelity Investments Retail Training Services
Fidelity Investments
82 Devonshire Street
Boston, Massachusetts 02109

First of America Bank Corporation Quality Service University
First of America Bank Corporation
108 East Michigan Avenue
Kalamazoo, Michigan 49007

Ford Heavy Truck University
Ford Motor Company
100 Renaissance Center
Detroit, Michigan 48243

General Electric Management Development Institute
General Electric
Old Albany Post Road
Ossining, New York 10562

Hamburger University
McDonald's Corporation
Ronald Lane
Oak Brook, Illinois 60521

Hart Schaffner & Marx University
Hartmarx Corporation
101 North Wacker Drive
Chicago, Illinois 60606

Iams University
The Iams Company
7250 Poe Avenue
Dayton, Ohio 45414

Skill Dynamics, an IBM Company
IBM
500 Columbus Avenue
Thornwood, New York 10594

Intel University
Intel Corporation
2565 Walsh Avenue
Santa Clara, California 95051

KPMG Peat Marwick Quality Institute
KPMG Peat Marwick
Three Chestnut Ridge Road
Montvale, New Jersey 07645-0435

MBNA Customer College (MBNA America)
MBNA America Bank N.A.
400 Christiana Road
Newark, Delaware 19713

Motorola University
Motorola Inc.
1303 East Algonquin Road
Schaumburg, Illinois 60196

Saturn Training Center
Saturn Corporation
100 Saturn Parkway
Spring Hill, Tennessee 37174

Southern Company College
The Southern Company
64 Perimeter Center East
Atlanta, Georgia 30346

Sprint University of Excellence[SM]
Sprint Corporation
2330 Shawnee Mission Parkway
Westwood, Kansas 66205

Sun U
Sun Microsystems
2550 Garcia Avenue
Mountain View, California 94043

Target Stores University
Target Stores (Division of Dayton-Hudson Stores)
33 South 6th Street
Minneapolis, Minnesota 55402

Walton Institute
Wal-Mart Stores, Inc.
702 Southwest 8th Street
Bentonville, Arkansas 72716-8074

Xerox Document University
Xerox Corporation
P.O. Box 2000
Leesburg, Virginia 22075

Notes

CHAPTER 1

1. Lester Thurow, speech, "The State of American Competitiveness and How It Can Be Improved," a Report of the Procedures from the Xerox Quality Forum II, sponsored by Xerox Corporation, July 31–August 2, 1990, Leesburg, Virginia, p. 14.

2. Lloyd Dobyns and Clare Mason-Crawford, *Quality or Else: The Revolution in World Business* (Boston: Houghton Mifflin, 1991), p. 125.

3. U.S. Congress, Office of Technology Assessment, *Worker Training: Competing in the New International Economy*, OTA-ITE-457 (Washington, D.C.: U.S. Government Printing Office, September 1990), p. 11.

4. Ibid., p. 12.

5. Ibid., p. 13.

6. Ibid., p. 11.

7. Anthony P. Carnevale, "What Training Means in an Election Year," *Training & Development*, October 1992, p. 46.

8. U.S. Congress, Office of Technology Assessment, *Worker Training: Competing in the New International Economy*, OTA-ITE-457 (Washington, D.C.: U.S. Government Printing Office, September 1990), p. 128.

9. Margaret Hilton, "Shared Training: Learning from Germany," *Monthly Labor Review*, March 1991, p. 33.

10. Ibid., p 34.

11. Michael L. Dertouzos, Richard K. Lester, and Robert M. Solow, *Made in America*. The MIT Commission on Industrial Productivity, (New York: Harper Collins, 1989), p. 87.

12. Ibid.

13. Ray Marshall and Marc Tucker, *Thinking for a Living* (New York: Basic Books, 1992), p. 44.

14. Michael L. Dertouzos, Richard K. Lester, and Robert M. Solow, p. 88.

15. Marshall and Tucker, *Thinking for a Living*, p. 58.

16. "Training and the Workplace: Smart Work," *The Economist*, August 22, 1992, p. 21.

17. Charles R. DeCarlo and Ormsbee W. Robinson, *Education in Business and Industry* (New York: Center for Applied Research in Education, 1966), p. 10.

18. Nell P. Eurich, *Corporate Classrooms*. The Carnegie Foundation for the Advancement of Teaching (Princeton: Princeton University Press, 1985), p. 48.

19. Robert Slater, *The New GE: How Jack Welsh Revived an American Institution* (Homewood, Ill.: Business One Irwin, 1992), p. 177.

20. Thomas Stewart, "GE Keeps Those Ideas Coming," *Fortune*, August 12, 1991, p. 49.

21. Ellen Randolph Williams, "Introduction to Quality University[SM], *American Express Quality University[SM] 1991 Catalog*, p. 1.

CHAPTER 2

1. Lloyd Dobyns and Clare Mason-Crawford, *Quality or Else: The Revolution in World Business* (Boston: Houghton Mifflin, 1991), p. 133.

2. Ibid., p. 134.

3. Robert Reich, *The Work of Nations* (New York: Knopf, 1991), p. 12.

4. Clay Carr, *Smart Training: The Manager's Guide to Training for Improved Performance* (New York: McGraw-Hill, 1992), p. 91.

5. Dobyns and Mason-Crawford, *Quality or Else*, p. 144.

6. Anthony P. Carnevale, Leila J. Gainer, and Ann S. Meltzer, *Workplace Basics: The Essential Skills Employers Want* (San Francisco: Jossey-Bass, 1991), p. 39.

7. *In Search of Quality*, video, volume 2. Enterprise Media: Boston, Mass.

8. William Wiggenhorn, "Motorola U: When Training Becomes an Education," *Harvard Business Review*, July–August 1990, p. 81.

9. Ibid., p. 82.

10. Ibid., p. 75.

11. Sprint's University of Excellence[SM] Business Case Analysis, November 20, 1991, Executive Summary, p. 1.2.

12. Peter M. Senge, *The Fifth Discipline: The Art and Practice of the Learning Organization* (New York: Doubleday Currency, 1990), p. 14.

13. Peter M. Senge, "The Leader's New Work: Building Learning Organizations," *Sloan Management Review*, Fall 1990, p. 1.

CHAPTER 3

1. Corning Core Competency Study, 1990, p. 10.
2. Corning Competency for Excellence Interview Questions, 1990, p. 7.
3. Ibid., p. 6.
4. William Wiggenhorn, "Motorola U: When Training Becomes an Education," *Harvard Business Review*, July–August 1990, p. 77.
5. Beverly Geber, "Saturn's Grand Experiment," *TRAINING*, June 1992, p. 31.
6. Saturn Customer Philosophy, laminated card distributed to all Saturn team members.

CHAPTER 4

1. Definition of Intel Value of Customer Orientation, as outlined in Intel Six Values Statement, March 1992.
2. Intel University Catalog, 1992, list and description of orientation seminars, p. 94.
3. Zandy B. Leibowitz, Nancy K. Schlossberg, and Jane E. Shore, "Stopping the Revolving Door," *Training & Development Journal*, February 1991, p. 43.
4. Ibid., p. 44.
5. Victor J. Danilov, *Corporate Museums, Galleries, and Visitor Centers: A Directory* (New York: Greenwood Press, 1991), p. 4.
6. Robert Slater, *The New GE: How Jack Welsh Revived an American Institution*. Homewood, Ill.: Business One Irwin, 1992), p. 261.
7. James Baughman, director of GE Management Development Institute, interview with author, November 13, 1992.
8. Marcia Heiman and Joshua Slomianko, *Learning to Learn on the Job* (Alexandria, Va.: American Society for Training and Development, 1989), p. 2.
9. Anthony P. Carnevale, Leila J. Gainer, and Ann S. Meltzer, *Workplace Basics: The Essential Skills Employers Want* (San Francisco: Jossey-Bass, 1991), p. 47.
10. Ibid., p. 48.
11. Michelle Cox, personnel manager, Corning Incorporated, interview with author, June 11, 1992.
12. Helene Cooper, "The New Educators: Carpet Firm Sets Up an In-House School to Stay Competitive," *The Wall Street Journal*, October 5, 1992, p. 1.

13. Helene Cooper, "The New Educators," p. 6.

14. Brian S. Meskal, "Just a Degree of Confidence," *Industry Week*, February 19, 1990, p. 66.

15. Myron Magnet, "The Truth about the American Worker," *Fortune*, May 4, 1992, p. 65.

16. Ibid., p. 67.

17. Carnevale, Gainer, and Meltzer, *Workplace Basics: Essential* , p. 11.

18. Gary High, "Lifelong Learning," speech at the American Society for Training & Development Conference and Exposition, May 31–June 5, 1992.

19. Glenn Rifkin, "The Loneliness of the Layoff Survivor," *New York Times*, January 3, 1993, Business Section, p. 1.

20. Apple's Employee Development Philosophy, Apple University Catalog of Services, 1992, p. 3.

21. Henry Levin, "Investing in People: A Strategy to Address America's Work Force Crisis," Commission on Work Force Quality and Labor Market Efficiency, September 1989, p. 103.

22. Ellen Graham, "Digging for Knowledge," *The Wall Street Journal*, September 11, 1992, p. B1.

CHAPTER 5

1. Ralph Clark, president of Skill Dynamics, an IBM company, interview with author, September 14, 1992.

2. Alan L. Wilkins and Michael P. Thompson, "On Getting The Story Crooked (and Straight)," *Journal of Organizational Change Management* 4, no. 3 (1991), p. 20.

3. David Armstrong, *Managing By Storying Around: A New Method of Leadership* (New York: Doubleday Currency, 1992), p. 7.

4. Case studies, Manager of Manager program, a leadership program offered to Motorola general managers, used by permission of Motorola University.

5. Ibid.

6. David Glass, Wal-Mart president and chief executive officer, and Donald Soderquist, Wal-Mart vice chairman and chief operating officer, message to shareholders, Wal-Mart Annual Report, 1992, p. 2.

7. Sam Walton with John Huey, *Sam Walton, Made In America* (New York: Doubleday, 1992), p. 156.

8. Bill Waers, manager of General Electric Answer Center, interview with author, December 1, 1992.

9. Barry Arnett, education consulting services executive with Skill Dynamics, an IBM company, interview with author, October 2, 1992.

10. *A Vision of IBM Human Resource Performance in the Year 2000*, IBM Corporate Education, January 1990, p. 15.

11. Ibid., p. 43.

12. Michael Rothschild, *Bionomics: The Inevitability of Capitalism* (New York: Doubleday Currency, 1989), p. 192.

13. Victoria J. Marsick and Karen Watkins, *Informal and Incidental Learning in the Workplace* (New York: Routledge, Chapman and Hall, 1990), p. 7.

14. David B. Youst and Laurence Lipsett, "New-Job Immersion without Drowning," *Training & Development Journal*, February 1989, p. 45.

CHAPTER 6

1. Gary High, "Lifelong Learning," speech at the American Society for Training & Development Conference and Exposition, May 31–June 5, 1992.

2. Beverly Geber, "Saturn's Grand Experiment," *TRAINING*, June 1992, p. 33.

3. SEMATECH Annual Report, 1991, p. 2.

4. SEMATECH Annual Report, 1991, p. 7.

5. John Markoff, "Environment is a Mission at SEMATECH," *New York Times*, October 5, 1992, p. D1.

6. William Wiggenhorn, *The 1991 Motorola University Year-End Report*, p. 14.

7. Jeanne C. Meister, "Retail U," *TRAINING*, March 1992, p. 56.

8. William Wiggenhorn, *The 1991 Motorola University Year-End Report*, p. 38.

9. William Wiggenhorn, "A Message from Motorola University Senior Management," *The 1991 Motorola University Year-End Report*, p. 2.

10. Gary Tooker, "A Message from the President of Motorola," *The Crisis in American Education* (Motorola Publication), p. 2.

11. La Mirada Visioning Conference, sponsored by Intel, Kyrene School District, and Arthur Andersen, January 13–14, 1992.

CHAPTER 7

1. Max DePree, *Leadership Is an Art* (New York: Dell Publishing, 1989), p. 23.
2. Jim Kinnear, president of Texaco, interview for Texaco StarQuality recognition video, October 1991.
3. Texaco StarQuality recognition training program, 1991.
4. Peter Senge, *The Fifth Discipline: The Art and Practice of the Learning Organization* (New York: Doubleday Currency, 1990), p. 235.
5. Gene Simpson, vice president and director of participatory management programs and master of ceremonies for Motorola Total Customer Satisfaction Team Competition, video highlights, March 30, 1991.
6. "The Intel Quality Award: Recognizing Top Performance," *Inteleads* (Intel in-house magazine), June 4, 1991.
7. Jon Madonna, chairman of KPMG Peat Marwick, welcome letter to all participants in the KPMG Peat Marwick Sharing Rally, June 3–4, 1991.
8. Sandy Frieday, Xerox human resource specialist, interview with the author, August 4, 1992.

CHAPTER 8

1. Thomas A. Stewart, "Brainpower," *Fortune*, June 3, 1991, p. 44.
2. Yuzo Yasuda, *40 Years, 20 Million Ideas: The Toyota Suggestion System* (Cambridge, Mass.: Productivity Press, 1991), p. 181.
3. Anthony P. Carnevale, "What Training Means in an Election Year," *Training & Development*, October 1992, p. 47.

Bibliography

Armstrong, David. *Managing By Storying Around: A New Method of Leadership.* New York: Doubleday Currency, 1992.

Bowsher, Jack E. *Educating America: Lessons Learned in the Nation's Corporations.* New York: Wiley, 1989.

Byrne, John A. "Paradigms for Postmodern Managers," *Business Week Special Issue: Reinventing America,* January 19, 1993.

Carnevale, Anthony P. "What Training Means in an Election Year," *Training & Development,* October 1992.

Carnevale, Anthony P., Leila J. Gainer, and Ann S. Meltzer. *Workplace Basics: The Essential Skills Employers Want.* San Francisco: Jossey-Bass, 1991.

Carr, Clay. "Should We Train and Was It Successful?" *Performance & Instruction,* August 1989.

Carr, Clay. *Smart Training: The Manager's Guide to Training for Improved Performance.* New York: McGraw-Hill, 1992.

Cooper, Helene. "The New Educators: Carpet Firm Sets Up an In-House School to Stay Competitive," *The Wall Street Journal,* October 5, 1992.

Danilov, Victor J. *Corporate Museums, Galleries, and Visitor Centers: A Directory.* New York: Greenwood Press, 1991.

Davidow, William H. and Bro Uttal. *Total Customer Service: The Ultimate Weapon.* New York: Harper & Row, 1989.

DePree, Max. *Leadership Is an Art.* New York: Dell Publishing, 1989.

Dertouzos, Michael L., Richard K. Lester, and Robert M. Solow. *Made in America:* The MIT Commission On Industrial Productivity, New York: Harper Collins, 1989.

DeYoung, Garrett. "Intel U Teaches Lessons You Never Learned in School," *Electronic Business,* October 15, 1990.

DeYoung, Garrett. "Reward Your Suppliers and They'll Reward You," *Electronic Business,* June 25, 1990.

Dobyns, Lloyd and Clare Mason-Crawford. *Quality or Else: The Revolution in World Business.* Boston: Houghton Mifflin, 1991.

Drucker, Peter. "Management in the Information Age," *The Wall Street Journal*, July 8, 1987.

Eurich, Nell. *Corporate Classrooms*. The Carnegie Foundation for the Advancement of Teaching. Princeton: Princeton University Press, 1985.

Feder, Barnaby. "At Motorola, Quality Is a Team Sport," *New York Times*. January 21, 1993.

Geber, Beverly. "Saturn's Grand Experiment," *TRAINING*, June 1992.

Gery, Gloria. *Electronic Performance Support Systems*. Boston: Weingarten, 1991.

Graham, Ellen. "Digging for Knowledge," *The Wall Street Journal*, September 11, 1992.

Hauser, John R. and Don Clausing. "The House of Quality," *Harvard Business Review*, May–June 1988.

Heiman, Marcia and Joshua Slomianko. *Learning to Learn on the Job*. Alexandria, Va.: American Society for Training and Development, 1989.

Hilton, Margaret. "Shared Training: Learning from Germany," *Monthly Labor Review*, March 1991.

Kanter, Rosabeth Moss. "Change: Where to Begin," *Harvard Business Review*, July–August 1991.

Kinzer, Stephen. "Germans' Apprentice System Is Seen as Key to Long Boom," *New York Times*, February 6, 1993.

Leibowitz, Zandy B., Nancy K. Schlossberg, and Jane E. Shore. "Stopping the Revolving Door," *Training & Development Journal*, February 1991.

Lemonick, Michael. "Tomorrow's Lesson: Learn or Perish," *Time Special Issue Beyond the Year 2000*, Fall 1992.

Magnet, Myron. "The Truth about the American Worker," *Fortune*, May 4, 1992.

Markoff, John. "Environment Is a Mission at SEMATECH," *New York Times*, October 5, 1992.

Marshall, Ray and Marc Tucker. *Thinking for a Living*. New York: Basic Books, 1992.

Marsick, Victoria J. and Karen Watkins. *Informal and Incidental Learning in the Workplace*. New York: Routledge, Chapman and Hall, 1990.

Meister, Jeanne C. "Retail U," *TRAINING*, March 1992.

Meskal, Brian. "Just a Degree of Confidence," *Industry Week*, February 19, 1990.

National Center on Education and the Economy. *America's Choice: High Skills or Low Wages*. Rochester, New York, 1990.

Peters, Tom. *Thriving on Chaos: Handbook for a Management Revolution.* New York: Knopf, 1986.

Prahalad, C. K. and Gary Hamel. "The Core Competence of the Corporation," *Harvard Business Review,* May–June 1990.

Raia, Ernest. "1991 Medal of Professional Excellence: Motorola," *Purchasing,* September 26, 1991.

Reich, Robert. *The Work of Nations.* New York: Knopf, 1991.

Remenschneider, Connie and Robert Hall. "Quality Service University: First of America Takes Action for Service Improvement," *Bank Marketing,* November 1991.

Rifkin, Glenn. "The Loneliness of the Layoff Survivor," *New York Times,* January 3, 1993.

Rothschild, Michael. *Bionomics: The Inevitability of Capitalism.* New York: Henry Holt, 1990.

Schor, Juliet B. *The Overworked American.* New York: Harper Collins, Publishers, 1991.

Senge, Peter M. *The Fifth Discipline: The Art and Practice of the Learning Organization.* New York: Doubleday Currency, 1990.

Senge, Peter M. "The Leader's New Work: Building Learning Organizations," *Sloan Management Review,* Fall 1990.

Sherman, Stratford. "A Brave New Darwinian Workplace," *Fortune,* January 25, 1993.

Slater, Robert. *The New GE: How Jack Welsh Revived an American Institution.* Homewood, Ill.: Business One Irwin, 1992.

Stewart, Thomas A. "Brainpower," *Fortune,* June 3, 1991.

Stewart, Thomas A. "GE Keeps Those Ideas Coming," *Fortune,* August 12, 1991.

"Teaching Business How to Train," *Business Week Special Issue: Reinventing America,* January 19, 1993.

Tichy, Noel and Stratford Sherman. *Control Your Destiny or Someone Else Will.* New York: Doubleday, 1993.

"Training and the Workplace: Smart Work," *The Economist,* August 22, 1992.

U.S. Chamber of Commerce, "Employee Benefits," *Survey Data from Benefit Year 1988,* Washington, D.C.: 1989.

U.S. Congress, Office of Technology Assessment, *Worker Training: Competing in the New International Economy,* OTA-ITE-457. Washington, D.C.: U.S. Government Printing Office, September 1990.

Walton, Sam with John Huey. *Sam Walton, Made In America*. New York: Doubleday, 1992.

Webb, David. "Suppliers Reeling from the Quality Onslaught," *Electronic Business*, October 7, 1991.

Wiggenhorn, William. "Motorola U: When Training Becomes an Education," *Harvard Business Review*. July–August 1990.

Wilkins, Alan L. and Michael P. Thompson. "On Getting the Story Crooked (and Straight)," *Journal of Organizational Change Management* 4, no. 3, 1991.

Willett, Hugh. "What Drives Quality at Intel?" *Electronic Business*, October 7, 1991.

Youst, David B. and Laurence Lipsett. "New Job Immersion without Drowning," *Training & Development Journal*, February 1989.

Yuzo, Yasuda. *40 Years, 20 Million Ideas: The Toyota Suggestion System*. Cambridge, Mass.: Productivity Press, 1991.

Zuboff, Shoshana. *In the Age of the Smart Machine: The Future of Work and Power*. New York: Basic Books, 1988.

Sources

INTERVIEWS

These are the people who generously gave of their time and knowledge to make this book a reality. Thanks to all of you.

Barbara Anders. Vice President, Human Resources, American Express

Barry Arnett. Education Consulting Services Executive, Skill Dynamics, an IBM company

Gary Aslin. Director, Xerox Document University, Xerox Corporation

Gail Baity. Manager, Strategic Corporate Education, Corning Incorporated

Edward Bales. Director of Education, Motorola, Inc.

David Basarab. Manager of Evaluation, Motorola University, Motorola, Inc.

James P. Baughman. Manager, Corporate Management Development, General Electric

John Boyles. Professor, Eastern Michigan University

Paul Brault. Manager, Supplier & Customer Training, Motorola, Inc.

Kenneth Breen. Manager, Benchmarking & Quality Education, Xerox

Margot Brown. Manager, Media Relations, Motorola Inc.

Lynne Cage. Manager Training & Development, Applied Magnetics Corporation

Vincent Cannella. Partner in Charge, Quality Service, KPMG Peat Marwick

Anthony P. Carnevale. President, Institute for Workplace Learning, American Society for Training & Development

Jeanne Chatigny. Program Manager, Texaco Quality Institute, Texaco Inc.

Ralph Clark. President, Skill Dynamics, an IBM company

David Connell. Dean, Southern Company College, The Southern Company.

Earl Conway. Former Manager of Quality, Procter & Gamble.

Gary Corrigan. Director of Customer Training, Dana Corporation

Michele Cox. Manager Personnel, Corning Incorporated

David Crowley. Communications Manager, Intel Corporation

Michael Cummins. Managing Director, University of Miami Quality Institute

Jim Cutler. Director, Apple University, Apple Corporation

Carson Daniels. Director, Customer Service, Olympus Corporation

Lance Davis. Director, PONSI, American Council on Education

Larry Davis. UAW Team Leader, Saturn Corporation

Steve DeMorro. Director, Squibb College, Bristol-Myers Squibb Company

Gail Digate. Principal, Leadership Learning Systems

Keith Dompier. Manager, Intel Quality College, Intel Corporation

Jennifer Ehart. Director, Sprint Corporation

Carlene Ellis. Senior Vice President, Human Resources, Intel Corporation

Maureen Erbach. Manager, Supplier Training, Allstate Insurance

Warren Evans. Manager, Quality Systems, Intel Corporation

Bill Faust. Program Manager, Leadership Development, Motorola University

Wendell Fletcher. Senior Analyst, Office of Technology Assessment

Steve Fraser. Manager, Leadership Development Center, Domino's Pizza

Sandy Frieday. Human Resource Specialist, Xerox Corporation

Larry Gilpin. Senior Vice President of Customer, Team, and Community Relations, Target Stores

Lisa Guillermin. K-12 Education Manager, Intel Corporation

Dave Hall. Corporate Director, Quality Technology, Intel Corporation

Tim Hammill. Manager of Customer Environment Education, Skill Dynamics, an IBM company

Mark Hart. Account Development Executive, Hart Schaffner & Marx

John Hess. Director of CMDS Team University, Computer Management Development Services

Gary High. Manager, Human Resource Development, Saturn Corporation

Annie Hill. CWA Representative, Communications Workers of America, AFL-CIO, CLC District 7

Paula Hill. Director, Southern Methodist University Business Leadership Center

Kenneth Hoffman. President and CEO, Hart Schaffner & Marx

Peter Huston. Director, Hart Schaffner & Marx University

Donna James. Vice President, Nationwide IPO University, Nationwide Insurance

Jeff Kahn. Director, Ford Heavy Truck University, Ford Motor Company

John Kelsch. Director, Quality, Xerox Corporation

Constantine Konstans. Director, KPMG Peat Marwick Quality Institute

Carol Kovacik. Coordinator, Quality Group, KPMG Peat Marwick

Larry Lateur. Dean, Dana Customer Training Center, Dana Corporation

Shelley Lauten. Manager of Cast Training, Disney University

Martin Lustig. Director of Quality Development, Sprint Corporation

Beth Luchsinger. Director, Banc One College, Banc One Corporation

Nick Maniaci. Manager, Quality Planning, KPMG Peat Marwick

Jerome Marxhausen. Executive Vice President, Hart Schaffner & Marx

Janet McLaughlin, Director, Corporate Education & Training, Corning Incorporated

Thomas McMullen. Manager, Texaco Quality Institute, Texaco Inc.

Julie Menard. Communications Specialist, Intel Corporation

Raymond Meurer. Bell Island Enterprises

Bunky Milton. Manager, Ford Heavy Truck University, Ford Motor Company

Sheila Murdick. Director, National Program on Noncollegiate Sponsored Instruction, Board of Regents of the University of the State of New York

Steve Neilsen. Managing Director Federal Express Leadership Institute, Federal Express Corporation

Larry Nelson. Human Resource Team Leader, Saturn

Roland Obstfeld, First Vice President, MBNA America Bank N.A.

Michael Oswald. Manager of Partnership Training, SEMATECH

Marty Raymond. Manager, Training and Strategic Implementation, Saturn Corporation

Connie Remenschneider. Manager, Quality Service University, First of America Bank Corporation

Deb Robbins. Manager, American Express Quality University^{SM}, American Express Travel Service

Jim Robertson. Manager, Motorola University Challenge, Motorola Inc.

Shirley Rogers. Dean, McDonald's Hamburger University, McDonald's

Wayne Rohrbaugh. Training Manager, McDonald's Hamburger University

Edward Runge. Manager, Management Resource Planning and Development, Xerox Corporation

Nancy Rus. Vice President and Corporate Director of Organizational Development, Motorola Inc.

Dennis Schaffer. Senior Training Manager, Texaco Quality Institute, Texaco Inc.

Mark Schrooten. Senior Instructional Design Specialist, American Express Quality University^{SM}, American Express Travel Service

Ken Schultz. Director of Business and Industry Institute, Mesa Community College

Larry Silvey. Partner, Arthur Andersen Consulting

Judy Simmons. Manager, Curriculum Development, University of Excellence^{SM}, Sprint Corporation

Gene Simpson. Vice President and Director of Particpative Management Programs, Motorola Inc.

Peter Smith. Director, Sun U, Sun Microsystems

Brenda Sumberg. Director of Quality, Motorola University, Motorola Inc.

Linda Thompson. Director, Amdahl University, Amdahl Corporation

Sue Thompson. Personnel Manager, Motorola, Arlington Heights plant

Jack Tootson. Director, Iams University, The Iams Company

Jane Truelove. Vice President, Fidelity Investments

Henry Turner. Employee Empowerment, Motorola, Arlington Heights

James Van Dyke. Associate Dean, Rio Salado Community College

Joe Walker. Manager of Education and Home Office Training, Wal-Mart

Pat Ward. Director, Ford Marketing Institute, Ford Motor Company

Richard Ward. Director, Intel University, Intel Corporation

Weintraub, Robert. Education Consultant, Skill Dynamics, an IBM company

Leslie Wemyss. Assistant Vice President, MBNA America Bank N.A.

Robert B. Wilcox. President, Wilcox & Associates

Bud Wurtz. Organization Development Specialist, Sprint Corporation

Calley Zilinsky. Director, Fox Valley Academy of Quality

Monica Zontanos. Director of Client Services, Rio Salado Community College

Index

Other books of interest to you from Irwin Professional Publishing . . .

QUALITY MANAGEMENT
Implementing the Best Ideas of the Masters
Bruce Brocka and M. Suzanne Brocka

By assembling over 30 proven TQM strategies, this short course in quality makes it easy to match the right improvement method to your company's needs. You'll find 75 ideas to jumpstart and maintain a TQM campaign, new TQM tools that improve product and service end value, plus a dozen managerial techniques to enhance productivity. (408 pages)
ISBN: 1-55623-540-2

GLOBAL QUALITY
A Synthesis of the World's Best Management Methods
Richard Tabor Greene
Co-published with ASQC Quality Press

Finally, a book that organizes the chaos of quality improvement techniques! Greene compiles 24 global quality systems, the 30 characteristics they share, plus 8 new business systems into this convenient reference. Also reveals 7 new quality improvement techniques being tested in Japan! (884 pages)
ISBN: 1-55623-915-7

MANAGEMENT OF QUALITY
Strategies to Improve Quality and the Bottom Line
Jack Hagan
Co-published with ASQC Quality Press

Now you can understand how to *profit* from quality with this easy-to-read, strategic guide. Hagan demonstrates how to view the quality improvement process as a business—and manage it for success. You'll find dozens of step-by-step guidelines for planning, implementing, and sustaining your organization's quality improvement efforts. (210 pages)
ISBN: 1-55623-924-6

THE CORPORATE GUIDE TO THE MALCOM BALDRIGE NATIONAL QUALITY AWARD
Proven Strategies for Building Quality into Your Organization
Marion Mills Steeples
Co-published with ASQC Quality Press
Forward by Robert W. Gavin
Chairman of the Executive Committee, Motorola Inc.

The insider's guide to the coveted quality award! Marion Steeples—a member of the Baldrige Board of Examiners since the award's inception—explains the major categories and their requirements, lessons learned from the winning companies, how you can cut development and production costs, streamline processes, and enhance worker moral. (358 pages)
ISBN: 1-55623-957-2

Available in fine book stores and libraries everywhere.